Research methods for English language teachers

JO McDONOUGH
Senior Lecturer in English as a Foreign Language, University of Essex, UK

STEVEN McDONOUGH
Lecturer in Applied Linguistics, University of Essex, UK

A member of the Hodder Headline Group
LONDON • NEW YORK • SYDNEY • AUCKLAND

To the memory of
DOROTHY MARTHA GLADYS JEPSON
1905–1994

First published in Great Britain in 1997 by
Arnold, a member of the Hodder Headline Group,
338 Euston Road, London NW1 3BH
175 Fifth Avenue, New York, NY 10010

Distributed exclusively in the USA by
St Martin's Press, Inc.
175 Fifth Avenue, New York, NY 10010

British Library Cataloguing in Publication Data
A catalogue record for this book is available from the British Library

Library of Congress Cataloging-in-Publication Data
McDonough, Jo
    Research methods for English language teachers / Jo McDonough.
    Steven McDonough.
        p.   cm.
    Includes bibliographical references and index.
    ISBN 0–340–61472–2 (pbk.)
    1. English language—Study and teaching—Foreign speakers–
    –Research—Methodology.   I. McDonough. Steven H.   II. Title.
    PE1128.A2M384   1997
    428′ .0072—dc20
                                                            96–35143
ISBN 0 340 61472 2 (pb)   CIP
ISBN 0 340 69223 5 (hb)

Typeset in 10½/12½ Ehrhardt by Saxon Graphics Ltd, Derby
Printed and bound in Great Britain by J W Arrowsmith Ltd, Bristol

Table of contents

Preface

'Research' and 'teaching' are in many ways quite different spheres of activity, each adhering to its own principles, procedures, objectives and methodologies. Indeed, the two terms have often been polarized, contributing to the unhelpful and rather tired distinction between 'theory' on the one hand and 'practice' on the other. In recent years, however, the interface has been both challenged and productively explored by practitioners in the field of ELT: there is a growing literature on the research carried out by teachers and on the kinds of models from which such research is drawn.

The present book is intended as a contribution to this literature. Its primary addressees are English language teachers in their everyday professional context. It is based on the view that teachers have a huge number of issues and questions surrounding them in that context; that there are available many appropriate research techniques for exploring those issues; that professional researchers and teachers have much to say of interest to each other; and that it is nowadays not unusual for English language teachers to pursue periods of training and professional development away from the classroom and thus sometimes to enter temporarily a different value system.

Teacher research has become something of a 'buzz' word. Although this book is divided into two sections, one that is largely concerned with 'principles' and another with 'method', we have attempted to show how these two aspects are linked. The principles informing the kinds of research with which teachers are becoming increasingly familiar have powerful derivations and long histories in other disciplines, in the social sciences as well as in general education; and research methods and techniques are themselves not free-floating, but are embedded in debates about philosophies and paradigms, and about how the social world might be construed. We hope, simply, that readers will find here some stimulus, or support, for exploring their own ideas and questions about teaching and learning, and will wish to peel away some of the layers of both content and method that have fascinated us.

Jo and Steven McDonough
University of Essex
1996

Acknowledgements

We are grateful to Longman Group UK Ltd and L. van Lier for permission to reproduce the box 'Types of research' from *The classroom and the language learner*, 1988, p. 57.

We particularly wish to acknowledge the ideas and hints and feedback from many colleagues and students over the last few years. We are also grateful to Dilly Meyer for helping us to prepare the final manuscript. Only we are to be held responsible for the outcome.

Introduction: setting the scene

This book is about teachers and research, more specifically about the relationship between them, and with the primary focus on teacher-initiated and teacher-executed research. It is therefore not in itself intended as a general manual covering all research topics and techniques of relevance to language learning and teaching (there are indeed many pertinent titles that do precisely this), which would include, for example, second language acquisition (SLA) research, needs analysis, programme evaluation, language testing and a number of other major areas. Our perspective does not, of course, exempt these from discussion, but they are drawn on in so far as the teacher may, in senses which it will be important to define, harness and make use of them. The book is embedded in the profession of Teaching English as a Foreign Language (TEFL), from which examples and case studies will be taken. At the same time, however, a great many of the issues and methodologies discussed derive from a broader educational base, and by implication from a diversity of philosophies, disciplines and procedures.

The book has been written in order to bring together the possibilities for research inherent and feasible in the English as a Foreign Language (EFL) classroom, and the range of approaches and techniques available to teachers for carrying out or being involved in such research. Thus the starting point and, we hope, the conceptual coherence offered, is the simple question of what practising teachers can actively do to try to develop a 'research stance', and to solve some of the open questions in their classroom environment. We would wish to argue that this is broad-based and not restrictive, first because of the number of topics that can in principle be the focus of attention, and second because of the wide range of research methods that can be called upon.

This view, then, is underpinned by several assumptions:

- The frequently cited dichotomy between, on the one hand, teaching as a 'practical activity' and, on the other, research as a 'theoretical' endeavour is regarded as unhelpful.

- Furthermore, although there are some plausible reasons as to why teachers may often feel alienated by conventional research outcomes and approaches, it is argued that researcher-generated research is not by definition irrelevant, and that teacher-initiated, applied, and even pure research paradigms can and should be brought together more than is currently the case. Teachers, as we shall see, can even change camps during the course of their careers. What is feasible therefore in principle includes understanding and applying pre-existing research results as well as possibilities for reciprocity and collaboration.
- On a cautionary note, however, the potential tension between a definition of teaching as 'action' and of research as 'understanding' cannot be fudged: much of the debate about action research, for example, revolves around this apparent conflict, as is signalled in its very name.
- It is clear that teachers have both explicit formulations of, and implicit attitudes to, issues and events in their own professional lives which a research perspective is able to address within the reality of the classroom context.
- These 'issues and events' potentially include aspects of the classroom, groups and subgroups, individual learners and their own purposes and agendas, the teacher's personal-professional development, the wider management and administrative context, syllabus and materials, collaboration with others, change and innovation, and are not restricted to the apparently dominant research concern of how language learning takes place, however important that is and, indeed, however much teachers might be able to contribute to it from sources and resources as yet not fully tapped.

The major and obvious question that is still begged is, of course, that of what is meant by the term 'research'. The beginning of an answer, albeit evasive, is to say that it depends on why we want to know: to the extent that reality is a personal and social construct, there is no exclusive and definitive answer. Nevertheless, definitions abound, and we offer a small selection here just to establish an initial framework (to be firmed up in Chapter 3 by when some key implications and manifestations will have been discussed). Brumfit and Mitchell (1989: 6), for instance, start with the idea that 'a "researching attitude" may be defined as the systematization of curiosity', a view echoed by Boomer (1987: 9) who writes: 'Research is simply institutionalised and formalised thinking. It is doing self-consciously what comes naturally'. Nunan (1992b: 3) offers the following more concrete definition: 'Research is a systematic process of enquiry consisting of 3 elements ... (1) a question, problem or hypothesis

(2) data (3) analysis and interpretation of data'. This is a useful view but, as we shall see during the course of this book, further questions will be raised as to whether all three are in fact necessary, and if so in what varying sequences they might appear in any individual research design. Stenhouse (quoted in the Rudduck and Hopkins, 1985, collection of his writings) considers that 'research should underwrite speculation and undermine assertion' and, more contentiously (Stenhouse, 1988) 'using research means doing research'. A broad view is taken by Stake (1995: 97): 'Research is not just the domain of scientists, it is the domain of craftspersons and artists as well, all who would study and interpret'. *The Guardian* (8 November 1995) has yet another perspective: 'reform [in education, law, social housing ...] without research is a dangerous exercise'. As a final quotation for purposes of this introduction, Hopkins (1993: 9) conceives of research – by teachers – as 'systematic self-conscious enquiry with the purpose of understanding and improving their practice'. There are obviously a number of recurring thematic strands here, particularly to do with formalization, self-awareness, change (Hopkins' 'improvement'), questioning and accessibility. A short brainstorm for the term 'research' among the authors' colleagues and students turned up similar points, and revealed a number of beliefs and assumptions: systematization; problem or data first; the testing of hypotheses; proof; objectivity; research relevance; replicability; going public on outcomes; accountability; and the distinction between research, evaluation and development.

Clearly, there is a multiplicity of perspectives which are not amenable to a ready-made definition nor to a consensus. For the moment, then, the reader is invited to note the range of associations of the term, perhaps to add his/her own to the list, and then to hold in at least temporary abeyance any firm commitment to one particular view.

This book is divided into two main sections. The first part is concerned with 'approaches': it is primarily concerned to examine the various interpretations of the notion of research in a teaching context, and to relate the discussion to the broader framework of research issues and traditions. Chapter 1 is largely descriptive, using a few disparate but typical EFL teaching situations to illustrate the contexts in which research issues might be formulated as well as to give examples of teachers carrying out research projects of their own. Chapter 2 attempts to delineate the 'teacher researcher' notion, with its possibilities and limitations, and looks too at the central concept of 'action research'. Chapter 3 then broadens the discussion, reviewing a range of possibilities for defining research and evaluating ways in which particular research paradigms and procedures can be said to reflect attitudes to the discovery and applicability of knowledge. It will also unpack the terminology of 'quantitative' and 'qualitative' research. Chapter 4 is concerned with a number of key research principles, and examines the extent to which different kinds of research address them, paying particular attention to the controversial issue of whether research outcomes need to be generalizable. Looking ahead to Part 2, Chapter 5 examines possible areas of research focus for the EFL teacher, and considers the processes whereby research questions and topics might be generated.

The second part of the book is directly concerned with both topics and methods. After a scene-setting chapter, each subsequent chapter discusses and exemplifies research techniques that we argue are considered appropriate and feasible for the English language teacher, taking into account the qualitative–quantitative spectrum and arguing that no one method, whether experimental or descriptive or anything else, is automatically to be preferred or has a monopoly on the truth. It all depends on teachers themselves – their values and objectives, their working environment, their views of their own role, their underlying professional attitudes, and what they want to know.

Part 1: principles and perspectives

1

Teachers in action

Introduction

A worldwide profession like that of TEFL is much too richly diverse to be neatly captured in an introductory chapter of this kind. Rather, the aim here is to offer a small variety of teaching situations – 'instances' – which, if not representative, at least give a flavour of teachers' working environments and professional concerns. These 'instances' are not case studies carefully chosen to illustrate models and possibilities for teacher research, and much of the rest of this book is anyway given over to this goal: indeed, in a number of these instances, 'research' is not obviously centre-stage at all. Our starting point, then, and a theme that underpins our arguments throughout, is a belief that research in language teaching must be predicated on an understanding of a wide range of contextual variables that will interact with and even determine both research perspectives and research methodology: they may of course also help to explain an absence of any research interest by participants whatsoever.

We hope to be able to show from the six instances briefly described a little later in this chapter that research possibilities for English language teachers can be seen on a broad spectrum. At one end there are well-formulated research questions which are then implemented as a concrete set of procedures with an actual research outcome. At the other end, and undoubtedly representing the majority of teaching situations, research remains an unrealized potential, though we would argue strongly that this research potential is in fact inherent by definition in every context, because no classroom and no group of people working together is without problems to solve, questions to resolve, grey areas to clarify and development areas to pursue. We have seen in the introduction to this book that a minimalist view of a 'research stance' requires the systematization and formalization of professional issues out of the complexity of day-to-day action: the idea that research possibilities are embedded in any teaching situation is well expressed by Fujiwara (quoted in Richards and Lockhart, 1994: 81), a teacher who writes: 'It is only when I look at these visions [of the class] that I can begin to analyze why I am doing what I'm doing ... so my planning process is based on layers and layers of assumptions, experiences and knowledge. I have to dig deep down to find out why I make the decisions I do.' We shall also come to see this spectrum as the book develops in terms of the crucial concepts of 'reflection' and 'action'.

We now turn to a short discussion of teachers' roles and contexts, which leads to the illustrative 'instances' each with a short commentary. In the final part of the chapter we draw out their key implications as far as research is concerned.

Context and roles

The notion of a 'context' is at the same time a simple and yet far-reaching one. It provides a framework in which to describe the diversity of approaches and methods in language teaching and their more specific and local inter-pretations (see, for example, Richards, 1985). It goes some way towards explaining the possibilities open to teachers, their freedom to manoeuvre, as it were, as well as the inevitable constraints and pressures upon them. It is through this route crucially linked to the teachers' perspectives on research, whether in terms of research opportunity, content areas, or methods accept-able and available. To stress the importance of contextual reference points for a great deal of the research activity carried out by teachers is also to confront directly such problematic and controversial issues as generalizability and validity. Definitions of 'context' also connect paradigms in educational research to their foundations and derivations in sociology and anthropology. We shall be exploring these broader areas of principle in subsequent chapters in this part of the book, and the implications of what Bryant (1993: 3) neatly refers to as the 'reading of settings'.

Context

For the moment it will be useful to note the very large number of factors operating at national, institutional and classroom level (Malamah-Thomas, 1987) that cluster together in various permutations to give each context its own particular set of characteristics. There are factors to do with the set-ting itself, which include:

- source of policy decisions
- status and training of teachers
- role of English in the country and the curriculum
- time available
- physical environment of classroom and school
- student: teacher ratio
- class size
- resources available
- anticipated methodology
- choice or imposition of coursebook

and so on. Other variables concern the learners themselves, for example:

- proficiency levels
- age
- interests
- motivation and attitude
- needs and goals
- learning styles
- mother tongue.

(For a fuller discussion, see McDonough and Shaw, 1993.)

Roles

Although a teacher's role is unlikely to be unique, it will clearly be influenced and in varying degrees determined by the nature of the context in which he/she works. All human beings (except presumably hermits and recluses) operate within a 'role set' inhabited by others (Handy, 1985), and a teacher's typical professional role set will therefore include colleagues, students, senior staff, secretaries, technicians, parents, sponsors and so on. This interactive network affects not only the details of a job specification but also individuals' perceptions of their roles.

Role theory is a complex subject, and this is certainly not the forum to elaborate on it. An awareness of 'role' is, however, important for the present discussion because a teacher's professional activities – research possibilities therefore included – are conditioned by what is expected of them and how they see themselves, through sociocultural norms, rules and regulations, attitudes, status and training. Classroom interaction patterns, for instance, may be based on a norm of social distance between teachers and learners (Wright, 1987; see also Richards and Lockhart, 1994), or alternatively one of a student-focused environment, so the kinds of issues that might be prioritized and investigated by teachers are likely to be very different in each case. Again, the apparently straightforward matter of where research is initiated and how it is subsequently pursued will be related to the teacher's position in the educational hierarchy, as will the associated possibilities for change and innovation.

This, then, is the framework for teachers' professional actions and assumptions, and a starting point for an assessment of the relative importance and appropriateness of different approaches to research in TEFL. The 'instances' that now follow are intended to show that typical teaching situations have research implications of many disparate kinds, determined to a considerable extent by the variables of context and teacher role. The authors offer a brief commentary to accompany each, and readers might also wish to draw their own implications. (It must be added here that no one type of situation is necessarily restricted to, or characteristic of, a particular geographical area, and no such implication is intended.)

Instances

For each of the instances described here the authors offer a brief commentary, intended simply to highlight points that seem to us to stand out: readers, of course, may well make other inferences.

Kenji Matsuda has taught in a Japanese Junior High School for eight years. He teaches for about 18 hours per week, Monday through Saturday, and, like all his colleagues, has a range of ancillary duties related to the smooth running of the school. There are regular staff meetings, and quite a lot of the time is spent discussing the new syllabus and the revised coursebooks that accompany it. This new syllabus derives from a policy decision made at Ministry of Education level that the country's English-language programmes should be designed to introduce a more communicative methodology into the school system alongside the rigorous teaching of English grammar. Examinations nevertheless remain an important element. KM uses both English and Japanese in the classroom, the latter particularly as a metalanguage for classroom instructions and linguistic explanations, as well as occasionally for the translation of new vocabulary. There are 35 students in his class. He sometimes has the opportunity to work alongside a native speaker Assistant English Teacher (AET), who visits the school for two weeks every three months on a peripatetic basis and who acts primarily as a language informant and 'resource person'. KM is occasionally required to attend talks at a local teachers' group, the most recent one given by a teacher just back from a training course in the USA. KM is himself interested in this scheme, arranged at Prefecture level through the Ministry.

Comment: On the face of it, KM's working environment is relatively constrained, and overtly 'top-down' in the sense that main course materials derive from centralized decision-making. Examinations are important. This teacher is also very busy 'at the chalk face' for six days a week. There is nevertheless some space for interpreting the national syllabus, and plenty of opportunity for peer contact and dissemination of information within the school and also locally. A chance for 'time out' to study abroad may be available, and it is noticeable that KM would be motivated to take advantage of this.

Ann Barker worked for several years on short contracts in various European countries and then, after successfully completing the RSA Cert TEFLA,[1] was offered a longer-term post in a private language school in Oxford teaching 25 hours per week. The school mainly organizes year-round courses for adults, with a big summer programme for younger learners. Management is currently looking at the possibility of developing

---

[1] Royal Society of Arts Certificate in Teaching English as a Foreign Language to Adults. One of a small number of initial qualifications for teaching EFL, and now administered by the University of Cambridge Local Examinations Syndicate.

more specialized programmes, particularly – following suggestions made by teachers informally and at staff meetings – in English for doctors and for business purposes. Within the school's budgetary constraints, some teachers may be given a reduction in teaching load in order to develop these new courses. AB's original background in nursing makes her an obvious candidate to contribute to this initiative. The school is a member of ARELS[2] and of the local EFL teachers' association, so it is at least possible to find out what other language schools offer in these areas, with obvious commercial restrictions. The school does not belong to any other national organization, and does not subscribe to EFL publications such as the *EL Gazette* or *ELT Journal*, so access to a broader information base is somewhat limited.

Comment: AB is on quite a typical EFL career track for native-speaker teachers, moving from the gathering of some limited experience (probably immediately after graduation) to an internationally accepted qualification, the first step on a recognized route into the profession. She has an interesting background in a different work area which, juxtaposed with TEFL, suggests a possible niche in ESP (English for Specific Purposes). It is worth noting that the school is willing to provide development opportunities, though so far in a rather limited way, and also that management is responsive to proposals from the teachers' group – an incipient symbiosis of individual and institutional opportunities.

Irina Petrov is one of 10 English language teachers attached to the Engineering Faculty of a large city university in central Europe. Other big departments, such as the School of Medicine, also have their own language teaching staff. There is no one section in which all English teachers of the university are based, with its own premises and resources. IP teaches for 16 hours per week, with an average class size of 15–20, although this is likely to increase. Students range from first year undergraduates to postgraduates (and even staff) hoping to spend a period in an English-speaking country. There is a growing demand for English throughout the country, following the rapid pace of political and social change in eastern and central Europe. IP is expected to produce her own teaching materials geared to the needs of engineers. She typically writes tasks and exercises based on readings taken from subject-specific textbooks, sometimes drawing on English language teaching material published some years ago and focusing on specialist terminology. The only material otherwise available is a small collection of commercially produced coursebooks donated by publishers or bought from the Faculty's limited budget. IP has once visited the UK, on a three-week Summer School for teachers.

---

[2] Association of Recognised English Language Services, the largest national organization of language schools in Britain.

Comment: There are a number of attractive aspects to working in a situation like that of IP. There is a clear subject-specific focus and therefore an obvious direction for research and development; students are highly motivated; and hours of work and class size are at the moment manageable, leaving time outside formal contact hours for course and materials planning. At the same time the environment is professionally narrowed by the lack of feasibility in making contacts with English teachers in other fields, and there is not yet either a clear policy for materials purchase and development, nor an opportunity for IP to follow a systematic course of training in this area. Expectations and reality may not be entirely in line with each other here.

Antonio Lopes is a tertiary-level college teacher who has just returned to Brazil after spending a year in Britain completing an MA in TEFL on a scholarship from the British Council. During his year away he studied a wide range of subjects, from principles of language and language learning through to more applied areas of methodology. He became particularly interested in reading skills, and hopes eventually to develop his small-scale MA dissertation into a research proposal for a PhD, which will involve large-scale sampling and statistical analysis of data. Meanwhile, he has returned to his old job, which involves teaching English to young college students. The college itself is one of several in the region that has been instrumental in implementing a major ESP reading project, which has also attracted a lot of external and consultancy support. Staff are encouraged to participate in the project, to attend and give presentations at relevant conferences, and to contribute to publications. If AL manages to achieve his ambition of gaining a PhD, he will be eligible for promotion to the university, where his job specification will include a research requirement in addition to classroom teaching.

Comment: AL has had a major opportunity to work in his own field at quite a high level away from the day-to-day rigours of the classroom, to come into professional contact with ELT worldwide via his peers on the MA programme, and to deal in theories and ideas not always directly related to his work that may simply have been stimulating for their own sake (for some people: for others they may have been felt to be 'irrelevant'). He has obviously become interested in research methodology as such, partly motivated by the career structure in his own country and the existence of a major and well-established project.

David French is an expatriate teacher working in a medium-sized language school in Korea after a degree and experience in other parts of the world. His contract obliges him to teach a variety of classroom courses mainly for adults wishing to pursue business opportunities abroad, and some who are candidates for proficiency tests enabling them to study in North America and Australia in particular. It also requires him to engage in research and development in areas which should loosely be of commercial benefit to the school, and a small part of his working week is reserved for such activity. Many of the courses lead to external certification via the Test of English for International Communication (TOEIC), the Test of English as a Foreign Language (TOEFL) and to a small extent the International English Language Testing System (IELTS), and company sponsors also specify relevant competence which they wish their employees to attain. The school is well resourced, with materials from foreign publishing houses mainly in the USA. There are adequate but not purpose-built teaching rooms, and plenty of educational technology in the form of language laboratories, video facilities, computing services and a self-access centre.

Comment: For some, DF has an enviable work situation. However, the company's enlightened policy on research and development does not include research training, and the busy timetable makes collaborative projects with other teachers very difficult to organize. Consequently initiating and sustaining a research project within the school involve major headaches and difficulties, leading to a degree of frustration among those who are interested. Time out in the form of a course of study leading to a higher degree affords time for re-appraisal and re-orientation, and the nurturing of a researchable project.

Carol Turner teaches English as a Second Language as a special needs teacher in a provincial English town. She is attached to the Local Education Authority and goes into whichever schools in the area require her expertise to give additional help to the pupils who have language problems. There is a substantial number of ethnic minority families in the district and some of the children are losing out on mainstream education because of their difficulties with English. Most of the children need help with their reading proficiency, some also have difficulties with oral work. She mostly works with individual pupils but runs some group sessions in a couple of schools she visits. As a special needs teacher she works with pupils identified as needing her expertise by the schools concerned, but the nature of the job is peripatetic and she is a (welcome) visitor rather than a core member of staff at any of the schools. She works with the pupils for as long as is necessary to return them productively to the mainstream classes. She has access to all the relevant records, and is able to consult the teachers and the parents concerned. She rarely teaches a whole class, but is often invited to staffrooms to advise.

Comment: CT, who has a rather special kind of experience, has the opportunity and the inclination to do research in her situation, but the very opportunities offered by her peripatetic access to all the schools in her district mean she has very little time. Her own position has been under threat from budgetary constraints and education cutbacks, but the problems her learners have do not go away, and neither has the number of such disadvantaged learners reduced. She sees scope for research into both the individual students' learning difficulties and into the institutional system of support for such pupils in the area.

Patterns of research: implications

The professional world of teachers encompasses many and varied attitudes, behaviours, expectations, actors, possibilities, pressures and constraints. Any specific research profile will therefore inevitably be linked at the least to questions such as who initiates the research; who carries it out; how if at all its outcomes are reported; its content and focus; where it takes place; how many people are involved; what the control and decision points are; its timescale; its funding source; and its possible applications. We argue, then, both here and subsequently, that research involvement by practising teachers is not restricted to any one particular paradigm, but can take place along a number of different and interacting dimensions. We offer in this section an overview of what can and does happen: Fig. 1.1 is an attempt to sum up the discussion in diagrammatic form rather than offer a comprehensive model, and anyway does not at this stage include much comment on methodology.

We use simple present forms in opening assertions in the interests of being straightforward, but they should be taken to stand for what is both actual and potential.

1. Research is sometimes carried out by external agents. These may be officially appointed, perhaps by a Ministry of Education, to undertake a large-scale project across a number of schools. These 'agents' may alternatively be university-based researchers who visit an institution just to collect data, initial formulation and subsequent analysis and write-up being done elsewhere. Teachers are often the objects of such research rather than participants, and may well not have sight of the final outcome. There are, however, many examples of this 'outsider research' that involve teachers more closely both in formulation and direction – if not in conception – allowing, as it were, their voices to be heard. (The work of Allwright, 1988, is an example of this and, as we shall see later, belongs in a tradition of largely naturalistic and interpretive research.)

2. Research is initiated at a higher administrative level outside the institution but is actually carried out by its staff *in situ*. This is often the case in a centralized education system, where national or local government specifies what it wants to find out (such as the efficacy of communicative teaching methodology, or the merits and drawbacks of newly introduced materials). In this case particularly there is an obvious issue of the 'ownership' of research topic

and methodology, in that these are largely out of the control of individual teachers. In some ways KM fits into this perspective.

3. Research is initiated by teachers themselves perceiving queries, problems and gaps in their own practice and setting about finding solutions. Choice of topic and methodology are then up to the individual. This may, either entirely or more usually within limits, be

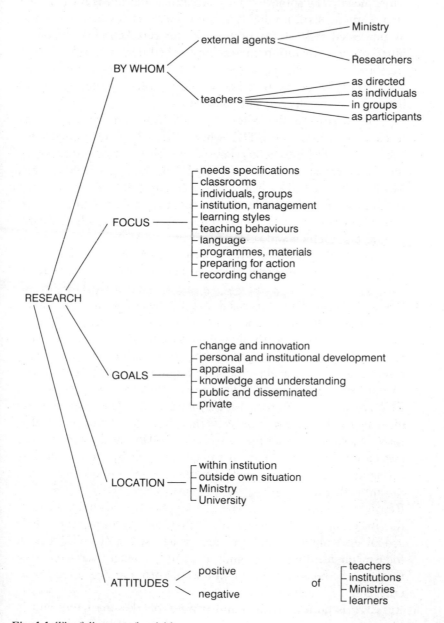

Fig. 1.1 The full range of variables

supported by the employer, perhaps to the extent of providing facilities, funding, or some teaching time off in lieu. The institution may
actually encourage research by teachers, both for their and its own
benefit, whilst not making it mandatory. AB is one of the teachers
who works in this kind of environment, where 'bottom-up' opportunities are available.

4. More negatively, some working situations discourage a research
stance among staff, implicitly if not even overtly, whether because
of perceived lack of time, attitudes to 'research' in relation to
other duties, disruption to teaching schedules, hierarchical bar-
riers and so on. This particular scenario is wryly documented by
Walker (1985: 192–3), together with a list of suggested strategies
to circumvent such apparent constraints.

5. Equally negatively, the whole idea of 'research' is rejected by
teachers (even, as with DF, where the school encourages it),
because they feel it to be 'irrelevant' to their practice and as something that 'researchers' do – the 'big R', in Boomer's (1987) terms.
More particularly, they lack a broad and articulated view of what
research is and what it can do for them – and what they can do
which will 'count' as research. This perception, which compart-
mentalizes teaching and research, is significant and widespread. It
has also been pivotal in the re-orientation of educational and
applied linguistic research that we start to explore in detail in
Chapter 2.

6. Research is sometimes carried out by teachers working alone,
sometimes with one or more peers in a research team, and sometimes collaboratively with outside researchers where the differing
perspectives come together in the formulation of an agreed
research agenda. Learners, too, may be included in the enterprise.
(A number of possibilities for such two- and three-way research in
ELT are set out in Nunan, 1992a, for example.) It is characteristic
of many teacher-research projects that they are institutional rather
than individual, sometimes involving collaboration across state
and national borders. Many of the benefits felt by the participants
accrue from the experience of working on common problems with
distant colleagues.

7. Research, as was flagged in the introduction to this book, takes as
its object of study classrooms, individuals, groups, the whole
school environment, management styles, self and colleagues; it
focuses on learning styles and strategies, learner characteristics,
teaching methods and behaviours, whole programmes or compon-
ents, language, materials and so on.

8. Research is both individual and private, on the one hand, and in
the public domain, on the other. In other words, teachers may

undertake an investigation for themselves in their own classroom, or they may consider the outcome or indeed the process to be of sufficient interest to share with others in an appropriate forum – meetings, conferences, journals and the like.

9. There are many possible motivations for undertaking research, including a wish to effect change and innovation, however small-scale, course evaluation, personal or institutional development, or simply a desire for knowledge and understanding. Some externally controlled research is, of course, also driven by an appraisal ethos where staff themselves are monitored, evaluated and judged.

10. Teachers also do research outside their working environment by, for example, undertaking postgraduate study at Masters or PhD level. Such research may or may not be directly related to their own situation and may or may not be intended to be taken back and applied there. In AL's case, the study period abroad has served pragmatically to satisfy promotion chances and to feed directly into an ongoing large-scale project, but also more broadly to encourage personal intellectual development. Such research may not, however, always be done entirely on a teacher's own volition, in the sense that it is just another requirement attached to their job description. Moreover, to the extent that it forms a research training, the methods and format required of a doctoral candidate may or may not be suitable for conducting contextual research in a working teaching environment.

Conclusion

This chapter has attempted to locate the discussion of appropriate research methods and to follow it within a view of the language teachers' world, with particular reference to English as a foreign/second language. It has recognized the diversity of that world by a small set of examples of teachers in action, who are of course fictitious, but who exhibit characteristics of context, opportunity and motivation which will be recognized by a number of real acquaintances and former students of ours. These examples could easily be multiplied, but they serve to illustrate several important features of the role of research and the attitudes of teachers and employers to research in the real world of institutional language teaching in many countries. Even these six examples show a striking diversity of opportunities and facilities for doing research, and incidentally of the roles of higher qualifications in this area. Some working contexts allow access to a single kind of classroom, others to a variety; some to one kind of course and teaching style, others to a variety. Some institutions are willing to sponsor research and give time but wish to see a tangible benefit, usually in terms of income or perhaps prestige; some regard research as a waste of income-generating time. Some teachers have the opportunity but no motivation for research, others motivation but no clear idea of what to do; others have projects they would like to follow but no opportunity.

Put another way, the chapter has tried to highlight the significance for what follows of such terms as the following.

Ownership

Who owns the ideas and the results of research? How does a classroom teacher come to feel ownership of a curriculum change?

Initiation

Getting a piece of research off the ground, having the idea, persuading colleagues to collaborate, obtaining sanctions and access from authorities, requires more time and energy than many teachers can spare.

Control

Both in the sense of taking control of one's own teaching situation, to the extent that is feasible, and in the sense of the discipline and stamina necessary to carry out a research project.

Relevance

Much Research with a big R is perceived by practitioners as irrelevant. This may be because the original connections of the research with practice have disappeared, or because it never originated in a classroom problem but within a related discipline. Teacher research can address relevant problems in their own context.

Subjects

This may refer to topics of interest, or more perniciously to the people from whom data is elicited.

Change

Much teacher research is about effecting and documenting change, in practice, in institutional systems, in methods.

Knowledge

All research is about finding out new knowledge; whether it is highly context-specific or generalizable depends on the aims and the methods of the research.

Discussion notes

NB Both here and throughout the book, discussion notes are offered simply as a stimulus to thinking further about the issues. They are not intended to be worked through rigorously, and should be regarded as an 'optional extra'.

1. Try to briefly describe your own teaching context or one of which you have experience along the lines of the six 'instances' set out in this chapter. Then construct your own commentary, highlighting both the most interesting and indeed frustrating aspects of the job, and then reflecting on the research opportunities inherent or perhaps explicitly available in that situation. If you are working in a group together with other teachers, you might find it fruitful to have someone else read and comment your own 'instance', and to do the same for them.

2. What is your own position in relation to the much-quoted idea of *research relevance*? For example, do you have experience of research either yourself or as done by others? Do you feel that for teachers in our field there is some kind of sliding scale of 'relevance'? And – if so – what kinds of topics would fit in at various points of your personal spectrum?

2

The teacher researcher in focus

Introduction

A view of the teacher as an extended professional whose portfolio of activities can in principle encompass an enquiring attitude leading to research is an intuitively attractive one. In its most basic formulation, it carries the clear implication that 'research' is not only something that is done 'on' or 'to' teachers, but is also an undertaking in which they can themselves be actively involved, by for example identifying interesting or problematic issues and topics, choosing suitable investigative instruments, and pursuing answers and outcomes. Teachers are therefore more in control in such a perspective, closer to the sources of decision-making and – in the current jargon – have greater 'ownership' of their own professional environment.

We shall see in subsequent chapters of this part of the book that research by teachers, both in practice and in its theoretical underpinnings, is complex and indeed controversial, directly impinging on such fundamental research questions as validity, generalizability and the nature of its contribution to a wider store of knowledge. These chapters will also comment more fully on derivations from research in anthropology and social science in particular. First, however, it is necessary in this chapter to show that research by teachers is embedded in a number of broader traditions in education, and in the course of the present discussion we shall be concerned with the much-mentioned question of the relationship between 'theory' and 'practice' and the 'relevance' of the former; with the nature and role in research of teaching conceived of as 'action', and with the possibilities inherent in teacher research for effecting educational change.

The present chapter, then, is largely descriptive and historical, the delineation of a concept. First of all we set the scene by examining the crucial notion of 'reflection' in helping to define what is meant by research in a practical professional context. There follows an overview of the background to some of these arguments in mainstream education, including the important tradition of 'action research'. The last main sections of the chapter discuss and illustrate teacher research in our own field of ELT, including an examination of how key concepts have started to permeate teacher training and education programmes.

Action and reflection

Brumfit and Mitchell, in their introductory chapter to a collection of papers that takes a very broad view of research possibilities in language classrooms, make the following assertion: 'There is a particularly strong contradictory pull [between research and teaching] in that research is a type of contemplation ... while teaching is a type of action' (1989: 10). This is a standard and much-cited polarization (and incidentally represents a view to which the Brumfit and Mitchell volume does not on the whole sub-scribe): it places the terms 'action' and 'contemplation' (or 'reflection'), teaching and research, in two quite distinct and incompatible universes. We can, on the one hand, visualize a teacher whose only concern is to follow a real-time lesson plan to take his or her lower intermediate class through to the next level, and, on the other, a researcher using amassed data to develop some new element in the theory of second language acquisition. This is, of course, a caricature of a situation in which teacher and researcher appar-ently have no meeting place and quite different agendas.

The following section shows how the terms 'action' and 'reflection' have been not only juxtaposed but amalgamated to provide a principled founda-tion for research by teachers: the whole, in other words, will be seen to be more than the sum of its two constituent parts. The argument hinges around the idea that reflecting on action allows the development of a crit-ical distance from the real-time action itself.

Research as reflection

The terms are now considered here specifically from a practitioner's per-spective. An obvious starting point for exploring the interface between action and reflection is teachers' professional knowledge about the central aspects of their jobs. The preceding chapter offered a range of possible 'action contexts' for the ELT profession, from which it can readily be gleaned that teachers 'know about' coursebooks, other materials, audio-visual resources, syllabuses, proficiency levels, examinations, working with colleagues, classrooms, methodology, individual learners, and many other aspects. Bolster (1983) characterizes the nature of much of this kind of knowledge as 'idiographic' and 'particularistic', primarily concerned, in other words, with the uniqueness and specificity of events and individuals in one's own professional context – although knowledge of materials, or examinations, and so on is of course potentially transferable and not only situation-specific. Teachers, then, are not on the whole concerned with large-scale comparisons across different situations. Rather, as Bolster (1983: 298) puts it: 'Every teacher ... knows that although there are many similarities between classes, each group has its own special characteristics, and that successful teaching requires the recognition ... of this uniqueness.' This should not be taken to imply that teachers are by definition unable to deal with other kinds of knowledge, merely that everyday professional life has certain typical epistemological attributes.

It is essentially from this knowledge base of everyday action that Schön (1983) developed his seminal theory of the 'reflective practitioner' in the book of the same name. His work, although concerned with the professions in general, has been extremely influential in the formulation of the teacher-researcher paradigm because it lies at the root of the idea that reflection is much more than just 'thinking about': he has shown that it can be rigorously conceptualized to provide firm and appropriate research principles that are in tune with the teacher's reality. Schön is critical of a view (of 'technical rationality') that assumes that theory merely needs to be applied in order to be of use to practitioners on the grounds that 'there is a swampy lowland where situations are confusing messes incapable of technical solution' (p. 42). He argues instead not that scientific method is inherently 'wrong' but that the unique and the particular are best dealt with by converting a professional's tacit *knowing-in-action* to an explicit *reflection-in-action*, so that 'when someone reflects-in-action, he becomes a researcher in the practice context' (p. 68). This is the amalgamation referred to at the beginning of this section, where doing and thinking are interwoven. There are parallels here with Giroux's (1988) view of the teacher as a 'transformative intellectual', a participant engaged in critical thinking: he argues strongly in favour of 'theory' to 'enable teachers to see what they are seeing'. In terms of our own profession this might imply, for example, a teacher becoming interested in the learning habits of an individual and carrying out a case study (and then perhaps others), when a more generalized theory of second language acquisition patterns would be less obviously applicable. Part 2 of this book will be exploring in much more detail the translation of these general principles into viable research methodologies: reflecting is the basis for research, not the research itself.

Theory, practice and relevance

It might be useful to take a brief pause for thought at this point. On the face of it, the dialectical relationship of *research* to *action* that has just been briefly outlined seems to challenge head-on the frequently referred-to, almost clichéd dichotomy of 'theory versus practice'. It is also common to describe it as a relationship of *reflexivity*, where elements are mutually illuminating (see, for example, Bolster, 1983; Hammersley and Atkinson, 1983). The dichotomy, on the other hand, is usually expressed in negative terms, and can be experienced as resistance to what is perceived as professionally irrelevant: a lecture on schema theory (for instance), however intellectually stimulating, does not inherently reach the teacher *qua* practitioner in his or her day-to-day sphere of action, nor are articles on universal grammar (for instance) of obvious immediate applicability when planning tomorrow's lesson for the lower intermediate group working through *Headway*.

The situation described here, however, is still not entirely straightforward. First of all, there are increasing signs that the reflective paradigm is itself forming the basis for a new and unhelpful dichotomy where teacher research (or 'action research', as will be clarified in the next section) is being advocated *in opposition to* researcher research and technical rationality. We discuss this in more depth in Chapter 4. Second, if the notion of reflection in action as the basis for research on practice does challenge researchers to redefine relevance and application, at the same time it undermines an attitude to teaching that sees it merely as 'craft knowledge' to be acquired as a set of usable techniques: in our own field, how to set up a role play, or deal with errors, or activate grammar, and so on. This point is particularly well made by Elliott (1991: 45–8). In a short chapter entitled 'The theory-practice problem', he tries to explain why teachers feel threatened by theory. (1) It symbolizes the power of the researcher to define valid knowledge (2) this knowledge is often couched in the form of generalizations so that localized experience is invalidated; and (3) there is an implication that teachers are inadequate because they do not conform to idealized models of curriculum. There is, however, a sting in the tail in Elliott's argument, because 'theory' and 'research' protect teachers' practices as individual realms of private, esoteric, intuitive craft knowledge, and it is precisely these conservative values that are also threatened by what he calls 'the new concept of professionalism embodied in the action-research movement', the 'counter-culture to the traditional craft culture', and the complex belief systems that are built up to become part of the professional ethos. What Elliott is taking issue with is the idea of craft knowledge as sufficient in itself, not of course with action-knowledge as generative and as the basis for research. Furthermore, this 'idiographic' kind of knowledge is concerned with skills and techniques, but also with the judgement needed to apply them appropriately (Pennington, 1990). From another perspective, it can also be classified into subject-matter knowledge (grammar, functions, topics, situations and so on in our field) versus content-independent 'action system' knowledge (Day, 1990). In other words, we need to be wary of regarding 'craft knowledge' as a monolithic concept. Elliott's view resonates in Schön: 'When practice is a repetitive administration of techniques to the same kinds of problems, the practitioner may look to leisure as a source of relief, or to early retirement; but when he functions as a researcher-in-practice, the practice itself is a source of renewal' (1983: 299).

To return now to the central purpose of this chapter, it will be useful to recap the arguments for teacher-initiated research, because they are a starting point both for the remainder of this largely descriptive chapter, and for our subsequent discussions on the parameters of research as a concept. These advantages are clearly set out in Beasley and Riordan (quoted in Nunan, 1989: 17–18) and are cited (almost) in full here:

- It begins with and builds on the knowledge that teachers have already accumulated.
- It focuses on the immediate concerns of classroom teachers.
- It matches the subtle organic process of classroom life.
- It builds on the 'natural' processes of evaluation and research which teachers carry out daily.
- It bridges the gap between understanding and action by merging the role of researcher and practitioner.
- It sharpens teachers' critical awareness through observation, recording and analysis of classroom events.
- It helps teachers better articulate teaching and learning processes to their colleagues and interested community members.
- It bridges the gap between theory and practice.

A short educational excursion

The teacher-researcher movement has a much longer tradition in mainstream education than in ELT: as long ago as 1970, for instance, Cane and Schroeder published a monograph analysing via questionnaire data the kinds of research teachers would like to see carried out and ways in which they might themselves become involved. Although their work focused as much on teachers having a say in research done by others as on the teacher as active researcher, it laid important foundations for subsequent developments. It is, then, the educational background that has largely provided the feeder into current work in ELT, and this section will now set out some of the key factors in that process.

In the UK, probably the major figure in stimulating both the principle and practice of teacher research was Stenhouse, formerly Professor of Education at the University of East Anglia (itself one of the best-known centres internationally of applied educational research). As expressed in his seminal book *An introduction to curriculum research and development* (1975), Stenhouse was very critical of an end-product, objectives model of education because 'it assesses without explaining' (p. 120). He advocated instead a process perspective which takes knowledge as 'the focus of speculation, not the object of mastery' (p. 85), in other words as evolving rather than preformed. From this he developed a view of the teacher as an extended, not a restricted, professional, engaged directly in the discovery and creation of knowledge through the medium of the school curriculum and their own involvement with it. Research, then, is 'the means towards a disciplined intuition, fusing creativeness and self-criticism' (p. 223).

A great deal of the discussion of teachers as researchers has been clearly allied to the concept of action research. Although this linkage is a rather loose and somewhat diffuse association rather than an equation, so much educational research has been carried out under this heading that it will be convenient to conflate the terms at this point as essentially belonging within the same paradigm.

Action research: background and principles

The field of action research is a broad and complex one, and there is only space here to pick out the features that have been most salient in educational terms, although its philosophical underpinnings and its expression in research methods will be evident in subsequent chapters. The term itself is usually attributed to Kurt Lewin, a German social psychologist who, working in the USA in the 1930s and 1940s, sought to develop a research methodology based on people's real-world experience that he felt experimental methods were unable to address. He is particularly quoted for his work with factory apprentices, where he was able to show the highest level of output in the subgroup that was allowed to formulate its own 'action plan' of production: this was felt to provide a persuasive argument in favour of group decision-making (Adelman, 1991; McNiff, 1988). Lewin was also concerned with other kinds of social groups, including the subcultures of USA city life: it is important to note that action research has maintained this broad framework of reference, and is applied in many areas of work and social life as well as education (hospitals, prisons, and so on). Following Lewin, there has been much discussion of definitions and models of action research. Centrally, it is conceived in terms of a self-reflective spiral, or cycle:

Initial idea → fact-finding → action plan → implementation → monitoring → revision → amended plan → and so on through the cycle.

To put this briefly in context, in ELT this could be taken to mean, for example, that a teacher is concerned about apparently different uptake on coursebook activities, collects data via observation, field notes and questionnaires, decides to vary the sequence of presentation, monitors success rates and quality of response, and so on until some useful changes have been effected. (A useful discussion of the principal models – Kemmis and McTaggart, 1988; Elliott, 1991 – can be found in Hopkins, 1993: Ch. 4).

The most quoted (even over-quoted) definition of action research is that of Carr and Kemmis: 'a form of *self-reflective* enquiry undertaken by *participants* in social *situations* in order to *improve* the rationality and justice of their own practices, their understanding of these practices, and the situations in which the practices are carried out' (1986: 162, italics added). From this definition, at least indirectly, flow the essential characteristics of 'pure' action research:

- it is participant-driven and reflective
- it is collaborative
- it leads to change and the improvement of practice, not just knowledge in itself
- it is context-specific.

These by no means always obtain so strictly, which is one reason why action research and teacher research more generally often take on convergent characteristics.

Some applications

The educational literature contains large numbers of reports of teacher-research and action-research projects, both modest and ambitious. Many derive directly from teachers themselves (see, for example, the reports in Hopkins, 1993; Goswami and Stillman, 1987; Hustler *et al.*, 1986). Others – a little paradoxically perhaps – have been generated and run by educational researchers. Among the best known of these are the large-scale Humanities Curriculum Project, initiated in the 1970s by Stenhouse with the overall aim of changing teaching strategies to give pupils more involvement in their own learning. Another example is provided by the Ford Teaching Project (Elliott and Adelman, 1975; Elliott, 1991), primarily concerned with the implementation of discovery methods in the classroom; and yet another by the Open University/Schools Council *Curriculum in action* project (1981), concerned with the kinds of questions teachers can ask, and the techniques they can use, to investigate their own classrooms. A number of these researchers, particularly Elliott, were also instrumental in the foundation of the Classroom Action Research Network (CARN, University of East Anglia) which, as its name implies, disseminates information on teacher research.

Much of the educational research that we have touched on here is self-evidently concerned with teachers and learners in classrooms, often with microstudies of very specific aspects of this context. However, action research in particular is also concerned with broader curriculum issues, and often with the administration and management of schools and institutional change (Hutchinson and Whitehouse, 1986; Lomax, 1990).

To take us into the final section of this chapter, it is instructive to note the kind of language used to explain the central tenets of action research. A glance at the extensive literature reveals such terms as:

- empowerment
- hierarchy
- power
- emancipation
- subversive
- change
- *status quo*
- enfranchisement
- reactionary
- intervention
- destabilization.

This, then, is some of the thinking that has informed mainstream national education and its associated training patterns. We now turn to an examination of the implications for ELT.

Teacher research and English language teaching

The purpose of this final section is to chart some of the ways in which the teacher-research ethos has come to be expressed in the teaching of English as a foreign/second language. Partly because of the nature of ELT as a worldwide profession operating in an enormous variety of different political, social and cultural contexts, it is, as we tried to portray in Chapter 1, a many-headed hydra with obvious problems of generalization compared with the national education system of any one country. Clearly the influence on ELT of the 'applied linguistic' tradition has been of paramount importance in terms of the design of teaching programmes, and it is part of the job of this book to explore possibilities for the uptake by teachers of this kind of research. For the purpose of the present chapter, however, we shall look, first, at the 'reflective' paradigm with particular reference to teacher education, and then at how this has been harnessed to the development of and research by practising teachers, often by invoking action research explicitly. We conclude the section by commenting on some of the more problematic issues raised in the transplanting and application of teacher-research and action-research models in ELT.

Reflective models in language teacher training

It is usual to make a distinction between 'teacher training' and 'teacher education', often in parallel to pre- versus in-service training. Looked at in another way, teachers are expected to acquire both a trainable 'repertoire of skills' (Pennington, 1990) and more generatively the educated judgement to apply and transfer those skills. Elliott comments more critically on the mechanistic aspects of competency-based training, quoting Pearson's distinction between 'habitual' and 'intelligent' skill knowledge, the latter allowing for discernment, discrimination and intelligent action. Since a 'reflective' view has influenced both areas, they are conflated here as 'training': in any case Bolster's (1983) analysis of the nature of teachers' knowledge as the basis for research remains appropriate whether that knowledge is already acquired or embryonic. Language teacher training programmes, then – whether short courses, introductory, or at advanced postgraduate level – are likely to contain a variety of types of input from explanation of techniques ('craft knowledge'), such as use of visuals, or using class readers, to information on applied linguistic research outcomes ('technical rationality'), such as the psychology of learning, linguistics, sociolinguistics. Increasingly, however, attention is being paid to the kind of perspective outlined in the preceding sections of this chapter.

Wallace (1991), drawing directly on the work of Schön, puts forward three current models in language teacher training: (1) the essentially imitative Craft Model, when trainees learn from experts; (2) the Applied Science Model (Schön's 'technical rationality'), a one-way procedure often leading to the much-criticized separation between research and practice; and (3) the Reflective Model, where knowledge is experiential rather than received. Although he argues that all three are necessary, particularly the reciprocity between (2) and (3), he is mainly concerned to explore the potential inherent in (3), and much of his book is an attempt to establish this as a coherent framework for training: 'research' is then seen as a logical extension of reflective practice. One might consider, for example, training procedures for the introduction of communicative methodology, or for teaching reading comprehension (see Fig. 2.1).

It is Wallace's contention that *reflective* training would be concerned both with a critical evaluation of techniques in context, and with an understanding of the reciprocity of received knowledge and classroom experience (1991: 55).

	Communicative methodology	Reading comprehension
Craft knowledge	Pair/group work Role play Building conversations Question and answer Useful phrases Games	Pre-questions Use of pictures Guessing in context Predicting Skimming and scanning Jumbletexts
Applied science	Semantico-grammatical categories Notions, functions Text and discourse Theories of communicative competence	Schema theory Psychological processing models Top-down/bottom-up strategies Perception and cognition

Fig. 2.1

A comparable approach is offered by Richards and Lockhart (1994), essentially a pre- and in-service training manual for reflective teaching. It starts from the assumptions that teachers 'know' a great deal about teaching, that their practice is based on many assumptions and beliefs, in other words that all teachers have a 'personal construct' but that 'unaware' experience alone is insufficient for development. Arguing for the central importance of critical reflection, they identify the range of the language teacher's domains of operation and propose a variety of approaches to enhance practitioners' explorations of their own teaching. These approaches – observation, questionnaires, audio and video recording, diaries – are among those discussed in Part 2 of this book. There are many other reports in the ELT literature of the use of the reflective paradigm in teacher training: see for example Swan (1993); Belleli (1993); Ellis (1993); Thornbury (1991).

Any discussion of teacher training programmes has implications at some point for the nature of supervision of trainees and the supervisor's role, and there are a number of interesting ways in which reflective approaches can be incorporated in this area of activity. Obviously a major goal of the supervisor-supervisee relationship is the learning and improvement of practice – action knowledge – rather than the formulation of overt research plans, but again the notion of reflection-in-action potentially allows the development of a research stance as an integral part of training. Handal and Lauvås devote a whole book to the relationship between supervision and reflective teaching. Their main thesis, and one which has clear kinship with the educational framework and the notion of a 'personal construct' outlined in this chapter, is that 'every teacher possesses a "practical theory" of teaching which is subjectively *the* strongest determining factor in her educational practice' (1987: 9). They promote a model of supervision derived from a counselling approach in which the starting point is this practical theory and teachers' own professional conditions: teachers then retain some control over, and ownership of, the whole process. Smith (1995) discusses an experiment in introducing guided and self-directed reflection as part of a teacher-training course. The course involved diary-keeping, planned time gaps between supervision and feedback for self-reflection, and involvement in action research. Smith comments on the enthusiasm of the trainees and on the levels of reflection they achieved: from practical solutions through theoretical questioning to changing attitudes or general educational orientation.

This view is echoed strongly in the related notion of 'clinical supervision', carried out by systematic observation and following a cyclical process of pre-observation (the 'planning conference'), observation, and post-observation (the 'feedback conference'). It is a model that is essentially collaborative rather than more traditionally directive, involving supervisor-trainee teacher in formulating together a hypothesis about problematic areas in the teacher's classroom practice, analysing the lesson, and proposing changes that could be implemented in future classes. The procedure is rooted in the teacher's own needs and problems, and can lead to the systematic investigation of aspects of teachers, learners, classrooms – to research in the sense that the term is used throughout this chapter.

Research and teacher development

'The shift in terminology from "education" to "development" is significant because it marks a shift in perception.' Although Swan (1993: 243) is here talking about student teachers specifically, she is indirectly making the more general point that teacher research has taken much of its impetus from the congruence of 'reflection' and 'development'. Over the last decade or so, the notion of teacher development has become prominent in ELT: it portrays teachers as active and questioning professionals willing to reflect and change in a long-term way over the course of their whole careers and not only when engaging in explicit training programmes. This whole area has been incorporated into various teachers' organizations, one of the largest being IATEFL (The International Association of Teachers of English as a Foreign Language). IATEFL has a number of Special Interest Groups ('SIGs'), one of which is concerned with Teacher Development (TD) (McDonough and Shaw, 1993). Its regular newsletters give a flavour of the wide range of professional-personal areas which its title subsumes, including cooperative development, training programmes, attendance at workshops, action-research projects, self-understanding, research with large classes, staff development, learning a new language, and many more.

Somewhat more recently, the linkage between teacher development, teacher research and action research in ELT has been made increasingly explicit, in particular by making connections with parallel trends both within and beyond education. The most concrete and significant illustration of this is provided by the collection of conference papers entitled, with deliberate ambiguity (if a little grammatical inaccuracy), *Teachers Develop Teachers Research* (Edge and Richards, 1993). (The second 'TDTR' conference was held in 1995 and, at the time of writing, a third is planned for 1997.) The collection - like the subsequent conferences – incorporates reports on small-scale, personal and collaborative projects by ELT practitioners, but also discusses principles and definitions, as well as drawing on teacher-research traditions in mainstream education and staff development patterns in, for example, large multinational companies.

The current burgeoning of teacher research in ELT has, not surprisingly, an international dimension: just the few publications cited in this section so far describe work being undertaken in – for instance – Poland, Romania, Cuba, Britain, Uruguay, Estonia, Sweden, Austria, Argentina ... the list could be considerably extended. Further instances are provided by the extensive work carried out in the USA, both in ELT and in mother-tongue education (Chamot, 1995; Goswami and Stillman, 1987; Green and Wallatt, 1981; Strickland, 1988). Australia has been particularly prominent in the development of large-scale, collaborative teacher-research projects, to a large extent in the context of the Adult Migrant Education Programme (AMEP), described by Nunan (1992a) in an extended case study. The collection *Teachers' Voices* (Burns and Hood, 1995) presents the published outcomes of a national action-research project designed to investigate the impact of newly introduced curriculum frameworks. Burns' introductory paper convincingly explains the reasons for the choice of the action-research model in a context of educational change, its associated methodology, and the constraints (of time, recognition, expertise) on practising teachers involved in such research.

There are, then, many instances of English language teachers worldwide becoming involved in research in their own contexts and classrooms, and it is clear that this is a rapidly growing field. At the same time, a number of practitioners have attempted to examine more broadly the principles on which research in ELT is based. Brindley (1990) sets out an ambitious 'research agenda' which, although intended initially to be applied in Australia, has wider implications. His paper, after rehearsing the background arguments in favour of teacher involvement, discusses TESOL research in terms of:

- initiation, execution and dissemination
- purposes
- recipients
- areas of study
- planning, data collection, monitoring
- follow-up

from the varied perspectives of teachers, learners and administrators.

For the practising teacher, these published reports of context-bound research projects make stimulating reading, and involvement in such projects is undoubtedly professionally and personally developmental. Nevertheless we leave this brief overview on a cautionary note (and one which looks ahead to Chapter 3 where the teacher-research ethos is examined more critically). It is simply this: in encouraging a research stance by teachers and arguing for its benefits, there is a need to be alert to the danger of establishing a research paradigm so 'alternative' that it fossilizes an either/or attitude in which researcher research is too often rejected. Brindley (1990: 8) makes this point almost in passing: 'Both "basic" research ... and "applied" research ... will have a role to play. Moreover, it is not as if the results of basic research are never mobilized to solve practical problems', and he goes on to quote Lett: 'applied research without a theoretical base can be random, inefficient and confusing, while basic research without the requisite applied research has little or no positive effect on practice.' We will examine this distinction more closely in Chapter 3.

Discussion

There are many implications to be drawn from approaches to research in mainstream education for the field of ELT, and we have also noted some aspects of the internationalism, even internationalization, of the so-called teacher-research movement. However, one of the central tenets of this kind of research, namely the importance of context, is at the same time problematic in evaluating research opportunities realistically. Chapter 1 outlined just a few of the working environments and roles of English language teachers, and the concomitant differing possibilities inherent in those contexts for doing research or simply expanding one's professional activities. ELT takes place in private institutions, colleges, universities, primary and secondary schools throughout the world, so we are inevitably dealing with an enormous diversity of culture, social structures, political institutions and educational frameworks that is very different from the kind of national system from which much of teacher and action research is derived. No one interpretation of the paradigm can therefore be universally applicable or generalizable, nor is the paradigm itself necessarily a panacea always leading to growth and innovation.

A little earlier in this chapter, we noted some of the terminology that is typically used to characterize action research – empowerment, destabilization, change and the like. Indeed, it is one of the goals of action research in particular to challenge entrenched structures of power and authority, to subvert autocratic and top-down decision-making procedures, and 'to [emancipate] individuals from the domination of unexamined assumptions embodied in the *status quo*' (Crookes, 1993: 131), a clear echo of Freire's (1972) radical position. Clearly, however, this view of research is not value-free but heavily value-laden so, given that values differ across contexts, self-evidently cannot be directly transplanted.

Even Somekh's (1993: 37) apparent compromise position would be inappropriate in many contexts: 'To have an impact on institutional development, individuals at different levels in the formal and informal power hierarchies need to carry out action research collaboratively. Although this is clearly much easier to establish in democratic institutions, the problems in establishing some form of collaborative action research in a more hierarchical institution need to be balanced against the difficulties in bringing about development and change by any other means.' Teachers work within different kinds of management and institutional structure, and the locus of change varies accordingly. In Kenji Matsuda's situation, for instance, the fact that decisions about innovations in syllabus are made at Ministry level does not invalidate changes made in that environment, nor does it necessarily mean that individual teachers cannot undertake investigations into the pedagogy of their own classrooms. Conversely, a situation where a teacher can more readily effect changes does not necessarily mean that those changes will be appropriate and effective. Roberts (1993) rightly stresses the need for more empirical studies to evaluate the efficacy in context of the theoretical claims made for self-directed classroom-based research. He offers two such studies – one carried out in the UK, the other in Israel – that lead him to be cautious, though not pessimistic, about its general applicability. His mixed bag of conclusions is worth summarizing:

- Collaborative action research is just one of several processes that can enable teachers to look productively at their own action.
- Change throughout a whole school via teacher research depends on the extent to which teachers have the power (*sic*) to effect it, and is only partially under teacher control.
- Teacher research can be illuminative for the classroom context even if outside change is imposed at other levels.

In the worldwide profession of ELT, the nature and focus of teacher research, whether actual or potential, are clearly widely divergent, with very variable 'freeroom' (Handal and Lauvås, 1987). It will depend on such interwoven factors as the management structure of institutions and educational systems, on culturally and socially determined beliefs, assumptions and expectations, on teacher training patterns, on resources available, on opportunities, and on self-perception. Within each local interpretation, teachers can, as we have seen, investigate classroom interaction and behaviour, individual learners, colleagues, self, syllabuses and materials, whole school policies and so on, whether those investigations are intended to further knowledge and understanding, or whether they are more interventionist and oriented to change. It will be our task in Part 2 to explore the methodologies available for doing this.

Conclusion

This chapter has explored some key notions in the development of teacher research in English as a foreign language. The contrast between 'action' and 'reflection' was shown to be only apparent, and Schön's resolution of this in the concept of 'reflection in action' was taken to be a keystone supporting the whole venture. Teacher-initiated research in this tradition was seen to have established and venerable roots in mainstream education, and both the advantages and some dangers of this approach were aired:

on the positive side:

- the immediate relevance to classroom teachers' problems and modes of work
- the bridges built between theory and practice
- the development of critical awareness
- the appropriacy for subtle processes lived through by the participants
- the challenge to the comfortable 'craft knowledge' view;

and on the minus side:

- the unhelpful growth of oppositions between research by teachers and by researchers
- the difficulties of evaluating its ultimate effectiveness as an agent for either personal or institutional change.

The chapter then briefly reviewed the work in mainstream education using action research, and pointed out the aims, some of the achievements, and some of the language, of these mainly large-scale curriculum innovation projects. A major section of the chapter was devoted to the use of teacher research in English language teaching, bearing in mind particularly the worldwide nature of the enterprise and its involvement in so many different cultures and educational systems. We saw how the principles of reflective training are being applied by several different training-programme designers, and looked at examples of research by teachers working individually, institutionally or in teams, which have been carried out and are currently in progress in many countries. Finally, the problem of cultural and situational effectiveness of teacher research in worldwide ELT was raised. It may be difficult to introduce an approach whose power for innovation and change may be feared by local and governmental authorities, but its capacity for stimulating local change may yet be preferable to either conservatism or the importation of culturally inappropriate methods via the 'applied science' model of training.

Discussion notes

1. Assuming that research by teachers is a possibility in your own teaching situation, enumerate what you consider to be the main variables that would affect the kinds of topics that could be addressed, and the ways in which research could be implemented. For example, what can be done may be affected by factors such as the amount of responsibility you have; patterns of cooperation with colleagues; contacts outside your own institution; or the question of how change in policy and methodology comes about, and who initiates it.

2. To what extent is the specific concept of *action* research feasible in any working context(s) with which you are familiar? Is such an attitude an integral part of your professional environment, or is it regarded as undesirable in terms of the *status quo*?

3. Even if you do not label yourself as a 'researcher', what are the kinds of classroom-related and other professional issues on which you mainly find yourself reflecting? On individuals in your class? On your own teaching style? On the materials available to you? ... and so on.

3

What is research?

Introduction

In the last chapter, we saw that many teachers do have the motivation to do research, and the problems that need research, and that some teachers have the opportunity to do so. This chapter first steps back from the classroom to examine general ideas about what research means in various real-world contexts, and then looks at what research specifically in language teaching does, and what special characteristics such research displays. In what follows, we will compare and contrast views of research in other fields; evaluate common views about research in language teaching; discuss the contrast between basic and applied research; look at the relative importance of description and intervention in the context of the problem under investigation; and explore the differences between quantitative and qualitative kinds of research both in terms of methodology and also in terms of underlying assumptions. This will be followed in Chapter 4 by a fuller account of the criteria by which research itself is evaluated, with some discussion of how 'teacher research' compares with research by researchers (usually in universities), on those criteria. Chapter 4 will then go on to deal with some important general principles of research design.

General views

The view of research implicit in the foregoing chapters has been one of professional enquiry. In other fields, the term 'research' has other senses. One could draw a crude (and probably ultimately invalid) distinction between two senses of the word *research* in the ordinary language. In the first sense, the outcome of research is the establishment, publicizing, or utilization of something that somebody – not the researcher or the person commissioning it – already knows. In the second sense, the outcome is knowledge nobody had before. This is the general aim of academic research. The word research is used in different fields in one or other of these senses, and in some fields in both senses. The title of this book uses the word in this second sense: however, teachers may be involved in research in both senses in their professional lives.

Some examples of the first sense are the following:

Fiction

For many novelists, it is essential to prepare for their writing by researching the background in which they wish to set their narrative for accuracy of description, sensitivity to atmosphere, history of the period in which their fiction takes place and authenticity of the language. The final criterion for them is the authenticity and artistic conviction of the final product in their readers' eyes. Research in this sense may take many forms, and involve considerable expense in terms of effort, time, and money: but the originality of the novel does not lie in the research but in the artistic creation for which it provides a background.

Journalism

For journalists, especially in investigative journalism, long periods of time are spent researching their stories to uncover facts and secrets which their editorial policy judges to be in the public interest, and in cross-checking what they are told or discover to establish its truth. This is not usually new truth, but information otherwise not public or deliberately withheld by another person. For them, the final criterion of truth may be bound up with legalities: the laws of libel and slander, or the Official Secrets Act.

Police work

For the police, there is an obvious parallel between preparing a case against a suspect by detective work and research in this first sense: the criminal they seek has a secret which the police are bound to uncover. Here again, the criterion of validity of the research is circumscribed by the law: laws of evidence, police procedure, protection of the rights of the innocent, the criminal and the victim. However, it is interesting that in this connection the language prefers the term 'detection' or 'investigation' to research.

Business and commerce

In the commercial world, much money is invested in product development and even sponsorship of basic research, and here one is referring to the second sense as described above. However, research is also conducted into the people who will buy the products: market research. Market research is used to establish what can be sold and who will buy it, how a product can be packaged, advertised and priced to make it commercially attractive, and, linked to advertising campaigns, even to create a market – to persuade people to buy something they did not know they wanted. The final criterion for research in this field is not therefore simply truth – the description of a market situation – and the authentic expression of that truth, but also the success of an intervention or manipulation of the market measured usually in profit terms.

Some obvious examples of research in the second sense are the following:

Medical research

In the medical world, research is conducted at many levels, and, apart from the commercial aspects of competition to sell drugs, it includes methods of assessing diagnoses and treatments, drug development, side-effects, methods of general practice, methods of surgery, epidemiology and common and rare illnesses. This is research in the second sense: to find out things nobody knew before. The final criterion is the discovery of new truths, but also the translation of the new truths into practical treatments, and the developments of economies of scale so that the treatment is available for the largest number of people. Here ethical considerations receive a great deal of attention, both in terms of the human patients and the animals which are used for trials, but the ethics of research are important generally as well, as we shall see in greater detail later.

Science and technology

Everyone naturally associates research with science and technology, white coats and laboratories, but it should be remembered in this context that advances in the sciences are not restricted to the discovery of new facts: advances in theory development and in research methods and approaches occur in parallel. It is of course a commonplace, though nevertheless important, to highlight the ethics of the development of scientific knowledge, both in the process of gathering the knowledge and in the fields of application.

Before we turn to language teaching and language teachers, this simple-minded survey of research in other fields has shown that 'research' is used both for the discovery and publication of concealed knowledge and for the creation of new knowledge. There are different kinds of criteria which depend on the field; it is also involved in intervention and manipulation of its sphere of interest; and it raises considerable ethical implications both in the process and in the applications.

Language teaching

Language teachers also do research in the first sense, but do not tend to call it research, though what they do is analogous to what a journalist or doctor does in preparing for their professional activity. They have to:

- scan textbooks and libraries for appropriate examples of the language and targeted exercises to include in their intended lesson plans
- find materials for conveying the points they wish to make
- locate appropriate texts and examples
- check their understanding of grammatical, pragmatic and cultural descriptions in preparing explanations
- find out why students have made certain kinds of mistakes and why they have behaved in certain ways, and
- look for remedies.

In all of this they are guided by what will work with their particular students in their context. This is very like what a journalist, novelist or market researcher has to do, or even a general practitioner choosing an appropriate treatment for a patient with a particular set of symptoms and prehistory. It is concerned with detection, with authenticity, with utility, and in a sense with product development, if the teacher's classroom activity can be seen as a product which is delivered to the students.

This kind of 'research' (sense 1) usually lacks the elements of originality, innovation and theory-building which characterize research in the second sense. The argument elaborated in Chapter 2, however, strongly suggests that language teachers are uniquely placed to be involved in research in this second sense as well. There are many questions about language learning and teaching which can only be answered by investigations conducted in the normal context of teaching and learning. But getting involved in research (2) also incurs risks – of adding commitments of time and application, of altering the teacher researcher's conception of their professional activity, of challenging their understanding of their own and their students' context of work, of changing that context from the inside. As Elliott (1991) has said, such risks may be seen as threatening or be welcomed by the teachers themselves, their students and their employers, and therefore most teachers will want to undertake this kind of research with good preparation and a clear idea of what is going to be involved.

But what sorts of activities would be classed as this kind of research? Sometimes prospective research students propose course development projects as research for the degree of PhD, and they are often refused. Course development, though clearly an activity many teachers engage in outside their classroom teaching hours, and which may, obviously, involve innovation in many ways, is not primarily geared to discovering new knowledge, but rather, to encouraging the best performance out of the students.

However, the process of course development may, perhaps even should, involve research activity in three areas, because course development which is based on empirical evidence ought to be more successful. These three areas are needs analysis, delivery and evaluation. In each of these areas a teacher may simply use a pre-existing or even prescribed method, questionnaire or performance indicator to gather the information identified as necessary for the development of the course, or may approach the problem in an altogether more imaginative way which may be indistinguishable from the procedures of research in the second sense outlined at the beginning of the chapter.

Common views of what research in language teaching does

As part of a course in applied linguistics and English language teaching we regularly ask experienced teachers how they conceive of research, and we have polled teachers at an international conference on the same question (McDonough and McDonough, 1990). There are, of course, as many answers as there are respondents, but they tend to group around a number of popular issues. Attitudes to research in language teaching can also be sharply contradictory, with widely differing views between individuals, and sometimes within the same individual until he or she has sorted out a coherent view, usually after some experience of reading relevant research, for example on an MA course. Here follows a selection:

'Research is systematic and is based on data'

This attitude provokes several interesting questions. The reference to systematicity could imply the application of coherent theory, but it is more likely to mean the use of a more or less meticulously planned method for carrying out the research. The belief that research is based on data begs questions about what actually counts as data: numbers, statements, questionnaire responses, errors, learner language, but perhaps also pictures, films, videos, tape-recordings, or even feelings and emotional encounters.

'Research uses experimental methods with treatment and control groups'

The identification of true research with experimental methods as used in the hard sciences or in laboratory psychology which involve controlled comparisons is a frequent attitude. It presumably excludes description and classification as valid kinds of research, since it depends on comparison. Contemplation of the many difficulties of executing such a model of research in normal classrooms probably means that this attitude correlates with a belief that research is actually irrelevant to the normal professional activities of a teacher.

'Research involves a hypothesis which is then tested'

Again, this quite sophisticated view reflects an important traditional principle: that research, as perhaps opposed to mere curiosity, requires a formal statement, graced by the technical word hypothesis, whose truth is put to the test. Pushing this notion further it is possible that this attitude underlies one of the distinctions between teaching and researching highlighted by Cohen and Manion (1989: 229) where they posit that 'research values precision, control, replication and attempts to generalise from specific events. Teaching, on the other hand, is concerned with action, with doing things, and translates generalisations into specific acts'. Cohen and Manion make this point in a discussion of action research.

This attitude also illustrates a frequent preference for traditional types of research rather than some of the principles of qualitative research, in particular the idea that theory can be derived from data collected.

'Research is objective'

The quality of objectivity usually refers to imperviousness to the actions or judgement of the researcher, that is to an external reality which is independent of the wishes or hopes of the person in the situation. Again, much of the methodology of traditional quantitative research is intended to ensure that the results and interpretations of the research hold good whoever actually performs it. Objectivity also suggests that those results and interpretations gained from one context of research will be true of others: therefore objectivity and generalizability are closely related. However, to the extent that objectivity involves a denial of the individuality of the participants, much activity by reflective practitioners and action researchers challenges the doctrine of dissociation between the roles of active participant and objective researcher. The roles and the individual ways the participant, here the teacher researcher, carries out those roles within the context in which the research takes place become a factor in the research itself.

Basic and applied research

Basic research is often described as research without immediate practical utility, driven only by the advancement of theory, whereas applied research involves some kind of applicability. Sharwood Smith suggests that there are two strands of second language acquisition research, a pure and an applied one. Pure SLA develops a body of knowledge about second language learners because it is 'interesting as a phenomenon in its own right' (1994: 4). It may make reference to, borrow theories and methods from, and expect to influence theoretical developments in a variety of other disciplines, such as linguistics, sociology and cognitive science. Applied SLA would, for Sharwood Smith, constitute an answer to the question 'What does second language research have to say to language teachers?' Applied research may develop along at least three different kinds of path, all of which have been used in language education at some time:

1. The application of research results and the theory they support to the solution of language teaching problems. A distant example of this is afforded by the development of pattern drills on the basis of learning experiments in the behaviourist tradition (Rivers, 1964); a more recent example is the adoption of schema-theoretic reading exercises (involving extensive pre-text exercises, the application of background knowledge) on the basis of research on second language readers (Carrell and Eisterhold, 1983).

2. A second view of applied research suggests that what is applied is not so much the products of existing research but the methodology of obtaining those results. Thus, much applied psychology research takes the 'scientific method' as embodied in experimental psychology and applies it to problems of human performance in the real world.

3. Yet a third view argues that applied research – which should be distinguished from action research (Cohen and Manion, 1989: 218) – develops its own body of knowledge and theory-building for its particular set of problems. It is this approach which blurs the distinction between basic or pure research and applied research, for the set of problems which the applied research is designed to help solve do not admit of a more basic approach. Research on and by the participants in language teaching can be of this third type, since it can be argued that only the kind of research which satisfies the conditions of validity and contextual relevance can be appropriate for the peculiar circumstances of the problem set we are trying to understand.

It is therefore suggested that the activities of classroom language teaching and learning contain the kind of challenge to our understanding and therefore to our attempts to introduce change and innovation which can only be resolved by doing research on and in those activities, using methods which are appropriate to those research aims and the problems under study. Neither the extrapolation of knowledge from 'pure' research, like comparative or universal linguistics, or learning behaviours in specially designed situations, or second language acquisition in other contexts (for example, naturalistic or self-taught) nor research 'applying' methods found appropriate for other kinds of problems, whether psycholinguistic, or sociological, or hard science, are likely to adequately represent the essentials and the variability of the problem.

Description and intervention

Whatever the planned, or unplanned, utility of the research-based know-ledge might be, it is usual to distinguish two kinds of aims, or possible routes to the common goal of improving understanding. These two are, broadly speaking, description and intervention. Much research proceeds by intervening in the activities or processes in question by manipulating the variables that can be identified and attempting to isolate the influence of one or more on the process. As we discuss more fully in the next section, experimental methods in particular use a variety of techniques for separating out the variables in a situation so that the conclusion about what affected what can be drawn. For example, if one wanted to know whether success in reading a foreign language was more likely for learners who were good readers in their mother tongue, a way of distinguishing good and bad readers in each language, perhaps by a test, would be required. Foreign language reading would be termed the Dependent Variable, mother tongue reading the Independent Variable. Simple counting of the frequency of people who were good or bad readers in both compared to those whose reading scores were very different in each language might answer the question, as in the following:

	good L1	bad L1
good L2	*a*	*b*
bad L2	*c*	*d*

To uphold the conclusion that good L1 reading is important for good L2 reading it is obvious that you would want to find a larger proportion of people in cells *a* and *d* than in cells *b* and *c* – more people in whom reading proficiency in their two languages was similar than people who were good in one and bad in the other. This difference in proportions can easily be evaluated using statistics, but the important point here is the immediate association between the evaluation of this interventionist technique (of isolating reading scores) and measurement by the use of tests for estimating the values of the dependent and the independent variable.

However, there would be other factors involved which might prevent any conclusion from such a simple procedure. These other variables could be confounded with the independent variable so as to bring into question the certainty of the connection apparent from the figures. Such 'confounding variables' may arise from characteristics of the people themselves (in the imaginary example one would be reluctant to accept the conclusion if it was discovered that all of the people in cells *a* and *d* were also teachers of reading but none in cells *b* and *c* were), or characteristics of the situation. Again, in our imaginary example the conclusion would be unsafe if it was discovered that the people had performed the reading tests in different places under different lighting conditions, noise levels, as individuals or groups, taking different completion times and so on. In the design of interventionist research, controls and counterbalances (which we will look at in detail in Chapter 10 on doing experiments) are built in, by using randomization, careful measurement of confounding variables and strict adherence to procedure, in order to allow the conclusions to be unambiguous.

Sometimes, this kind of research, when applied to language teaching and other educational problems, leads to procedures which distort the situation in which the research is being conducted. Green's (1975) study of the efficacy of language laboratories required both groups of children to go from school to the university where the language laboratory group performed lessons in the laboratory and the comparison (or 'control' group) did ordinary lessons – but in what was for them an extraordinary situation. The reason was to control for the possible confounding of any benefit accruing from the actual language laboratory teaching with the general excitement of being chosen to go off to the university for a research purpose. Thus, the learners' personal and educational context is controlled and counterbalanced so that particular effects can be made manifest.

Descriptive research, on the other hand, aims at making explicit the significant effects within the context itself. To this end the research attempts to provide a rich account of the whole situation rather than minimizing it. There are two reasons for this. The first is that in most educational situations the list of possible confounding variables is so large, with some systematic and some unsystematic ones, that realistic and satisfactory control and counterbalance are nearly impossible. The second, and more positive reason, is that it is increasingly realized that individual effects which can be isolated rarely work alone: therefore the pattern of context in which they are embedded is all important.

Context

The importance of the role of 'context' in formulating the teacher-research paradigm has appeared several times in the discussion so far, both explicitly and by implication. We have, for instance, considered both the concrete contextual variables at play in teachers' working environments (Chapter 1), as well as ways in which the notion of context can be linked to the nature of professional knowledge and to issues of specificity and generalizability (Chapter 2). A simple example will serve to illustrate.

One of the authors went to the classroom to prepare for the next lesson (an EFL Study Skills class for students in university). The previous teacher had not cleaned the whiteboard, on which the following was written:

> nationality
> naturalized citizen
> miso soup
> he is a descendant of the Emperor
> invisible

Although the present writer knew the group taught by her colleague very well, it was nevertheless impossible to reconstruct except in the vaguest terms what had been the substance of the lesson. Clearly the teacher had not merely stuck to a fixed lesson plan (the 'objectives model'), but had also responded to what Richards and Lockhart (1994: 84) call 'the interactional dynamics of the teaching-learning process', thus creating a *uniqueness* of context for this particular lesson. Calderhead (1987, quoting Doyle) offers six features of the classroom environment that are relevant here. It has:

1. Multidimensionality   2. Immediacy   3. Simultaneity

4. Unpredictability   5. Publicness   6. History

In this view, then, reality is seen not as fixed and stable but as socially constructed, so what Sevigny (1981: 72) calls the 'social order' – in our case, of a classroom – is perceived as 'an emergent phenomenon'. This view is echoed by Erickson and Schultz (1981: 148), who describe social contexts as 'interactionally constituted environments' where there is a constant process of change and re-adjustment.

This perspective has a long pedigree in social science, through such major related traditions as ethnomethodology, phenomenology, grounded theory, and symbolic interactionism. There is no space here to go into such a rich and complex field in any detail, but the importance and attractiveness of these traditions for educational research should not be underestimated. Herbert Blumer, for example (quoted in Hammersley, 1989), who is particularly associated with symbolic interactionism and the Chicago School of social science, wrote that meanings are not fixed and universal but variable, 'fabricated through the process of social interaction'. In this view (as Denzin, 1970, underlines) social life is in a state of flux, and open to multiple perspectives and interpretations. It is, as he says, 'a world that refuses to stand still'. Not only, as we shall see in Chapter 4, does this throw a problematic light on standard research questions of validity and reliability: it is also likely that the view it encapsulates will be recognized by the majority of teachers as what happens in their everyday reality.

Normative and interpretive research

In the previous section, two modes of research were described briefly. The distinction between them is not just methodological, that is to say not just a question of selecting the most appropriate method for the subject under study. It is not merely a question therefore of 'horses for courses'. Van Lier (1988: 57) sets out the various types of research in a useful table, in which two dimensions of control and structure give four broad types: measuring, controlling, watching, and asking/doing. His table is reproduced in Fig. 3.1 for illustration.

Van Lier's dimension of 'control' is roughly equivalent to what was described above as description versus intervention; his dimension of

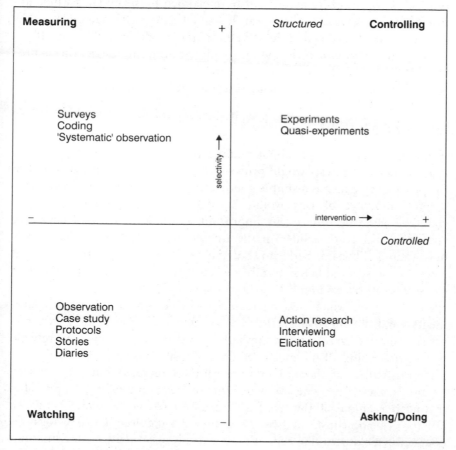

Fig. 3.1   Types of research (Reprinted by permission of Addison Wesley Longman Ltd.)

structure is roughly equivalent to the traditional distinction between quantitative and qualitative approaches. We now turn to this difference, but widen the discussion a little to take into account the implications of the parallel but slightly more general terms 'normative' and 'interpretive'.

Normative approaches

Normative approaches can be characterized by the following:

- description by numbers
- significance in terms of probability
- use of experimental or quasi-experimental designs
- generalization from sample to population
- the search for causes.

Typically, as Cohen and Manion (1989) point out, they have been associated with large-scale research, with 'objective' judgements made by researchers from the 'outside', and have claimed to isolate facts which are true of more people than the research was actually performed on. In addition, it is usually claimed, at least in experimental designs, that the effects isolated are causal in nature, and although with certain designs this is precluded, the eventual goal of such research is to come up with valid cause-and-effect relations like those sought in the natural sciences.

Description by numbers

In our imaginary example about reading proficiency in the previous section, we noted that tests would probably be used to give a measurement of the proficiency either as a simple good versus bad judgement or as a score.

One advantage of this would be that such measurements can be counted, and this reflects an important assumption of the normative approach: that truth resides in the degree of agreement between many observations. Thus it is better to take many measurements of the same trait from one person and better to take measurements from many people than to use one-off observations. Procedures such as finding the mean (or average – the figure which best characterizes agreement of all the measurements) and the deviation (the degree to which those measurements actually do not agree) can be applied to find the most valid and reliable way of describing all the measurements by using just one or two figures. Such manipulations allow a kind of truth to be revealed, but notice it may be an abstract truth, one for which no real example exists. A (probably mythical) example of this is the description of the 'average' family in Britain as being constituted by 1.5 adults, 2.4 children and 0.5 dogs. Of course, such a description represents, probably accurately, the fact that not all nuclear families consist of two adults, that there is a range of offspring numbers from none to double figures, and about half the families own a dog: but equally obviously no family answering that description will ever be found.

Significance in terms of probability

Technically, the 'significance' of a result is the likelihood that it could have been produced by chance, rather than by some systematic influence. (Whether the systematic influence was what the original hypothesis or theory said it would be can only be determined by the design – hence the controls and counterbalances mentioned in the previous section.) In experimental, survey, and correlational designs as used in psychology and psycholinguistics, therefore, the definition of a fact is a matter of likelihood, of distinguishing 'fact' from 'accident'.

Use of experimental and quasi-experimental designs

Normative research typically uses designs which attempt to identify independent and dependent variables and incorporate controls for systematic confounding variables, known features which might bias the results, such as previous learning experience, language proficiency level, intelligence, sex or whatever, and counterbalances like randomization for unknown but suspected variables.

The search for generalization from sample to population

The aim of this kind of research is to make generalizations, and find evidence from the particular sample studied to the population of people at large, or at least to some recognizable subset of them, like people in the same kind of learning situation elsewhere in place or time. In itself this aim is shared by most kinds of research including, as we shall see, qualitative methods. However, there are two rather serious problems with it for language teaching and teacher research. The first is that the quality of the generalizations possible, given the inevitably narrow data base in the language arts, tends to be restricted. McLaughlin (1987: 155, Table 7.1) lists 10 generalizations based on second language research which he sees as hypotheses which the general theory of second language acquisition he seeks must explain. However, close inspection shows that they are all remarkably vague, and he himself points out 'there is not universal agreement as to their status'. Second, practitioners wishing to act on these kinds of generalizations for another group of learners in another place have an almost impossible task relating the general to the particular.

The search for cause

Van Lier (1989) criticizes normative approaches for espousing a positivistic belief in determinism – that is to say, the search is for causal effects,
and the test of the search is the success of the prediction. If, therefore (to
use one of his own examples), you can say that a particular strength of
wind will cause a tree to fall down, you can test this by observing the effect
on an experimental tree of winds of different strengths. He points out that
even classical physics is hard put to it to guarantee such a prediction,
because the causal chain is complicated, involving characteristics of the
wind, the tree itself (age, type of wood, foliage, health), the soil it is
planted in, the proximity of other trees and objects causing eddies and so
on. He also points out that such a causal model is irrelevant in language
teaching because teaching does not cause people to learn anyway.

With these arguments he criticizes a whole tradition of research on
teaching which endeavours to specify elements of the process – teaching –
which affect the product – learning. However, it is still legitimate to ask
why as well as how things happen, and he distinguishes between causes and
reasons. Such a distinction takes us into the realms of rather abstruse philosophy except for the parallel distinction between explanation and prediction. The failure of many kinds of theory to predict in all real-world
circumstances (meteorology is one familiar example) is not held to be a
major critique of the theory since in general terms the theory may well give
satisfactory explanations. Prediction is, however, not necessarily a tougher
criterion than explanation: we can all predict that a child will acquire the
language of its environment but nobody can yet explain how. Skinner could
predict with some accuracy the learning curve of an animal in a Skinner
box but could not explain it in terms other than his predictions.

Interpretive approaches

In this category are often collected together a number of research traditions which actually differ considerably among themselves as to their
major assumptions and fields of interest and applicability, favourite data
types and methods of analysis. They are participant observation, symbolic
interactionism, ethnography, ethnomethodology and others. However, the
contrast with the normative approach highlights the shared features of
these traditions. Many of these features hold considerable attraction for
research in language teaching and learning, collaborative research and
research by teachers, since they suggest alternative solutions to the problems of context, generalizability and confidence in the conclusions, and
offer canons of methodological rigour to the investigation of local and
often small-scale problems of learning communities. After the main characteristics of this kind of research have been described in what follows, a
further section will point up some interesting parallels in the two

approaches which exist despite their very different origins and basic assumptions. Later, in Chapter 4, the increasingly frequent strategy of using elements of both approaches will be discussed under the heading of triangulation.

Ethnography

As Watson-Gegeo (1988) points out, ethnography has become, for some researchers in language learning, almost a synonym for qualitative or interpretive research, although this assumption is in fact unwarranted. Brown (1984) also introduces a distinction between experimental and naturalistic research in language learning, and discusses ethnography as an important variety of naturalistic enquiry. Following Ochsner, she presents a useful tabulation of the contrasts between experimental and naturalistic research which, although polarized, clarifies the comparison. This is an excerpt from the tabulation:

Experimental	Naturalistic
Nomothetic	Rational
Empirical	Qualitative
Quantitative	Grounded
Scientific	Ethnographic

Van Lier (1988; 1989), as already mentioned, has performed an ethnography of classroom language learning and discusses ethnography, if not as a synonym, then perhaps as an emblem of interpretive or naturalistic research. Watson-Gegeo and Van Lier highlight several principles in ethnographic research which are explored in what follows: the 'emic' principle, which refers to the 'rules, concepts, beliefs, and meanings of the people themselves, functioning within their own group' (Van Lier, 1989: 43); the 'holistic' principle, by which ethnographers attempt to understand phenomena in connection with the location and situation of those phenomena and not abstracted from them; the accent on 'context', as described earlier in this chapter; the use of 'grounded theory'; and the idea that the process of research should be open and explicit about its procedures and design decisions.

Participant research

Many, but not all, of these qualitative approaches claim the virtue of the researcher being a participant in the situation being researched as compared to an 'objective' outsider. The participant observer may be a researcher who takes a role within the community being studied, as in the anthropological tradition stemming from Malinowski, and much ethnographic work; or may be a 'natural' participant in the situation like a teacher – or a student, for that matter – who adds to their normal role that of data-gatherer and analyst. The fieldwork involved will be intensive, conducted according to rules of evidence, and reflective. However, being a participant observer does not necessarily guarantee privileged entry to the most appropriate interpretation: indeed, it could be a disadvantage requiring considerable effort to overcome, because, as Erickson (1986: 121) says, everyday life is often 'invisible' to us precisely because it is familiar, so to pose the question 'what is happening here?' is to pose a considerable challenge. What is commonplace to the participant may be problematic to the researcher who aims to produce a plausible interpretation of a whole situation. However, Erickson also points out that the participant observer is in the best position to note 'concrete details of practice' – in other words a fully detailed record of actions which can be used to provide the data for interpretation.

Local and non-local organization

Interpretive approaches deal particularly with what actions mean to the people who engage in them – with the local meanings (an example of the 'emic' principle). Thus, such research is necessarily situated in natural groupings: real classes, normal school organizations, rather than concocted or randomized organizations and assignment to treatment group for the purpose of control or counterbalancing of 'confounding variables'. That is, however, not to say they do not pay attention to more general meanings, which are non-local meanings. Interpretations of a particular context and what cooperative action means to the participants in it is both to be compared to similar actions in other contexts – 'how do they do this elsewhere?' – and used to illuminate those other contexts as well.

Generalization

It might be thought that an approach relying so heavily on the explication of context and the local meanings of action could not produce useful generalizations. Interpretive research indeed does aim to uncover generic, universal features of the phenomenon in question through comprehensive and detailed study of individual contexts, of 'local microcultures' – a classroom, or learning group. Erickson compares such 'concrete' universals with the 'abstract' universals produced by statistical research: 'The paradox is that to achieve valid discovery of universals one must stay very close to concrete cases' (1986: 130).

The search for meaning interpretations

This research tradition looks at the ways in which the participants interpret their own situation to themselves and to each other. Thus, what contributes to achievement is seen in the pattern of interaction between more or less skilled teachers and more or less skilled learners and how the learning community utilizes its resources. Connected with this distinction is that between behaviour and action: a billiard ball might be said to behave in a minimal kind of way as a result of forces on a flat bed; but a learner is acting in the situation and making sense (or failing to make sense) of it. 'The billiard ball does not make sense of its environment' (Erickson, 1986: 137).

Qualitative data

It follows from the above that the kinds of data collected are very different to those in normative research. Whereas normative research requires a numerical evaluation, qualitative research usually gathers observations, interviews, field data records, questionnaires, transcripts, and so on. The range of data is wide, but this also requires rules of evidence so that rigour is preserved. This comprehensive attitude to data also means that it is typical for qualitative data collection choices to evolve, as in the action research spiral (Chapter 2), as insights and tentative conclusions by the researcher indicate the need for other confirmation.

Plausible interpretations

To ensure plausibility, there have to be rules of evidence. Erickson (1986: 140) gives a straightforward description of five rules, here reproduced as positive statements.

1. Evidence must be adequate in amount to support interpretations. Central importance is given to complete and detailed observation.
2. Evidence should come from a variety of data types. Reliance on one type can miss important features and, more seriously, leave conclusions unvalidated.
3. Data must have good 'interpretive status': in other words, researchers have to guard against misunderstanding features in the data, because of inadequacy of amount or even deliberate misinformation.
4. Disconfirming evidence should be included and actively sought.
5. Discrepant cases should be analysed carefully. Qualitative research uses discrepant case analysis as a powerful antidote to looking only for evidence to support the researcher's conclusion.

Ethical considerations

Qualitative research is not alone in valuing ethical considerations highly. However, arguably, this tradition has formulated more explicitly than others how research ethics work, both (a) to protect the validity of the research – for example, the achievement of good data by recognizing that data provided by informants is owned by them, and its use is with their permission only; and (b) to protect the participants of the research through rules of confidentiality and consent to particular uses of the data.

Some parallels between normative and interpretive approaches

Despite the many deep differences, it will be realized that both traditions share a number of concerns, but provide different solutions.

In both, there is a concern for quality of data: in normative research it is expressed in terms of pre-testing the research instruments and tests for validity and reliability, in interpretive research in terms of quantity and variety of data types.

In both, there is a concern for potential falsification. In normative research, this is enshrined in the use of empirical data to reject a null hypothesis; in interpretive research, it is expressed as the search for disconfirming evidence and 'discrepant case analysis'.

In both, there are procedures for determining what is significant, but in the former the significance of a finding lies in probability, whereas in the latter, it is a question of revealing the universal and generic from comparisons of data sets which are as complete as possible.

Conclusion

This chapter has attempted to follow through and extend the issues raised in the discussion of teacher research in Chapter 2. It has in a sense stepped back a little, in order to look at some of the key concepts that inform teacher-initiated research, together with their derivations and background, as well as to set this particular orientation to research within a broader definitional framework. Since methods and techniques do not exist in a vacuum, this exploration of the paradigms themselves, and their implications in general terms for language teaching, are also a necessary precursor to the whole of Part 2 of this book.

The chapter began by invoking a simplified but convenient distinction between two senses of the term 'research': uncovering and perhaps reinventing the known world, and discovering new things. We then reported some commonly expressed views from teachers on the assumed criteria for research in language teaching. This led to a more detailed exploration of some familiar and often polarized terms, in particular:

- basic (or 'pure') versus applied research
- interventionist versus descriptive approaches
- normative versus interpretive traditions, in particular the much-

quoted quantitative/qualitative distinction and the nature and role
of ethnography

as well as the pivotal notion of 'context' within the interpretive dimension
of social science and educational research.

In the course of the discussion, we have suggested that, although these
represent apparently very different ways of seeing the world, it is not
always helpful to see them as mutually exclusive forms of knowledge, and
the methodology used for a particular research undertaking may well combine facets of each. Nevertheless, an understanding of the epistemological
distinctions is important when making informed and reasoned choices
about research content and method.

Discussion notes

1. What are your own associations of the term 'research'? To what
   extent are they comparable to those listed as quotations in this
   chapter?
2. Can you identify areas of 'applied research' that in your opinion
   have had a direct impact on aspects of methodology, or materials?
   (For example, many coursebooks claim to derive activities directly
   from research on reading comprehension, or discourse analysis,
   and so on.)
3. Do you think that teachers typically make 'causal' judgements
   about ways in which their learners learn (or apparently fail to
   learn?)

4

Principles and problems: what makes good research?

Introduction

The first, and largest, section of this chapter discusses some 13 features which are traditionally associated with good research, and attempts to explain them. They fall loosely into four groups, concerned with the initiation and undertaking of research, the internal workings of research, the applications of research, and one all-pervading issue: the ethics of research.

There are many areas in which these features are potentially in conflict, for example, the tension between confidentiality of data and publication, or between sensitivity and objectivity, or between originality and research history, or between contextual accuracy and replicability. The quality of research can therefore be seen to some extent in the adequacy and sincerity of the compromise chosen by the researcher.

The second section compares various actual research traditions, mainly the normative and hermeneutic as introduced in the previous chapter, and the research that can be performed in the academic context, often in pursuit of higher degrees, and participatory research by teachers in their own context. Each kind of research has its own advantages; no one tradition or situation can claim supremacy over the others in all circumstances.

The third section considers some important issues in research design, and explores the advantages and some dangers in the use of confirmatory strategies such as triangulation and multitrait, multimethod research.

Features of good research

The following 13 features seem to fall loosely into four rough categories, and we shall deal with each of them in turn.

First, there are features to do with the initiation and undertaking of research – the *interest, originality, specificity* and *publication* or dissemination of the research questions and findings.

Second, there are features of the design and methodology of the research – the *sensitivity, objectivity, validity* and *reliability* of the methods chosen, and the key principle of *falsifiability*, which applies to hypotheses, conclusions, and theories equally.

Third, there are features concerning the application to other situations, of practical exploitation, use in effecting change and innovation, and of further or parallel research – *replicability, generalizability* and *utility*.

Last, there is the question of the *ethics* of research and how the participants' rights are affected, how both the quality of the research data and the confidentiality of disclosures made by respondents may be protected.

Initiation and undertaking of research

1. Interest

It need hardly be said that good research is interesting to somebody. Although interest is a notoriously difficult concept to capture on paper, in research terms it often has to be defended explicitly, and in writing. For example, it might be necessary to persuade an authority to make time or funds available for doing the research, or argue for a proposal for higher-degree research at a university. The reasons for finding something interesting might obviously be anything, for example:

personal
- an observation of something unexpected or incongruous
- difference between two versions of the same event
- a difference in the reception of the same lesson by two parallel groups

arising out of something read

- a prediction from an established theory
- implications from a description of someone else's research
- an unexplained result in previous work
- a puzzle unexplained by existing theories and ideas about learning
- a discrepancy between normal assumptions (for example, from a methodology text) and actual outcomes

based on possible consequences

- the pay-off from adopting a new approach in terms of efficiency, use of resources, cost, and so on
- the inside story of the implementation of a new decision.

As we shall see in Chapter 5 when discussing the generation and development of research ideas, the original idea that sparks off the venture may evolve as a result of subsequent consideration of what has already been established about the problem in the extant research literature, or from the preliminary results of the actual research. However, the original interest, if strong enough, will remain to guide the execution of the research and help to anchor the results and interpretation in the original question: and also to motivate the researcher in the depressing times when all seems data and no sense.

2. Originality

This quality is closely allied to the first, though it is possibly even more elusive. The original contribution in much published research is in fact quite small. While it would be everybody's dream to come up with a totally new explanation to account for a totally new set of data about a question nobody had thought of before, in practice it does not work out like that. Originality may reside in any one, any combination, or (rarely) all of:

- a new question
- new data – perhaps from a different kind of class, a lesson within an education system not previously researched (for example, trying out writers' conferencing in a school system where it had not been evaluated before)
- a combination of data – for example, adding interviews to observations
- a new theory or modification of theory
- evaluating a new teaching method or learning strategy
- a new analysis of previously obtained data
- using a recognized data collection method in a new context
- (even) replicating a previous study to compare the results and thus establish its generalizability.

3. Specificity

Empirical research of all kinds uses observations of specific events to uncover general principles. If a teacher was interested, for example, in how participation in class affects learning, then the teacher would want to be very clear as to what kinds of classroom behaviour constituted participation, what signs of learning to be looking for, and what indicators of a relationship between them to spot.

Cook (1986: 17–19) gives an illustration of the process of concretizing a general question into a specific question that can be answered, by increasing in eight stages the specificity of each concept, or operationalizing the general concepts (in his example, learning by speaking and learning by writing) by reducing them to actual tests and measurements (particular learners, particular tasks and achievement measures). Research in the normative tradition requires this kind of specificity, for otherwise no measurements can be taken. However, replacing a general concept like 'speaking' or 'participation' with a speaking test or an index of student turn-taking begs the question of how well the test or index chosen actually represents what the researcher wanted to enquire about. This 'method of detail' stands or falls by the appropriacy of the details chosen.

Qualitative research, however, requires specificity in a slightly different sense: specificity of context, a sufficiently detailed description of the personal, institutional, and educational context for the research to represent adequately the individuality of the situation. A qualitative approach to Cook's question might therefore look at different individuals in the same class and record all the different types of learning mode and spoken and written utterances produced by them and relate the observations to pupils' self-reports or interview data, placing the data in the context of the history of the class or the aims of the programme. This particular issue is crucial to the question of how research questions are generated, to be examined in Chapter 5.

4. Publication

Publication may seem a strange feature to be grouped under initiation and undertaking of research, but research activity needs publication and publications in two serious ways.

First, research ideas and ways of doing the research are often suggested by reading the professional literature. The originality of a piece of research is usually evaluated by how it compares with what has been done before on the topic. In a thesis submitted for a research degree, the literature review is an integral and necessary part: the issues identified and pursued by previous researchers and the methods they used are evaluated, and the thesis writer continues to demonstrate how the new research will contribute to the sum of knowledge. But, although research conducted by teachers in their own classrooms does not need to follow the same canons of display and presentation as a PhD, the topic is not usually without some kind of history. The teacher researcher will still want to know how other teachers' thinking compares with their own, how previous attempts to solve the problem have fared, what the results of similar studies have been, in order to make a judgement about the direction, methods and perhaps generalizability or at least transferability of their own research.

Second, any research requires dissemination through conference presentation or discussion or publication so that it may be evaluated by others. Public perusal, in particular peer perusal, is part of the process of validation. A teacher may discover to his/her own satisfaction that, for example, conferencing works reliably for their students learning to write in a second language. Until the details of the work are available for other people (in some suitable and accessible forum, it does not have to be a research journal in a university library!) no one else can question the methods used or check the plausibility of the conclusions: because of that, no one else need believe the research, and, crucially, neither can the researcher have confidence that his or her conclusions can be accepted.

Design and methodology

5. Sensitivity

Research aims to discover both broad generalizations and subtle differentiations. In language learning research there have been many attempts to demonstrate links between broad categories of personality and achievement, and concurrently there have been many investigations of individual learners following particular courses. Sensitivity is, however, more than a question of scale, it is primarily a question of quality of data, discriminatory power of tests, and the use of 'insider knowledge', particularly in the case of participant observatory research.

It may take some time to learn the skills necessary to obtain good-quality data: depending on the project, the researcher may need interviewing skills, practice in constructing questionnaires, careful observation and recording techniques, all of which we discuss in Part 2 of this book. Allwright refers to the problem of skill-learning time in his report of a workshop in 'exploratory teaching' (1993: 129–30); perhaps surprisingly, his workshop collaborators did not seem to regard it as seriously as he did. Perhaps their enthusiasm coloured their judgement, or perhaps they saw ways of incorporating research skill learning into the development of their teaching skills.

There have been a number of research projects whose inconclusive or disappointing results have been blamed on measures and tests that were too crude to show up the sought-after differences, particularly in the area of individual differences in learning. One such issue is the controversy surrounding the supposed advantage of extroverts over introverts in learning a foreign language (Skehan, 1989). Similar problems may arise when using standard tests as measures of achievement on a course: the unreliability of the tests may mask any true gains in proficiency.

As Burton and Mickan remark (1993: 113), discussing teacher's classroom research, 'the closeness of teachers to the events being researched' is a frequent argument for teachers to be involved in research. They identify particularly 'information from the front line: teachers are most familiar with the complex circumstances involved in the teaching and learning of languages; what they experience in classrooms is a direct source of information about language learning.'

This kind of closeness should promote sensitivity, but it is striking that later in their list of reasons for language teachers to do classroom research is 'learning through research: teachers' research promotes their own learning about what is happening in their classrooms, and their understanding of why it is happening; through research teachers hypothesize about their experience' (1993: 114).

Thus sensitivity to issues peculiar to language learning in classrooms is a great asset to the teacher as a participant researcher; but doing the research may be the best way of maximizing that sensitivity.

6. Objectivity

Classical research designs strive for the elimination from the results of an experiment of any biases from the researcher: the knowledge gained is seen as objective and independent of any particular human agent, with personality, emotions, career aspirations, hopes and desires. Thus, the message is important, not the messenger. It is obvious that in educational research as well, particularly in evaluation, the possibility of communicating to the learning group what the researcher wants to hear is only too open.

If a teacher wanted to compare, say, teaching via group discussion with teaching using video clips, and had strong reasons to prefer one to the other, his/her research might unconsciously lead the students to prefer the alternative he or she preferred by making it more interesting, being more relaxed in it, or devoting more time to it. An objective approach would build in safeguards against such 'experimenter bias', perhaps by substituting the teacher by others who did not have such preferences. However, any objectivity gained by using different teachers might be neutralized or at least compromised by the effects of disrupting the normal arrangements for the class or classes. Thus objectivity is a laudable goal, but so is contextual specificity: the problem is to satisfy both concurrently, not to sacrifice the one for the other.

One argument for action research is that it has typically accepted that the actors, including the researchers as observers, are an integral part of the situation being researched, not simply nuisances to be eliminated or controlled out of the way. Dadds (1995) argues that there are serious reasons concerning completeness of description and the recording of significant factors for participant observers or teacher researchers to carry out 'first-person research' into their own reactions to events, including even the recording of emotional reactions. This is one justification for treating diaries, which are the least objective of all data, as research data.

7. Validity

Suppose a researcher follows a particular student through a language course and beyond, perhaps into the community to look at language maintenance or success in a job requiring that language. The researcher observes the student in the class, holds interviews, records achievement scores, takes into account scores on IQ and individual difference measures, reads his diaries, observes him after the course. Two questions immediately arise out of any description the researcher writes:

1. Does the interpretation of all this data accord with reality – presumably the student's reality in this case?
2. Is it possible from this interpretation to suggest that other students in similar circumstances might learn, react to the course, meet problems after the course, in the same way?

Question 1 is a question of internal validity, or credibility; question 2 is one of external validity, or generalizability. Another illustration of internal validity is afforded by a famous study of learner strategies, the 'Good Language Learner' study (Naiman et al., 1975). In this, a number of kinds of data taken from school learners of French, by observations, mental tests and interviews, were related to achievement via two kinds of tests: a standardized listening comprehension test and an 'oral dictation' task in which the student has to repeat sentences spoken by the teacher. The extent to which the reader will accept Naiman et al.'s conclusions is dependent on how happily they accept the validity of measuring language by those tests. Thus, validity is essentially to do with credibility, which is the term used by Lincoln and Guba (1985). However, an even stricter criterion of validity can be entertained, namely that research needs to be credible not only to consumers but also to the original participants in the situation under review. How this might be achieved is a separate question.

8. Reliability

In any kind of measurement, reliability concerns the confidence the user can have that the measure will give the same answer given the same thing to measure. For example, nobody would trust a language test that produced wildly different answers if given to the same person twice, just as one would expect a pair of scales to weigh a pound of sugar as a pound, however often one weighed it. In practice, of course, no one expects the complicated data arising out of language learning situations to be as reliable as a pair of scales, partly because it is just a different order of complexity and partly because lots of the data are not, in any meaningful sense, measurements. In language proficiency testing, for example, there are recognized procedures for estimating how unreliable the test score is: that is, what its range of accuracy or 'spread of error' is. If a test score only claims to be reliable within two scale points either side of the actual score (imagine a score of 50 ± 2), it is effectively saying that it cannot guarantee that the true score of that testee is any particular one between 48 and 52, but the best obtainable estimate is somewhere in that range. To put it another way, there are limits within which a test receiver can be confident the true score lies, and statistically those limits can be given a quantity, like 68 per cent, 95 per cent and 99 per cent confident.

To take a non-measurement example, a researcher might wish to ask pupils to write diaries: but there is no guarantee that the picture of the class so gained will be the best possible, simply because some of them may not cooperate, some may lose them, or not be in class on the day they are collected. Data-collection procedures all suffer from problems of reliability, which, again following Lincoln and Guba, might more appropriately be glossed as 'dependability'.

Another instance of reliability concerns data analysis. Just as essay marks might be made more reliable by double marking, so coding, or labelling, a sequence of classroom moves, or themes occurring in an interview transcript, may be made more reliable if the task is done by two or three people independently and the decisions with the least agreement rejected.

However, we should bear in mind Elton's (1995) stricture that there is no contest between validity and reliability: validity is far more important. He relates a tale about a scientist who looked for the watch he had lost not where he had dropped it but under the table lamp, because that was where he could see best – clearly a reliable, well-illuminated situation, but doomed to failure.

9. Falsifiability

Knowledge develops by finding interpretations and understandings which supersede older interpretations, understandings or descriptions (loosely, theory), and empirical research is used to provide evidence to support that development. A classical principle in empirical work is that progress comes through finding evidence that tells us that a theory is wrong, not simply by finding evidence which confirms what was already thought. For this to be possible, a theory (again, without attaching any technical sophistication to this term) needs to be sufficiently precise to be capable of being shown to be wrong. A theory which says 'sometimes x happens and sometimes y happens' cannot be falsified unless it can state the conditions producing outcome x and distinguishes them from those that produce y. If this holds, a theory can be said to be falsifiable. Obviously, it is a measure of the strength and importance of a theory that it may take a very long time and much ingenious research effort to prove that it is wrong, and replace it with another that accounts for the new evidence plus all the evidence that the older theory accounted for. This principle is the reason why most statistical research attempts to reject a null hypothesis (that, for example, there is no difference between two treatments on some measure) by showing that the average difference observed is so unlikely by chance that it must be true. However, although falsifiability is a respected goal, it has been argued that in reality most research efforts proceed by confirming existing notions: by looking for supporting evidence. Change comes about when the search for confirmation in fact produces a build-up of anomalous and disconfirming results which then provoke a switch to a new, more widely applicable theory. In language learning research a number of authors (McLaughlin, 1987; Ellis, 1994) have pointed out that the principle of falsification is often ignored, or at least not fulfilled.

Schumann (1993) explores the implications of this principle for language learning research, and similarly concludes that it is not feasible in most situations to adhere to it. The problem is a general one. As we saw in Chapter 3, naturalistic methods also look for discrepant cases or evidence disconfirming their interpretations in order to test and refine those interpretations for the most accurate statement possible; but they are necessarily dependent on what data might occur naturally since they do not manipulate the context for the purpose of the research.

Applications to other situations: three aspects of transferability

10. Replicability

A piece of research will be highly valued if it is so clearly reported that somebody else can do the same thing again and obtain the same results. Accurate reporting of a piece of research is therefore not just a matter of good manners: the practical possibility of repeating the research means that it is open to a test of reliability. In fact, replication studies are surprisingly infrequent in the standard applied linguistic literature, and at least one author (Brindley, 1990) has argued that this reduces the value of the literature. Naturally, there is a *prima facie* conflict between replication and originality, and it is understandable that people looking for a research topic (discussed in much greater detail in Chapter 5) prefer to go for what looks like a new thing to look at rather than repeating someone else's work. However, to repeat someone else's study in a new situation on the basis of an explicit and complete report is itself a useful activity, and if the results are different, interest will be high. The replication issue therefore touches directly on other features mentioned here: originality, reliability and falsifiability. Furthermore, there is a genre of research, called, by Cohen and Manion (1989), 'meta-analysis', which is related to the replicability issue, but which involves comparing as many studies as possible of a particular phenomenon to establish the general tendency and the weight of evidence. In language learning studies there have been several: Peal and Lambert's (1962) examination of cognitive deficit in bilinguals and Long's (1983) examination of studies comparing 'instructed' and 'natural' language learning are often quoted as examples. The significance of replicability depends, however, on another factor: the uniqueness of teaching/learning situations. Doing the same kind of observation in a class of, say Algerian learners in Algeria, Japanese learners in Japan or a multilingual group in Bournemouth may not produce the same results: that cannot mean that the three observations are any less valid. Thus, in context-bound research, failure to replicate does not of itself invalidate. However, this problem gives a very strong reason for reports of how the research was conducted to be as complete as possible, so that the crucial differences in the contexts may be identified. (For further discussion, see Chapter 13 on case study research.)

11. Generalizability

In one sense, all research is about making significant generalizations (i.e. the most general and accurate statement possible) about some problem area. Educational research and research in language learning situations are no exception. Thus, a linguist will be looking, for example, for the most economical way to capture grammatical regularities in a rule, or the set of primary and secondary meanings of a word in a lexical entry; a classroom researcher will be looking for the most important features of the classroom situation and how they interact. In this sense, research works from the particular, specific data, to general statements that data can support. In applied linguistic research, much activity has been devoted to seeking the 'conditions' in which language learning generally occurs – Spolsky devotes a whole book to it (1989). 'Condition-seeking' research, often with regard to individual differences like aptitude, motivation, and so on, has attempted to establish general statements (Skehan, 1989). There is another sense of generalization, to another context or situation, which is much less congenial. As we discussed in Chapter 2, in many cases teaching requires this kind of generalization: taking principles derived in one situation and generalizing them to new situations. This sense is more properly a matter of 'action' than 'research', and therefore will be discussed later under 'utility'. Here we should explore a little deeper the notion of making general statements in context-bound research and research conducted by participant researchers. The purpose of this kind of research is to achieve deeper understanding of those particular contexts; such an understanding involves, necessarily, recognizing both what is special and unique and what is characteristic, normal and commonplace. Erickson (1986), in discussing qualitative research, draws a rather surprising parallel between this aim and that of a linguist looking for universal principles of language, and describing particular languages. His point is that, in both cases, the universal and the particular are established by exact and complete description of the phenomena concerned. This point will be taken up in Chapter 13 where the notion of naturalistic generalization is discussed in relation to case study research.

12. Utility

The second, and in one way more practical, sense of generalizability mentioned above refers to the utility of the research. Can the findings be used, either in the future in the immediate context, or applied to other contexts? Commonly, there are two general positions on this. One is that empirical research findings are in fact of little practical use: 'The application of basic research findings to professional practice is always a risky business. This is no less true in the case of language education ... research findings are often too incomplete and limited to indicate substantial and unqualified practical implications' (Beebe, 1988: 106). The other is that the function of research is to help us draw out assumptions which we can question: 'Research findings can challenge our sometimes complacent and poorly substantiated beliefs about the way learning occurs' (Beebe, 1988: 107).

Beebe's remarks were made in the context of the relationship between second language acquisition research and second language pedagogy and teacher training, and Ellis (1994) concludes his massive study of second language acquisition with a careful review of current opinion on this issue. Ellis notes in his final remark, after discussing various positions from 'don't apply' to 'go ahead and apply': 'Furthermore, some educationalists might feel that research undertaken by professional researchers will always be of limited value to language teachers and that a more worthwhile and exciting approach is action research, where teachers become researchers by identifying research questions important to them and seeking answers in their own classes' (1994: 689).

It may well be that the main utility of research is not the commonplace of direct application but the experience of challenged assumptions, which seem to make otherwise familiar situations more interesting, curious, and indeed less familiar. Research can put new perspectives on to old situations, which is exactly why it can contribute powerfully to innovation and the maintenance of innovation in context.

13. Ethics

There are, mercifully, few parallels in language education research with headline ethical issues in science such as military applications of nuclear physics, biology, or chemistry, or the use of animals in the drug and cosmetics industries. However, there are important ethical questions regarding the collection, interpretation and publication of research findings, which affect both the researcher and the clients or subjects who provide the data. These questions concern:

1. access to the situation in which the research is to take place
2. protection of the clients who provide the data
3. protection of the validity of the data collected

4. ownership of the data
5. agreements about disclosure and publication
6. codes of practice about generalizability and application in other contexts.

1. Access. In most language education situations, and in all institutional ones, some kind of permission is needed to carry out research. This permission can usually only be granted by a senior person who acts as a gatekeeper. One concern that such a person may have is, of course, that the research may interfere with the teaching and learning activity or, depending on design, disrupt the normal running of the institution beyond tolerable levels.

2. Clients need to be protected by assurances about all procedures to ensure confidentiality. These may be situations in which the researcher is vouchsafed private information concerning, say, opinions about another participant (the teacher, a fellow teacher, another student) which would cause embarrassment if passed to that person.

3. The data needs to be protected so that it is of the highest quality: simple procedures such as asking interviewees to vet a transcript, give permission for it to be used in specified ways, and so on, can ensure this.

4. Data provided by people in a social learning situation, an observation, or an in-depth interview, should be considered the property of the providers. Recently, this principle has even been incorporated in law.

5. None of the above would be possible unless some explicit agreement is made with the data providers or those responsible for them about the conditions of disclosure and publication. Publication and dissemination of results are themselves part of research, and the enterprise will not get off the ground unless the participants' agreement can be obtained on such conditions, whether open or restricted.

6. Some poor decisions about programme design have been taken in the past when choices have been made on the basis of inappropriate extension of research findings to new contexts. A code of practice designed to limit this kind of damage has been proposed by EUROSLA (the European Second Language Association), for use by its members, who are researchers. In the current climate, further initiatives of this sort are to be expected. Many social research organizations such as the British Sociological Association have established codes of professional ethics.

As mentioned before, these features of good research are not independent, they interact: the quality is in the balance and compromise. There may be tensions to be resolved for any particular piece of research between confidentiality and protection, and publication; between sensitivity and reliability; between originality and publication; between replicability and context-specificity; and possibly between validity and reliability in some cases.

Comparison of research traditions on these features

Educational researchers have used many research methods, as is evident from manuals such as Cohen and Manion (1989). Stenhouse (1975) points out that in geography, different projections of the earth are useful for different purposes – large-scale charts use the 'Mercator' projection for crossing seas and oceans and the 'Gnomonic' projection is used for small-scale harbour charts. Both suffer from the error of representing an irregular spherical surface in two dimensions, but that distortion is quantifiable. Thus different research methods serve different kinds of problems and different purposes. However, that is not a purely relativist position, for there are general criteria. How do the various research traditions compare? Hopkins' view is as follows (1993: 171):

> Criteria such as validity, reliability, generalizability, are necessary if teacher-researchers are to escape the sentimental anecdote that often replaces statistical research designs in education, and gives teacher-research such a bad name. Enquiry, self-monitoring, and teacher-research need to establish standards and criteria that are applicable to their area of activity, rather than assume (and then reject) criteria designed for different problems.

Without necessarily subscribing to the view that teacher research is often sentimental anecdote, we can, however, agree that appropriate standards can be established.

By and large, traditional numerical designs are good on objectivity, reliability, falsifiability and replicability, and weaker on interest and originality, context-specificity and utility. Qualitative approaches are good on interest, originality, sensitivity, context-specificity and validity. They are sometimes thought to be weaker on falsifiability and generalizability. Recalling the discussion of 'discrepant case analysis' in the last chapter, it is clear that qualitative designs do not have to be any weaker in falsifiability than quantitative ones.

The comments about utility and ethics apply in equal measure to both broad traditions; individual pieces of research may well have variable strengths and weaknesses in this regard.

Research by participant teachers and action research may be very strong on interest, originality, context-specificity, validity and utility, but weaker on publication, reliability and replicability. On publication, there is often a feeling that this kind of research may accentuate the uniqueness of the situation and play down the history of the topic as developed in other contexts. But there is also a danger of re-inventing the wheel, of unwittingly replicating, without reference to the history of thought which lies behind every research topic. A quotation from Bassey (1986: 24) may illustrate a prevalent attitude: 'The only reference to the educational literature is to P's source of inspiration. There is no tedious reference to queuing theory or to physiological explanations of fidgeting. Action researchers use the literature only to the extent that there is something significant and germane to the issue under study: they do not genuflect to Pavlov and to Piaget in order to impress their readers.'

In so far as this quotation puts a higher valuation on relevance and significance, it cannot be criticized: but the suggestion that a literature search, and the typical literature review that is normally part of a research report, are there to impress the readers cannot go unchallenged. A literature review is about writing the history (briefly, of course) of approaches to a subject and to the methodology of previous investigations to establish the crucial questions lurking under the surface. It is there to establish the ancestry and the originality of the new work.

Schecter and Ramirez (1992: 192) discuss their findings after studying a teacher-research group associated with their university in the USA, by monitoring meetings of the group and analysing the in-house reports of their work. It is therefore a kind of meta-analysis. They found a number of important differences between teacher researchers and university 'professional' researchers. The first of these concerned the role of the literature search: the university researchers, whatever research tradition they subscribed to, needed to demonstrate explicitly that their work contributed to an existing body of knowledge; the teacher researchers, on the other hand, quoted other people's work on their topics where it had been useful for them, but without undertaking systematic reviews. The second concerned reliability and validity judgements, in particular the role of personal experience. For the university researcher, this would not suffice; for the teacher researchers, it was regarded more highly, although many also attempted to support it by other forms of evidence. Third, they found that several pieces of teacher research did not 'address a problem' but rather took teaching methods and described their implementation and success. University research usually requires question areas to be painstakingly broken down into crucial problems or issues which the actual research can be performed on. A further very interesting point made by Schecter and Ramirez is the difference in standardization of forms of reporting, and that, as teacher research matures and becomes more widespread, so such standardization of rhetorical forms may increase. They describe the 'double narrative', i.e. the description of the research interwoven with the narrative of the researchers' development, and point out that a frequent style of reporting uses this, for the reason that teacher researchers are strongly aware of the reflexive relationship between the roles of teacher and researcher, which contrasts with the university researcher's claims of objectivity.

Aspects of design of research

It will be evident from the foregoing that there is no simple formula which guarantees good research, and there is no necessity for research to use only one method. In fact there are good reasons to incorporate several techniques in data-gathering. This allows the opportunity of greater credibility and greater plausibility of interpretation. For example, a researcher might decide to find out the opinions of a group of learners about a particular approach through a questionnaire, which would elicit easily countable answers on a range of standard questions, but supplement this either with interviews with a sample of learners or a content analysis of diaries written at the time of the introduction of the new approach. The two kinds of data, quantitative and qualitative, may coincide on a number of points, thus strengthening conclusions drawn from them, and diverge on others. In general, such a procedure is called triangulation – another term taken from geography, referring to finding an unknown position from the intersection of three compass bearings. Denzin (1978) argues that triangulation takes place in four different areas of the research effort: combining data sources, using comparisons of theory and individual accounts, using multiple methods, and several observers where possible. We return to this important concept in Part 2. An obvious example would be as follows: in a small-scale study of student opinion, a researcher might conduct both a session of individual interviews and a focus group discussion, in order to test the depths of feeling on particular points and its resistance to change in social interaction. In general, mixing methods of data collection aids validity (see Chapter 14 for a fuller discussion).

Methods of analysis may also with profit be mixed, to check on interpretation. In a study of students learning to write in a second language, a researcher might want to look at the written products both in terms of the frequencies of certain grammatical and rhetorical structures, and at the global impressions of comprehensibility recorded by a sample of readers. Some large-scale multimethod studies by academic researchers have reached the press (for example, Bachman and Palmer, 1982, on testing; Anderson et al., 1991, on test-taking strategies). Bearing in mind Schecter and Ramirez's (1992) point about the strength of the argument from personal experience, it seems that teacher researchers could profitably design into their research several kinds of data collection and analysis procedures to test and support their own convictions from experience.

A further problem in research design of any kind is the nature of any comparisons to be drawn. Purely descriptive research takes a situation and describes it: it is sometimes called 'one-shot' research. There may be a number of possible other comparisons. An example would be a time series in which the development of a situation over time is charted. Another would be the use of different treatments, either within the same person or group at different times, like a study of reading strategies for different kinds of text in a foreign language. In this case, there may be a need to control order effects, so that reading the different texts is not confused with reading them in a particular order. Another kind of treatment might require two different groups at the same time, as when two different classes are observed receiving the same lesson. Yet another kind of treatment comparison might involve two groups receiving different treatments, which becomes the classic 'Group A Group B' or 'experimental and control group' design.

Manuals of research design contain a large variety of possible design features which may get very complicated in order to allow unambiguous conclusions to be drawn: some of the more common ones will be introduced later. The main point to be drawn out here is that considerations of good design affect all kinds of research, by anybody engaged in research. An exploratory 'one-shot' design may be correct for the particular situation and purpose, but, if so, the researcher has to consider carefully the completeness and the quality of the data which she or he can use in the exploration, just as a researcher using a complex comparative design looking at changes over time in several treatment groups has to be careful that the data collected is in a form that will allow the planned comparisons actually to be made at the end of the day.

Conclusion

This chapter has introduced 13 key terms that are conventionally used to discuss and categorize the nature of 'research' as a concept, although they are not usually brought together in this way. We have, to put it another way, attempted to provide a metalanguage that can be used for talking about different approaches to research. It is probably true to say that *validity*, *reliability* and *generalizability* are those that surface most frequently – and often quite technically – in the literature on research method: nevertheless it is important to remember that each individual feature has its own kind of significance depending on the type of research project undertaken. Thus, for example, *falsifiability* is a major concern within a normative approach, *ethical* considerations play a large and explicit role in many interpretive traditions, and *publication* (not quite the same as going public) is a *sine qua non* in many academic contexts.

The 13 criteria have been proposed here as a framework for evaluating 'good' research. However, given our earlier descriptions of different, even competing paradigms, it should be clear that each criterion is open to different possible interpretations, and this we have tried to draw out in the course of the discussion. *Objectivity*, for instance, is a complex and controversial term, difficult to define and sometimes even rejected as a goal of good research. All the features set out here 'in principle' will recur in various ways in the subsequent methods chapters, as will the issue of mixing methods and the role of triangulation in data analysis.

Discussion notes

1. Taking any piece of research with which you are familiar (something you have done yourself or been involved with, either as participant or subject, or perhaps something you have read about), try to evaluate the extent to which the research addressed the 13 criteria. It may have done so explicitly, or alternatively some criteria may only have been implied, or been absent altogether.
2. Do you consider that certain criteria are best suited to certain kinds of research? For example, are some of them more applicable than others to an action-research approach?
3. How would you define the term 'objectivity'? We will see that it is an important one for several of the methods to be discussed.

5

Generating research

Introduction

This chapter is the final one in which research is discussed in terms of its underlying principles, though at the same time it is intended to provide a springboard for a subsequent exploration of the methods which operationalize those principles. The chapter is based on the assumption that a research stance is integral to the view of the extended professional that underpins this book, and not a kind of 'bolt-on extra' only obliquely related to one's everyday mainstream duties. Its central aim, then, is to examine the question of where research ideas come from, and the kinds of topics that might appropriately be addressed. By and large, for the purposes of the present discussion, we adopt the convenient position that content tends to go in search of method rather than vice versa, though we shall see later that this is by no means always the case either in theory or practice, particularly with data-rich sources. The approach taken here is intentionally an eclectic one, covering both research that is teacher-generated and executed, but also the use and uptake of research done by others.

We begin by reviewing some of the factors on which the origin and execution of research in a working context depend. This is followed by a run-through of the key elements in the debate about the relative roles of theory and data and their relationship to paradigm distinctions. The next section illustrates the kind of content that is nominated by (a small sample of) teachers of English as a foreign language. The chapter ends by asking how existing research might impinge on the activities of practising teachers.

Beginnings

In Chapter 1 we looked at some typical teachers 'in action' in their working situations, noting particularly the ways in which factors of context and role affect, constrain or facilitate their room for professional manoeuvre. A key point there was the assertion that all these teaching situations, however disparate, have an inherent potential for research to take place. This section is concerned, in fairly concrete terms, with how that potential might become actual. Let us therefore suppose that the teachers in action in Chapter 1 have, as it were, developed a research consciousness such that they are now working on specific projects. In other words we will tell a little more of the stories of a few of them, with a couple of new people interspersed to broaden the spectrum: the aim is to give a sense of the variety of ways in which a teacher might be stimulated to do research. There is of course a jump in logic here, because it will not be until the subsequent section that the genesis, sources and development of research ideas are more explicitly discussed.

Kenji Matsuda has now been on a six-month language development and teacher training programme in the UK. During his stay he was required (by the Ministry) to write a project directly addressing some aspect of his own situation. He chose to work on the methodology of vocabulary teaching. Now back home, he is linking his project work with everyday reality by analysing the set textbook and tabulating its methods of introducing and reinforcing vocabulary, and by selectively introducing new techniques then testing his class at regular intervals to see which methods encourage greater retention. He plans to persuade colleagues to try out something similar, and possibly to discover whether different methods, including use of the mother tongue, are suitable at different proficiency levels.

Anna Garcia is a Colombian university teacher of English with many years' classroom experience. The main part of her job is to teach reading skills to undergraduates in different subject areas. Although the materials used are relatively up-to-date in the sense of incorporating current views on the nature of comprehension, this teacher feels that her students' reading skills in English remain at a rudimentary level. She suspects that this may be related to, though not necessarily caused by, inefficient reading skills in Spanish, and in turn to the fact that language is typically taught in the schools as a grammatical system. She has managed to get a scholarship for a PhD to research this issue in depth. Her plans include an investigation of what other researchers have found, the development of instruments to measure reading efficiency in two languages, and an analysis of pedagogic practice.

Ann Barker's school decided to go ahead with its plans for more specialized programmes to run alongside its general English courses, both as whole packages and as part-course options. They have started with 'Business English' and 'Medical English', and AB, in view of her background, has been put in charge of the latter. Existing materials have been useful up to a point in getting started, but she is uncomfortable with them because they either overgeneralize or focus on one professional subgroup in a way that is not obviously relevant to another. She would therefore like to prepare in-house material that is more focused in terms of topics, skills, discourse and language structure. She has started by contacting her local hospital with a view to collecting (a) typical written data and (b) samples of spoken interaction, in the first instance as it relates to nursing staff.

Frank Jones works in a British university in the area of teaching English for Academic Purposes (EAP) to non-native postgraduate students. Together with a colleague he has completed a questionnaire-based study, involving about 300 students, designed to investigate the attitude changes of new students in relation to both academic and social-personal matters as they adapt to a new culture and progress through the academic year. Initially intended for internal university circulation, the results when reported at a national conference found sufficient resonance that colleagues in other universities are now seeking to replicate the original study and compare results.

Carol Turner has become increasingly interested in looking in more depth at the learning patterns of her pupils. She knows that she will have to set aside some time to review and update her earlier training in the teaching of young learners in general. However, she also plans to collect empirical data on her small groups in each school, and on individuals within them, probably by keeping a log over an extended period of time backed up with samples of the children's work. Her access to staffrooms means that she can liaise closely with mainstream teachers, who have agreed to make available the normal class work of CT's pupils and others, and to be interviewed from time to time.

Although these research instances are necessarily selective, we can now, so to speak, square the circle with Chapter 1 and briefly enumerate some of the parameters of research activity within the broader framework outlined there. (It is worth noting that Hopkins (1993) offers a comparable selection of case studies of teachers – he calls them 'reflective professionals' – carrying out research within mainstream education in Britain and Canada.)

All these teachers have made choices which, whatever the eventual outcome, have an organic relationship with issues that are pedagogically familiar to them. At least from their perspective, then, research entails questions of:

- methods choice (the substance of Part 2)
- focus and topics
- timescale
- time available
- participation (individual, collegial, collaborative)
- access (to institutions, participants, literature)
- scope
- review of the work of others

- outcome (personal/institutional change, interest, conference, higher degree . . .).

All these will surface in one form or another in subsequent chapters. There are also questions of:

- the initial stimulus for the research
- paradigm choice

which are both related to the wider issues of approach.

Approaches

The logical leap admitted to earlier means that we have not really enquired as to where these teachers got their research ideas from, nor how those ideas developed into a research plan. Behind this seemingly straightforward statement is a question that has been extensively discussed in our field (as in many others), whether in linguistics, second language acquisition studies, classroom research and many other areas. Any research undertaking therefore will need to have an angle, at least implicitly, on such a pervasive issue, not least because it is underpinned by basic choices in research philosophy.

Theory first?

The 'classic' debate is well covered in the literature. It is relevant here in so far as it points up the particular locus/loci for the kinds of research that teachers might do in the broad sense intended here, and because it taps into a long tradition of debate in the philosophy and practice of both the natural and social sciences from which even a small-scale and modestly conceived project cannot really be separated. We restrict ourselves here to a brief and very simplified overview: lengthier and accessible comment can be found in Allwright and Bailey (1991), McLaughlin (1987) and Seliger and Shohamy (1989).

A long-established, historically dominant view of research (albeit possibly as much honoured in the breach as in the observance) sees it as beginning from a theoretical position with the goal of testing out or refining that theory. It is an essentially 'nomological' approach that works from and towards the establishment of laws of varying degrees of specificity. Clearly it is an approach most closely associated with experimental science, with concomitant procedures of control of variables and the setting up of hypotheses. It is often referred to as 'hypothetico-deductive' or 'analytic', typified by a set of research stages algorithmically followed through on a 'if x then y' formula. Sharwood Smith (1994), for example, a second language acquisition (SLA) specialist, provides many illustrations of how much research in this area is concerned with theory-building and theory-testing, such as modelling the mental representation of linguistic knowledge, or the delineation of the concept of Universal Grammar (UG) (see Chapter 3 for a related discussion).

There is no reason in principle why a teacher should not undertake this kind of research, or find its ethos uncongenial, given a familiarity with the theoretical bases, though it may be more appropriately carried out in a context where it is the sole focus and where there is plenty of access to the literature, such as when working for a higher degree. For a number of reasons, however, a teacher's working life has a complexity that is different in kind from the undoubted complexity of the 'theory first' approach.

Sources of research ideas

First of all, the notion of 'theory' will probably have a different connotation from that of 'grand theory' and abstracted laws. As we have commented before, teachers' theory is more likely to consist of their personal constructs, assumptions and beliefs, all of which will be an amalgam of many factors – experience, value system, training, reading, other people, and so on. Second, a hypothesis can be formulated rather more loosely so that it becomes an idea that is a starting point to be tested out. Third, teachers in action are grounded in the context of their everyday practice, surrounded most obviously by raw data rather than overt theory, so that a qualitative paradigm – though by no means always qualitative method – is likely to be intuitively more appropriate. McLaughlin (1987) is one of several writers to explicate the data-driven, inductive approach to research which starts from empirical study (before, at least for the professional researcher, proceeding towards theoretical statements). This approach may also be referred to as 'bottom-up', or 'heuristic', generating hypotheses rather than testing them.

How then, in practice, might a teacher get started? Most likely it will be triggered by an aspect of practice, such as looking at a class, critical reflection after a lesson or while preparing one, or chatting with colleagues. Often there will simply be a sense of dissonance or unease with what Berthoff (1987: 33) calls 'tight schedules, leakproof syllabi, the instructor's manual, and the gilt-edged study guide' (and we can think back to Schön's 'swampy lowlands' instead). This unease may be formulated perhaps as:

- Why does the class not respond to (certain kinds of material)?
- How can I/we know (when best to switch to another activity)?
- I/she wasn't satisfied with (the way I handled the student's question).
- This coursebook has (inappropriate texts).
- X always goes his own way – it's really irritating.

- Does everyone else find (that the level is different from the test results)?
- What if (I do something different from what they're expecting)?

This kind of starting point has been formalized in terms of 'critical incidents' in teaching, moments or events which trigger a step-by-step investigation and understanding of aspects of one's practice (Tripp, 1993).

There are, of course, further sources from which ideas might derive. One is reading the work of others, or hearing a paper at a conference, possibly linking up with what was already a latent idea, or alternatively supplying a 'new' notion that an individual teacher finds stimulating enough to follow up. A paper on the nature of people's behaviour in 'natural' as opposed to pedagogically constructed groupings, for example, might trigger a fresh look at one's classroom practice in this area; or an article on 'display' questions might encourage a teacher to examine more closely the ways in which he or she poses questions.

Finally (for purposes of this section), and despite the frequent exhortation (Allwright and Bailey, 1991, for instance) that it is preferable to start with the focus provided by some kind of question, the data collected from, say, diaries, or from observation of recordings, and then reflected upon, can suggest topics for investigation for which other research tools are then invoked. Hopkins (1993) makes the point that research may start with 'closed' questions where a hypothesis or idea is already quite well formulated, but also with 'open' questions which begin either with data or with a broad area within which more specific issues will be identified and then explored.

Research in progress

One view of a research endeavour might be that it progresses systematically something like this:

hypothesis/idea→ choice of methods → investigation → results

Most researchers, however, whether they work within a normative or interpretive framework, are unlikely to be able to follow such a neat and logical set of stages: there will always be dead-ends, new data, data that do not seem to 'fit', uncooperative subjects/participants and much – fortunately – that is unexpected.

We have spent some time in this book so far setting out the qualitative research paradigm that, whatever the specific orientation, regards context and socially constructed meanings as particularly significant. Taylor and Bogdan (1984: 5) make the following point: 'Qualitative research is inductive. Researchers develop concepts, insights, and understanding from patterns in the data, rather than collecting data to assess preconceived models, hypotheses, or theories. They begin their studies with only *vaguely formulated research questions*' (italics added). This is echoed by Dillon (cited in Hopkins, 1993), who conceptualizes 'problems' as either existent, emergent or potential. Education, like the human behaviour it deals with, is a necessarily uncertain science, so that emergent questions will always need reformulation on the road to their increasing specificity. For example, a case study of an individual learner started only with his teacher's frustration at his apparent inability/unwillingness to learn. The teacher got interested, asked herself why this 'non-learning' was happening, then collected different kinds of data that gradually began to shed light on the problem which eventually became a reflection on evaluation procedures (McDonough and McDonough, 1993).

Seliger and Shohamy (1989) offer a common-sense model incorporating four phases of preparation for research in which systematic progression, a variety of starting points, and the possibility of changing direction, are all allowed for. The phases are:

- formulating the general question
- focusing the question
- deciding on an objective
- formulating the research plan (or hypothesis).

In this section we have put forward some possible starting points for research. We next survey by way of illustration the kinds of content that might provide the substance.

Content: teachers' choices

The purpose of this section is to set out some of the kinds of content that EFL teachers identify as being worthy of investigative attention. It would self-evidently be an absurd undertaking to attempt to give a comprehensive rundown of all possible topics and all known research projects by teachers going on in our field. So, short of an unattainable universality, we will mainly exemplify by using a specific circumstance in which teachers were asked to focus on themes of potential interest.

Themes

In the context of a postgraduate course module on research methods, it is arranged for the participants – all practising language teachers from a number of different countries and backgrounds – to observe ongoing English language classes in the same institution. It is not an exercise in observation as such, except for the instruction to participants (who go to the classes in pairs) that they should regard it as a descriptive and not an evaluative task, and should find ways of noting down as many of the class-room events as possible. Both conceptually and in terms of design, the exercise has obvious flaws: we are not concerned with possible research outcomes nor with the meaning perspectives of the observees, and the details of the methodologies of observation are consciously fudged so as to provide an easily managed vehicle to trigger focal topics. One further instruction reads : 'Generating issues for research involves noticing inter-esting events in the class. They may be interesting because you cannot immediately explain them, or because they illustrate familiar themes from your theoretical knowledge, or because they do not ..., or because possible explanations are unsatisfactory in the context you have observed.'

Here then are some samples of what these participants have found worth noticing.

- How to recognize/deal with 'false friends' in a multilingual class-room?
- What do students learn from listening to each others' role-plays?
- What is the role and value of reformulating learner responses?
- How do teachers change the way they use language with different addressees?
- What are the sources of misunderstanding in a lesson?
- Are the attention-seekers necessarily the strongest linguistically?
- The variable accuracy of explanation when teachers deal with vocabulary queries 'on the spot'.
- What does silence signify?
- What are the characteristics of good monitoring?
- Patterns of participation.
- How to deal methodologically with latecomers.
- Distinguishing and evaluating explanation versus discovery of meaning.
- To what extent do students do pair work according to the teacher's instructions?
- What do students get out of a lesson, and to what extent does this match with teachers' perceptions?

Comparable lists, though not drawn explicitly from observation, are to be found in Brindley (1990), Chamot (1995), Johnson (1992), Nunan (1989; 1992b) and Richards and Lockhart (1994). It is noticeable that the majority of themes that they (or their informants) nominate are likewise formulated as direct questions, such as 'What aspects of learner behaviour do I respond to?', 'Do I interact with some learners more than with others?' (Nunan), or 'How are objectives modified in the light of ongoing assessment?', 'What differences are there between the type of language produced by learners inside and outside the classroom?' (Brindley).

Even from this rather rough-and-ready list it is clear that there are a number of categories into which teachers' choices fall, including:

- class management
- learning styles and strategies
- teacher behaviour
- styles of language presentation.

To these might be added further categories and subcategories identified by the authors just mentioned:

- Testing and assessment
- Course evaluation
- Planning and setting objectives
- Talk and interaction
- Needs assessment
- Learner language

as well as more 'macro' issues such as sociocultural concerns and teacher training. The potential for topic selection is obviously considerable.

Specifying further

There are a number of reasons why the kinds of topics just touched on are unlikely to lead directly to a research project without further formulation. Some of these reasons – resources, timescale, likely goals, patterns of participation of those involved and so on – were listed earlier in this chapter as important factors affecting both approach and execution. There are three more specific reasons briefly commented on here: the first two relate loosely to what might be said to constitute 'researchable'.

First, some topics are clearly very wide-ranging, such as 'participation of learners', 'good monitoring' or 'what does silence signify?'. As triggers they are probably interesting: as 'emergent' issues they need to be further broken down, focused and modified, so that a tighter formulation becomes a more manageable undertaking. 'Participation of learners', for instance, may involve asking whether participation differs according to task type, nationality or proficiency, and possibly the interaction between them. This is related to the question of the feasibility and penetrability of the topic itself: 'teaching and learning grammar' or 'using the mother tongue', however central, are so large-scale that it is difficult to see how a way in could be found to investigate them at all. Nunan makes the further point that topics need to be worth addressing in the first place, and is tongue-in-cheek dubious as to whether 'a study to determine the number of Spanish interpreters who wear designer jeans' (1992b: 213) would be. Similar doubts – the 'so what?' problem – might be raised over a research exercise that collected numerical data for its own sake, for example the nationality, age and sex of students returning a questionnaire. Hopkins (1993: 64), albeit from an action-oriented perspective, advises: 'when choosing a topic or focus for classroom research, make certain ... that it is viable, discrete, intrinsically interesting, involves collaboration and is related in some way to whole school concerns.'

Second, any researcher will need to make a realistic match between topic and method of investigation. The postgraduate-teacher participants who provided the authors' list of topics (see previous section) were subsequently invited to shortlist themes of their own choosing and sketch out a possible research procedure, covering such questions as:

- What data would you want, and from what sources?
- How would you collect it?
- How would you analyse it?

For the record, one group chose 'the role of feedback and praise', 'how teachers adapt their language to different proficiency levels', and 'observable patterns of monitoring'. A range of methodology was proposed, including observation and recording of classes, interviews, coding and counting, and field notes.

Finally, some popular nominated topics have often been the subject of a considerable body of previous research, for instance teacher talking time (TTT), the treatment of learners' errors, turn-taking, and many more. We are certainly not suggesting here that the insights provided by a teacher-research project in such an area would not contribute 'new knowledge': on the contrary, and for the moment as an aside, there is much to be said for the establishment of collaborative research carried out by teachers and professional researchers in partnership. What this does suggest, however, is the need for both the availability of, and critical openness to, the existing literature, and it is to this point that we now turn.

Research and research: existing work

This section is in no sense intended as a review of areas of potential teacher-generated research lined up against what has already been done by others. Our concern here is to address the issue of the possible relationship between what a practising teacher might do within the main framework that we have dealt with so far – the context of their everyday professional work. The 'elsewhereness' of 'the big R' that we commented on in Chapter 2 is indeed often unattractive to practising teachers, partly it must be said because of a limited and limiting view of the nature of 'theory' and 'practice', and partly, to put it more positively, because different professionals (in our case teachers and 'academic' researchers) may quite properly have different agendas, expectations, procedures and targets. (After all, if I buy a motor boat I can't complain that it doesn't have sails.) It is nevertheless one of our contentions in this book that it would be both unrealistic and shortsighted for a teacher investigating a personally motivating topic to ignore the availability of existing work, even if that work were of background interest rather than direct application and even if – as is likely – that work will be harnessed to serve the teacher's own research goals. (The reciprocal, i.e. the researcher's need for a deeper understanding of practice, is itself far too often overlooked, and it is an important reason for teachers to produce powerful descriptions of their own teaching contexts for researchers to absorb. For researchers to give time to doing teaching will in certain circumstances be equally useful.) It is also presumptuous to suppose that teachers have no interest in background reading, only being focused on local concerns. In this section, then, we comment on ways of using the work of others, whether professional researchers or teachers, first from a particular perspective in teacher training, then from the point of view of the experienced teacher at work.

Theory through training

It is common practice in many teacher training/education programmes (see Chapter 2) that information is given, often in the form of lectures and set readings, about the established research base of the subject. In our field, of course, this would particularly be referred to as 'applied linguistics'. A typical programme, for example, would contain such topics (to take a few at random) as Communicative Competence, Universal Grammar, the Monitor Model, Errors and Interlanguage, Schema Theory, First and Second Language Acquisition, Discourse Analysis, Semantics and Vocabulary, and so on. In our view the appropriacy of this methodology as one segment of a training programme needs no defence if it helps to prevent the theory–practice disjunction from being perpetuated. However, there are other ways of looking at this such that 'teachers' theory' and 'researchers' theory' are more explicitly linked.

Marshall and Rossman (1989: 22) put forward this point of view: 'Personal, tacit theory and formal theory ... help to bring the question, the curious phenomenon, or the problematic issue into focus. The potential research moves from a troubling and/or intriguing real-world observation ... to personal theory ... to formal theory, concepts and models from literature ... which frame a focused research question.' This is by no means a universal or necessary procedure, but it is one that has a well-known parallel in the literature on teacher training in EFL, and it is worth setting out in a little more detail. Ramani (1987) seeks an antidote to the 'theoretical-input model', and finds one in an eight-stage procedure that encourages trainees to conceptualize and formalize issues in their own practice. The starting point is the trainees' 'pre-theoretical map', tapped into by inviting a pre-viewing discussion of personal criteria for evaluating a lesson which is then shown on video. The post-viewing discussion concentrated on eliciting sub-jective responses and then relating them to the established and agreed cri-teria. For example, by the end of this process the participants had foregrounded as worth commenting on the ways in which teachers ask ques-tions, and were able to formulate their observations quite sharply with the trainer as facilitator/reformulator. The final stage consisted of a handout from the trainer setting out the issues as the trainees had perceived them, and recommending relevant readings from the existing literature on the argument that these were now an organic part of the whole process. The whole procedure shows how trainees can begin with informal reactions to data, and work *towards* the personal 'discovery' of existing work. It also illus-trates how individual research can be related to a broader knowledge base.

Starting research – some brief case studies

It will be obvious from the above discussion that research plans do not spring fully fledged into existence. Before every piece of completed research there has been a long and often depressing period of change and development, often with discarded data and thwarted attempts at analysis. Imagine Anna Garcia, who wanted to investigate the English reading skills of her Spanish-speaking students and had a hunch that there was a con-nection with levels of reading skill in their native language. She also saw that some of the comprehension errors were motivated by grammatical ignorance. Her first research plan involved a contrastive analysis of the two languages, but then she realized that she was not going to be able to relate the results of the linguistic analysis to any reading ability measures. At this point, she began to read more widely in the professional literature on foreign language reading skills. This showed her some newer methods of describing reading skills, and also that other people, in this case in three different countries, had investigated first and second language reading ability. This reassured her that the topic was manageable, but she had not suspected that other people's thinking about it was quite so advanced, even to the extent of the existence of a theory, the 'threshold' theory of transfer of first language reading skills. She was at first daunted by the interna-tional dimension to her original problem, believing that it took her away from the possibility of improving the performance of her students in her own context. Then she realized that the work she had read was itself flawed and contradictory, so she decided to test out a modified 'threshold' hypothesis with her own students.

Anna Garcia's experience is interesting in the present context because of the role of the codified experience in the 'literature' in shaping her own research plans, and helping her to substitute something practical and manageable for the general and unworkable ideas she set out with. In her particular case, she obtained funding to go to Britain for research training.

In another case, a teacher wanted to introduce a particular technique which he thought would be advantageous: peer conferencing to improve pupils' writing skills. He had noticed that the pupils did not respond very effectively to their teacher's usual comments on their work and he wanted to evaluate this technique. Unfortunately, it had not been tried in his own education system, so he decided to research it in his own context to assess if it was worth recommending more widely. In his case, the literature on learning to write in a second language was remote because most of it concerned learning situations in countries where the role of the foreign language was very different from that in his own African context. However, it did give him hints towards the design of the research, for example what indications of improvement in the writing to look for, what comparisons to set up, and how to combine a numerical approach counting aspects of performance with a qualitative analysis of the actual peer conference sessions.

A third teacher's experience of starting research was different again. This teacher, working in a special kind of secondary school in a South American country, wanted to conduct an evaluation for the English for Specific Purposes component of the course. This component used a great deal of material originally developed for the university system in her country, in an internationally supported project. The university project had been evaluated, with positive outcomes, but there were obvious questions about its extension 'downwards' in the secondary schools. After much effort looking at ways of measuring achievement, resources, teacher training, costs and implementation, this teacher realized that she needed something much more focused and in one way less ambitious for her own project. She decided to focus on technical reading, and to compare reading strategies used by successful and unsuccessful students. For her method, she chose to combine two existing approaches she discovered in the literature: an 'introspective' approach called protocol analysis, and a quantitative questionnaire approach. Thus in this case, an explicit wish to replicate an evaluation in a new context turned into an original thesis which eventually won her a doctorate.

In each of these personal stories, there is a different outcome from the interaction between a teacher's original thoughts about the research topic, and the work of others that they consulted. The first teacher experienced some degree of shock that the question she had come up with in her own classes had been researched in other contexts at all; the literature she read showed that she was in touch with a widely recognized problem, but also that attempting to do something about it would require a greater degree of sophistication in analysis and design than she originally expected. The second teacher found that the question he wanted to ask was somewhat devoid of interesting and relevant prehistory in language-learning contexts similar to his own, and decided to extrapolate methods and insights from other cultural and educational contexts in order to establish a viable design, and in order to argue for the innovation on the basis of plausible comparisons. The third teacher found the literature in a particular area of enquiry gave her the means to develop a 'do-able' piece of research when she was beginning to despair that her original idea was too unfocused and difficult to carry out.

These three personal histories were based on the experiences of real people; in each case they were pursuing research in order to obtain a higher degree. As pointed out by Schecter and Ramirez (1992: see Chapter 4 in this book), this aim introduces a parameter of explicit incorporation of the researcher's work into the history of the subject which teacher researchers may not feel bound by. However, the teacher researcher may nevertheless experience the same sense of shock, surprise, lack of support, and stimulus for development in interacting with the relevant literature. In Chapter 6, some sources for literature search and ways of discovering what has been done about particular topics are listed.

Conclusion

This chapter has looked at where research ideas come from, how individuals begin to test their ideas and develop their own research programmes, and how those research activities relate to their normal professional lives. The chapter explored the variety of approaches that are possible, from testing predictions from established theory in one's own classroom, through the use of a teacher's own experience, to inductive or data-driven research in which explanations are sought for problems that are allowed to emerge, as it were, from data collected. The point was made that just as different groups have different ideas of theory, so they have different attitudes to the desirable degree of precision in the initial research questions. An overview of likely themes for research by English language teachers was offered, based on actual observation of classrooms. These themes are refined in discussion as the central issue which underlies the question is identified. Often, several apparently different questions mask the same issue, sometimes questions need to shift as the most important issues emerge. The strategy of training teachers to discover theoretical controversy through classroom observation – to develop an awareness of theory through educated observation – was discussed as a way of generating new research questions. Finally, some personal histories of teachers developing research programmes were given which illustrate the variety of effects that interaction with the history of their chosen topics can have – sometimes depressing, but mostly formative and encouraging.

Discussion notes

1. Reflecting directly on your own teaching situation and experience, what events, or incidents, can you identify that have given you a sense of 'unease'? These may be to do with individual learners, your own planning, the whole class, colleagues, materials and many more. When you have identified some incidents, choose one and try asking a series of questions about it, for example:

   - What exactly happened?
   - Why do I remember it?
   - Why do I feel it was important?
   - What did I learn from it?
   - Did anything change as a consequence?

   It is useful to work on these questions with a colleague.

2. In your reading of the published professional literature, what works (books, articles) have been particularly memorable or influential for you?

Part 2: topics and methods

6

Definitions and overview

This chapter is intended as a bridge between the two main parts of this book. It begins with a brief commentary on the relationship of research principle to research design, including some observations on the terminology involved, and then introduces the methods and techniques that will be discussed in subsequent chapters. The final section of the chapter suggests in practical terms some of the channels open to teacher researchers who wish to 'go public' and disseminate their own work to a wider audience, and read up on published work.

Principles, methods, techniques

A considerable proportion of this book so far has been spent on a discussion of the major paradigms underpinning educational research, their derivations (particularly in the social and natural sciences), and some of the key issues that arise as a consequence – how to approach fundamental questions of validity, reliability, generalizability and so on. On the face of it, it would seem intuitively sensible to assume that a particular orientation to research would have straightforward implications for design: a preference for a qualitative paradigm would, one might expect, lead to data-collection techniques at the naturalistic end of the spectrum and to interpretive rather than quantitative analysis. Thus, for instance, an interest in the 'local meanings' of participants in the classroom context (following Brown's, 1984, tabulation of the features of naturalistic versus experimental research touched on in Chapter 3) might involve selective non-evaluative observation triangulated by teacher and learner diaries; in-depth interviews and case studies might be preferred to questionnaires administered to large populations. There is obviously much logic in a research procedure that matches in kind, as it were, a research ethos and the dependent practicalities of its design.

However, a caution is also in order, and it is useful to make a parallel with language teaching here. Most language teachers will be familiar with the debate surrounding communicative methodology and its claimed advantages over the teaching of a language as a formal linguistic system through grammatical patterns (Widdowson's, 1978, well-known use/usage dichotomy). We know that a communicatively-based coursebook or lesson does not pre-clude systematic attention to grammatical exponents directly or indirectly related to the context of use. Likewise, a glance at a structurally organized textbook will almost certainly reveal opportunities for learners to practise the structure in a 'communicative' situation. In other words, the choice of a *principle* does not automatically mean that certain *methods* are ruled in or out, and so it is with research design. Erickson (quoted in Denzin and Lincoln, 1994: 213) points out that research is qualitative (or quantitative) because of its 'substantive focus and intent', not just because qualitative techniques are being used. Taking the example of narrative description, he argues that a qualitative researcher, on the one hand, and someone with a positivist, behaviourist orientation, on the other, if confronted with the 'same' phenomenon, 'would write substantively differing accounts of what had happened, choosing different kinds of verbs, nouns, adverbs and adjec-tives to characterize the actions that were described', reflecting varying degrees of research interest in the meanings of the 'actors' in the situation. We shall try to show as we work our way through the available methodology of research (for instance, coding systems in observation analysis, or content analysis of verbal data) that quantitative techniques are often used in an interpretive as well as a positivist framework without 'damaging' the para-digm choice itself. Marshall and Rossman's (1989: 42) common-sense advice is worth quoting here: 'Researchers should design the study according to the research questions they seek to answer.'

There is one further factor that requires comment: again there are rough parallels with language teaching. Many readers will be familiar with the three-stage model of course design associated with the work of Richards and Rodgers (1986, though they based their discussion on earlier work by Anthony). The model is intended to show how 'theory' becomes 'practice' through a process of increasing specificity and concretization. The levels are *Approach*, *Design* and *Procedure*. 'Approach' refers to general views – theories – of language and learning on which the next stage is based. 'Design' is the stage at which axioms at the first level are converted into syllabus and materials construction, and 'Procedure' refers to the practical techniques used in the classroom. Research, too, is often written about in a comparable way, a sequential distinction being made between interdependent levels:

Principle → Method (or methodology) → Technique

Taylor and Bogdan equate the middle level not so much with practicalities as with the logic of research design: 'When stripped to their essentials, debates over methodology are debates over assumptions and purposes, over theory and perspective' (1984: 1). Walker (1985) refers to 'methodology' in a similar way, and further distinguishes it from 'method'. Observation, or interviews, for example, would be methods in this definition, leaving the term 'techniques' to denote the details – in the case of observation, checklists, coding systems, descriptive strategies, and so on. As with much terminology, usage is often rather loose and interchangeable: we note the concepts here because they indicate a useful general framework for conceptualizing the whole research process. We shall ourselves approximate Walker's method/technique distinction.

Introduction to methods and techniques

The literature on research methods is extensive and growing. In the field of English as a foreign language alone, published work deals with language learning, often but not always from the perspective of applied linguistic researchers as much as teachers, and more specifically with what is potentially feasible for language teachers. (See, for example, Allwright and Bailey, 1991; Brown, 1988; Nunan, 1992b; Seliger and Shohamy, 1989). It is useful to set these alongside the more explicitly teacher-oriented work from mainstream education (for example Hopkins, 1993; Nixon, 1981; Walker, 1985), as well as standard reference works such as Cohen and Manion (1989). A typical profile of methods coverage would include at least the following, in no particular order:

- questionnaires
- interviews
- observation (direct and recorded)
- field notes, diaries, documents
- case study (not strictly a 'method', as we shall see)
- experiments
- think-aloud
- numerical analysis.

As we have often commented, choice of method and associated techniques will depend on many factors, often of a very practical nature (see Chapter 5 for a more detailed discussion). When we take into account that each of these methods is a 'composite', with considerable possibility for internal variation, then the permutations are many. For example, interviews can be structured, semistructured or unstructured and open-ended, and can take place between a number of different participants (learners, teachers, outsiders, and so on); observation can be evaluative, descriptive, or 'coded' in some way, as well as being carried out by different people with different purposes; and all methods can interact. Walker (1985: Chapter 3) is one of several writers to set out the advantages and disadvantages to teacher researchers in particular of some of the main methods, using data in the form of feedback from teachers participating in the Ford

Teaching Project (FTP). Just from his discussion we can invoke such considerations as the participants involved, their number and role; the amount of time needed; relevance and applicability; follow-up possibilities; bias and objectivity; equipment needed; research training needed; confidentiality; degree of specificity; administrative logistics; cost and scale. As Walker comments: 'The accumulation of this kind of practical knowledge provides an important background to decisions that need to be made concerning the selection of research methods when faced by particular research problems' (1985: 60).

In the chapters that follow, we look at the principal research methods and their associated techniques from the teachers' viewpoint, but at the same time discussing the varying extent to which they have been important in the research methodology of language teaching and learning more generally. There are, in other words, emphases on the frequency of use of methods depending on the type of research and the training of the researcher (observation and transcription, for example, being more widely used across the whole spectrum than diary studies). We begin in fact with observation in the language classroom, because it is particularly widespread and pervasive as a method. The subsequent chapters, to use Van Lier's schematization (1988, and quoted in Chapter 3 of this book), sit at various points within his two main parameters of intervention and selectivity and a fourfold division of methods into those that mainly involve one of *Measuring*, *Controlling*, *Watching* and *Doing/Asking*. Since we hold the view that all methods in principle should be available to teachers, the chapters are not to be seen as occurring in any systematic sequence. We therefore cover:

- observation
- diary studies
- numerical methods
- experimental methods
- questionnaires and interviews
- think-aloud and other introspective techniques
- case studies

and conclude with a chapter explicitly discussing some of the possibilities for combining methods. First, however, as a window on methods, a short digression on ways of informing others about one's research.

Out there: discovering other people's work and telling them about one's own

The point has been made several times, and particularly in Chapter 4, that research needs publication and dissemination both in its formative stage, learning from what other people have done, and as an outcome, telling others what the researcher has found. There are many different channels and modes of dissemination and discussion of research available. Here follows a necessarily incomplete list.

First of all, at the most local level, there are some schools and colleges that run in-house conferences, under the heading of 'staff development', at which there is the opportunity to invite outside speakers, and to present an individual's work – either in progress or as a final report – to colleagues. This opportunity does not exist in all teaching contexts. In many cases there are, however, in the local area, organizations or loose groupings of teachers who meet more or less occasionally to exchange views. Such teacher groups usually flourish longer if they are in contact with and can draw on the resources of regional or national organizations. Based in Britain, there is one large organization relevant to EFL teachers: the International Association of Teachers of English as a Foreign Language (IATEFL). This organization runs a large annual conference, publishes a newsletter, and offers a number of useful services. In particular, its members can join a number of Special Interest Groups or SIGs, which have special meetings at national and local level, and publish their own newsletters which are often hungry for copy from practising teachers engaged in research and development. The SIGs most obviously promoting research are 'Research', 'Teacher Development' and 'Testing'; but research features regularly in all the others as well. Outside the EFL field there are similar organizations for other languages, and for those interested in action research there is CARN, the Classroom Action Research Network. The United States' organization TESOL (Teaching English to Speakers of Other Languages) plays a local, national and international role, and many national organizations are themselves affiliates of the 'mother' TESOL. TESOL also runs a massive annual Convention, many Special Interest Groups, and promotes and aids more local events. The British Association for Applied Linguistics (BAAL) also runs an annual conference and promotes research on teaching languages. The addresses for these organizations are in the Appendix.

There are many publications which carry reports of research in language learning, teaching and education. The major international journals in the field are: *Applied Linguistics, English for Specific Purposes, International Journal of Applied Linguistics, International Review of Applied Linguistics, Language Awareness, Language Learning, RELC Journal, Studies in Second Language Acquisition, Second Language Research, System* and *TESOL Quarterly.* There are a number of journals which specialize rather more in teaching English as a foreign language and carry articles by teachers: *ELT Journal, Modern English Teacher, Practical English Teacher, Prospect,* and *The Teacher Trainer.* In the UK there is also a monthly newspaper, the *EL Gazette,* in which announcements of conferences are often made, and reports of interesting events in the field are carried, as well as some topic-based bibliographic articles. The addresses of the publishers of all these periodicals are in the Appendix.

For those with access to full library facilities, there are several useful sources of summaries of particular topics. An annual publication is the *Review of ELT* (Macmillan). There are *Dictionary of Linguistics and Phonetics* (Crystal, 1991), *A Linguistics Encyclopaedia* (Malmkjaer, 1993) and *Handbook of Applied Linguistics* (H. and K. Johnson, in press, Blackwell). A recent publication of relevance is *The Cambridge Encyclopaedia of the English Language* (Crystal, 1995). Most useful are the abstracting journals, such as *Linguistics and Language Behavior Abstracts* (published in the USA) and *Language Teaching* (published in the UK). These publish one-paragraph reviews of newly published papers in other journals, with full references, grouped under a whole range of key words. Both feature a regular spot for a commissioned 'State of the Art' article with an explicitly comprehensive bibliographic brief, so a glance at recent editions will produce detailed reviews of work in a multitude of topic areas. Full details of these are given in the Appendix.

In the UK, the Centre for Information on Language Teaching (CILT) maintains a register of ongoing language-related research projects, has a dedicated library and provides a bibliographic search service. In the United States, the ERIC (Educational Research Information Center) also provides a range of bibliographic services from short pre-prepared documents to full individually commissioned searches. Both of these can be accessed from abroad, though some of the services attract modest charges. Bibliographic searches through hard copy and electronic databases can also be commissioned through a local university library, again there are usually costs involved. These libraries also have the computerized database of 'Dissertation Abstracts' where unpublished graduate work can be accessed, usually going back to about 1985.

Rapidly increasing in importance and scope is the amount of information available electronically. At the time of writing, there is an explosion of interest and development available to those who have access to the Internet via e-mail or the World Wide Web. However, it can be quite frustrating to find that after some hours of 'surfing the net' either some crucial connection breaks down or there is no useful information at the end anyway. Enthusiasts claim that both of these problems will reduce as the technology improves and the quality of the information placed on the network gets better. Already, users of e-mail can sign up to a free electronic mail service, 'TESL-L', and a paper-free refereed journal, 'TESL-EJ' dedicated to English language teaching worldwide. Seedhouse's article in IATEFL Research SIG newsletter (1995: 6) explains lucidly how to do this. The instructions are given in the Appendix. Seedhouse points out that such resources give access to huge numbers of people, and in the case

of the journal promise quick returns – your work, if accepted, can be dis-
seminated within months rather than the typical two years of a conventional journal. Such resources can be used to find out if users are working
on similar problems, to get others to fill out your questionnaires, to get
volunteers for your research projects, and possibly to obtain other people's
opinions of your ideas.

Other material available on the Internet include even a Virtual Library,
run by Birkbeck College of the University of London, and Home pages
for organizations such as the British Council and IATEFL. At the time of
writing, there is not one for TESOL but it is being developed. Library cata-
logues can also be directly accessed. The IATEFL newsletters have
already carried useful articles by Seedhouse (1995) and Blackie (1995)
guiding potential users. The American ERIC organization can also be
accessed by e-mail. All these electronic addresses can be found in the
Appendix.

Information exchange is becoming easier and easier: naturally, no one will
confuse quantity for quality of information, and it must be most users'
experience of electronic information that there is a lot of dross to be waded
through before anything interesting crops up. However, as we saw in
Chapter 5, there are many ways in which other people's work and other
interested people can be useful to an enquiring teacher, and the information
explosion has to be welcomed: it means wider and easier access to other
people's thinking, their problems, and their contributions, for everybody.

7

Observing language classrooms

Introduction

'Observation', as it stands, is a monolithic label, a broad and even amorphous umbrella term subsuming many and varied purposes and interpretations. Hopkins (1993), for example, gives a positive sense of this breadth of application by describing it as a 'pivotal activity' with a crucial role to play in classroom research, teachers' personal-professional growth, and school development as a whole. Observation with its associated techniques is also often embedded in a larger-scale research plan as one method among others, when perhaps a variety of data sources is appropriate. Here, however, we take it as by and large discrete, returning to it in the final chapter in the discussion of ways in which methods might be used in conjunction with each other.

There are a number of categories into which the world of classroom observation is divided up in schemes proposed in the literature. To take just three: Wallace (1991) writes about system-based/ethnographic/*ad hoc* procedures; Hopkins (1993) has a more detailed breakdown into systematic/structured /focused/open observation; and Seliger and Shohamy (1989) encapsulate the same spectrum in a binary structured/open distinction. As we shall see, all such frameworks beg a number of questions, to do with the observer's degree of participation, the issue of 'objectivity', inductive (heuristic) and deductive (analytic) parameters, among others. The present chapter makes a straightforward distinction between 'systematic' and 'naturalistic' observation. We begin by attempting to delineate the term as a way of focusing on its specific role in research. There follows a discussion of the kinds of frameworks teachers might develop for structuring observations, and a comment on the development of coding systems for classroom-based research. After a bridging section on the interface between quantitative and qualitative approaches, we turn to the more 'open' methodology of descriptive observation. Throughout we take observation to be an intentional activity rather than a more reactive 'noticing' of classroom events.

Observation: uses and perspectives

Consideration of context, as discussed in Chapter 3, implies that any claim of typicality has to be taken with caution. Nevertheless, to provide a simple window on the classroom, we might agree that the following description of a segment of a lesson represents a reasonably realistic if unexceptional scenario for an EFL class in some parts of the world. (In the absence of other available means of presentation, a verbal description will have to suffice.)

> The teacher (T) has a lower-intermediate class of 16 students (Ss) aged 18–23 from a number of countries. This is the first lesson of the day. He chats a little about the previous evening's activities, then nominates a few Ss in turn to say what they did. He occasionally corrects past tense forms and pronunciation. He then asks them to open their coursebooks at the new Unit, which begins with a narrative about a family's experiences on their holidays. This is read aloud by Ss who self-select, and is followed by vocabulary checks: some Ss write down the new words, sometimes checking in their bilingual pocket dictionaries. The text is followed by questions, which T asks Ss to work on in pairs: some do so, others work alone. Answers are then checked in plenary. The coursebook has some grammar explanations and exercises which the class works through with T. For the final activity Ss listen to a cassette with two people talking in a question-and-answer format about an accident one of them had witnessed. Ss fill in details in a table as they listen. With a few minutes to go before the end of the lesson, T does a quick verbal test of irregular verb forms.

This is not in itself particularly illuminating, because there is no specification as to observer nor as to the purpose of the observation, so without this information there are many possible interpretations of what is going on. As Lincoln and Guba (1985) point out – and here we anticipate 'naturalistic' arguments about perspective to be addressed below – reality is constructed and interpreted differently by different individuals, whether the entity is (their examples) communism, good manners, God, Harvard University, the Middle Ages, urban blight, social science, trickle-down economics, Watergate ... and, we might add, a segment of an EFL lesson.

There are, then, at least three key parameters that need to be clarified. These are (1) the observer, (2) the goals of the observation, and (3) the procedures; in other words who?, why? and how?, which will in turn be determined by the nature of the setting in which the observation is taking place (see Chapter 1 for a fuller discussion of these factors; a useful discussion of the interaction of various features as applied to observation can also be found in Walker, 1985: 120ff). These are just a few of the possibilities under these headings, and the permutations are many:

Observer
Course director
Head/senior teacher
Colleague/peer
Trainee/junior teacher
New teacher
Researcher from outside the institution
External assessor

Goals
Placement of students
Evaluation of efficacy of materials
Apprenticeship for novice/trainee staff ('craft' learning)
Staff appraisal: formative/developmental
                    summative, e.g. management decisions on employment
Quality assurance and control
Personal development
Improvement in methodology

Procedures
Checklists and written criteria: observer-constructed; agreed in advance
with those observed; prepared by external agency
Audio- and video-recordings
Notes and logs
Participation/non-participation
With/without feedback.

Just this brief and selective overview should be enough to show that
'observation' is multifaceted, and without clear cut-offs between applications. Most combinations could in fact be invoked as a way of looking at
the EFL lesson described above. We now need to consider more specifically the uses of observation as a research tool.

Observation for research

Even with this apparent narrowing-down of the role of observation, there
remain many and varied possibilities for both approach and execution: the
research applications of observation therefore need to be situated in the
context of the lines of argument in the present book. Let us remind ourselves that we are concerned primarily with the kinds of investigations that
teachers can undertake as an integral part of their professional lives, but
also with the uptake, whether receptively or by application, of the work of
others (researchers, other teachers), and with what can be done when there

is an opportunity to take 'time out' to concentrate fully on a research project. Although teachers working directly from their day-to-day teaching experience may well feel more in tune with a naturalistic, interpretive research paradigm, the spectrum taken as a whole still encompasses many choices. The discussion in this chapter is restricted to observation carried out in the classroom itself, though of course there is no reason in principle why it should not be able to handle looking at staffrooms, shadowing individuals at work and so on, as indeed is often the case with, for example, participant observation studies.

A well-known volume in the educational literature on observation is entitled *Looking in Classrooms* (Good and Brophy, 1978). The overall tone of the book is prescriptive in that a major goal is to increase teacher awareness and effectiveness: nevertheless, the title is memorable and the preposition significant. Everyday language allows a number of possibilities: looking *in*, looking *at*, looking *for*, looking *with*, looking *into* ..., each reflecting a somewhat different orientation, as the work of Stenhouse (1975; 1985, in the Rudduck and Hopkins collection) reminds us. Researchers and policy-makers can look at teachers, who themselves can look at their learners or their colleagues; teachers can look with each other, or a researcher with a teacher; any of these people can look for something specific once the issue for investigation has been formulated; looking in can be done by someone standing outside, but also by an insider in the situation. Most of the approaches and attitudes discussed in Part 1 of the book should be recognizable here.

The main interrelated areas that the remainder of this chapter will be concerned with under the two headings flagged above (and they will of course recur in subsequent chapters) are simply:

- research in the interests of increasing knowledge and understanding of a phenomenon, or of creating 'new' knowledge, whether that knowledge aspires to be idiographic and particular, or transferable and general
- research undertaken explicitly to bring about change, innovation and action, often at institutional level; this is an important point at which research and evaluation clearly interact
- research for personal-professional development.

Within these broad categories, we shall need to invoke a number of further issues, including:

- the observer's role on a spectrum of objectivity–subjectivity, and the whole question of bias; degrees of participation/non-participation
- the role of those observed

- the nature of the data derived from observation and the timing of its collection; the use of data to trigger research questions versus its role in answering questions already formulated
- different ways of counting, systematizing and analysing data, and some of the problems associated both with selectivity and data reduction, and the converse of 'rich' data
- the nature of the setting itself, including the uses in research of the 'normal' classroom and opposed to the specially constructed or even the experimental.

Systematizing observation

Preliminaries

In this section we shall look at ways of observing classrooms which were very popular at one time and try to evaluate them as tools for teacher research. We refer to the use of preplanned observational categories, sometimes coding schemes, or 'systematic observation schedules'. To use them, the observer has to learn how to recognize instances of particular categories of classroom behaviour and note them down as they occur, either live or from some kind of recording. Clearly, observing one's own class is difficult, but not impossible, to reconcile with teaching it at the same time: the Open University's course on *Curriculum in Action* (1981) contains a video of several teachers doing just that. However, in practice, self-observation by teachers is likely to involve video- or audio-recording for later analysis, but collaborative observation – going into a colleague's class – is in some ways easier to conduct in real time.

Why systematize?

Earlier in the chapter an important distinction was drawn between observation as an 'intentional activity' and 'reactive noticing' of classroom events. The second is a necessary part of generating research questions (and of teaching anyway!); but intentional observation implies planning and the use of some previously established categories. The importance of systematicity was neatly put by Fanselow (1977) who devised a particular coding scheme called FOCUS, when he pointed out that we all see different features in the same scene and therefore give different accounts: in his view serious investigation needed agreement between observers on the basic categories involved. So systematicity implies prior decisions about what to record. Furthermore, it implies agreement or at least prior decisions about methods: when to record, for example:

- on a regular time base (every 3 seconds, 30 seconds, 60 seconds, and so on)

- using a recognizable boundary marker – like 'OK' – to signal a segment of a lesson devoted to one topic
- to categorize one turn of speaking at a time

and so on; and what kind of temporal information to record, such as frequencies or sequences.

Coding systems may be published and in widespread use, such as the venerable 'Flanders Interaction Analysis Categories' (FIAC) (Flanders, 1970) or the 'Communicative Orientation of Language Teaching' (COLT) scheme (Fröhlich *et al.*, 1985), or they may be set up for particular purposes by individuals.

The use of systematic coding schedules is therefore very much an elaborated checklist approach. Checklists are used to ensure that relevant steps are noticed and remembered, like a week's shopping list or a pilot's landing checks; but since they thereby systematically reduce the raw data, interesting events in that data that are not included on the checklist will not be noted.

The advantages of a coding system approach may be easily summarized as follows:

1. They are easier to use than on-the-spot description or paper recording.
2. The use of agreed and even published category systems enables comparisons with other studies and therefore generalizability.
3. They can be tailor-made for a particular problem.
4. Analysis can be by simple frequency counting and numerical analysis.
5. Patterns of interaction and development through time can be established.
6. Personal patterns of a particular teacher or learner can be established.
7. It is possible, indeed vital, to train observers in the coding system. A measure of reliability of the scheme is given by the relative ease different observers have in agreeing that actual behaviours are instances of one or other category.

The disadvantages of the use of coding systems in general are as follows.

1. They involve editing, i.e. reduction, of the data, in however systematic a way. Depending on the unit of analysis, for instance, taking a time base or a segment of a lesson, what is going on outside that unit does not count directly in the analysis. Thus, noting what is happening every 30 seconds essentially discards what has happened in the intervening time.
2. The categories are preselected, and may not be the relevant ones for the lesson being observed. Put more strongly, observation

schemes need to be validated against some independent criterion of relevance, of relation to achievement, or whatever. How otherwise do we know what the analysis categories are that are significant for learning? This has rarely been done even with category systems that are in widespread use.

3. Very often, observing a class using a categorical checklist cannot take into account relevant but unobserved shared knowledge among the actual participants. Thus going into other teachers' classes and using a systematic observation schedule can be blind to features of the history of that class and its institutional context which are presupposed by the participants themselves. This objection may not hold for observing one's own classes, but the use of 'insider knowledge' in interpretation has to be consistent and rule-governed.

Kinds of analysis

In looking for behaviours to slot into categories, the researcher is ultimately interested in what the observable behaviour tells him about something deeper: the aspect of learning or teaching under study. Categories vary therefore in the degree of precision they exhibit. A frequent division here is between high-inference categories and low-inference categories. Using high-inference categories, an observer has to make a considerable effort of judgement to decide whether a range of behaviours constitutes a category. A long-standing example of this is the first category of the Flanders Interaction Analysis Categories: 'Accepting the feeling tone of the students'. A teacher might do this either verbally or non-verbally; by a major or minor change from his/her planned lesson; by ceding turns of speech to a student expressing that mood; or by explicitly referring to the 'feeling tone' or ambient atmosphere. The observer has to make a number of judgements which concern the intention and probable outcome of the behaviour; the teacher's accuracy of perception of what the students are feeling; and a host of other context-bound variables to assign the event to a category. By contrast a low-inference category like 'hands-up' is relatively easy to code, but the later interpretation might prove more difficult. In particular, even with low-inference categories, the observer probably has to decide whether they are looking at something deliberate, possibly symbolic and meaningful, or accidental, unintentional and without symbolic significance.

Published or invented categories

There is no need to rely on published literature for categories: a researcher can develop his or her own for some particular research purpose. For example, a teacher researcher might be interested in the possible effects of different kinds of strategies for giving oral feedback or intervening about an error in spoken performance. Rather than taking a global category like 'praise' or 'criticism', a project might choose more detailed categories, as follows:

- identifying the location of an error by prompt or non-word – oh!
- giving a location by repetition
- giving a prompt
- asking a grammatical question
- asking a meaning-related question
- pretending not to understand the utterance containing the error
- asking for a translation
- giving a paraphrase
- asking for a paraphrase
- intervening immediately the error occurred
- intervening after the end of the student's turn to speak
- intervening at a topic shift boundary marker ('OK')
- non-verbal reaction such as gesture

and so on.

In other contexts, a teacher might want to develop a set of observational categories for events like 'handling questions from the class' or 'initiating a group work activity' or 'setting up a reading comprehension task' or 'giving grammatical explanations': in principle the possibilities are endless.

Experience of using the invented-category system would show how workable it was, and how consistent the researcher was in applying the codings; trying to teach somebody else to use it would help establish which categories were more reliable. The usual tests for reliability of coding systems is the percentage of agreement between independent coders (teachability), and the percentage of agreement between codings at different times by the same judge (consistency). Notice in this mocked-up suggestion there is still a considerable amount of judgement involved: even these are relatively high-inference categories. Another difficulty the researcher would have with these categories is time: since each of these may occupy one or even part of a turn of speech, recognizing and noting them may be too difficult for real-time work, and resort would have to be made to a recording and transcript.

A further set of decisions which would bear on the choice of categories would be their suitability for different kinds of participant groups. For example, the teacher researcher in our examples might be interested in:

- the teacher in a lockstep teacher-fronted class
- teacher–student interaction
- a selected group of students within a co-acting class

- a small working group of students in a group-work class
- the teacher working in turn with several groups working on the same or different materials.

Analysis of codings

Coded transcripts of classes can be analysed in several useful ways.

1. By counting *frequency*, in which the relative frequency of each kind of behaviour can be set out in tabular form and conclusions drawn from the overall picture. This might indicate, perhaps to the surprise of the class or the teacher, particularly favoured kinds of behaviour or mannerisms associated with a particular class, students or teacher; or might demonstrate the proportion of time spent on certain kinds of linguistic exchanges at the expense of others, or the proportion of time spent in the target language as opposed to a common language. Before drawing many conclusions it would be possible to check how any markedly over- or under-used behaviours compared with what chance would predict by using an appropriate statistical test (for the significance of proportions, see Chapter 9 on 'chi-square').

2. By finding *patterns*, in the sense that there may be certain sequences of behaviour that are characteristic of the lesson: e.g.

soliciting answers → nominating a pupil → receiving an answer → checking with another pupil → praise.

These patterns may be individual to a particular teacher or general depending on what is under observation. As the teacher researcher inspects the data for such patterns there will be two concerns in particular: first, to use any 'insider knowledge' carefully and defensibly especially when observing one's own behaviour or one's own class; second, to remember that one swallow does not make a summer, and not to believe there is a pattern until there are several examples of it.

Relationships with other information

Instances of particular codings, frequencies and patterns, are difficult to interpret only by reference to themselves. Lessons, in particular, usually have a planned structure which at the least can be compared to the actual sequence of the lesson to observe and explain differences. Lessons and their participants also have a temporal and a structural place in a programme or curriculum which itself may be significant in explaining what is or is not observed. Furthermore, lessons and the people co-producing them – the teachers and the students – have both individual and corporate histories, and any outside observer using a coding scheme may miss very important events by not knowing those histories. An inside, participant teacher researcher will probably know some of it, but it is a weakness of the method that there is no systematic way of including this kind of information. Lastly, behaviours which can be coded may be expressed in all sorts of different ways, both linguistic and non-linguistic, so some record of the type of expression might be kept, especially in the case of a language class. An important issue in many early language-classroom observations was simply how much, and when, and for what purpose, either teacher or students used their mother tongue or the foreign language.

Live observation or recording?

Any form of observation is going to introduce some distortion from normality. It is incumbent on the teacher researcher to satisfy himself or herself that any distortion is evaluated or taken account of. At its worst, the distortion of the data could invalidate the observations as a true picture of what normally occurs; at best, the amount and kind of distortion can be known and the conclusions modified accordingly. Sitting at the back of someone else's classroom – or of one's own while the students are working on their own – conducting an observation and marking down instances of particular events in code can distract the attention of students and teacher alike, however used they may be to the presence of another teacher in the class. Introducing a tape-recorder into the class to listen to later can also distract attention, and the recording can also distort: microphones are much more limited devices than the human ear, voices on the recording are much less easy to identify, and distant participants may not be picked up. However, such a recording can be used as a check on a coding conducted live, without necessarily writing a transcript. Writing up a transcript of an audio-recording makes it available for careful analysis, freeing the researcher from the constraints of real time, but it is itself a very time-consuming exercise, and naturally loses more information which may be necessary to decide between coding categories, such as intonation and other paralinguistic cues and non-verbal activities, unless the recording can be supplemented by field notes.

Video has naturally been used a great deal in observational work, but any fixed camera only sees what it is pointing at and a movable camera requires an operator who is necessarily editing the record as he or she chooses what to record. Even the comparatively simple problem of recording interaction between students and teacher in a teacher-fronted classroom is quite difficult to accomplish. Camera equipment in a class may also distract and possibly invite strange behaviour; leaving it unused for a time to let the class get used to it has been advocated. Siting audio- or video-recording equipment out of sight of the participants, as with the use of one-way vision screens set in classroom walls, can be criticized reasonably on ethical grounds. All the participants can be considered to have a right of consent to the research, so concealed observation may be interpreted as bypassing that right, unless the researcher reveals its existence and location – which rather negates the point of concealment in the first place.

Alternatives to coding schemes

Using a coding scheme or a systematic observation schedule, whether in real time or on a recording or transcript, is a way of separating out significant events from the mass of data, spotting patterns, and arriving at an interpretation of the structure of what has been observed. It necessarily involves reducing the data by some preconceived plan, hence the checklist of categories. The validity of the resulting interpretation has a lot to do with the validity of the coding categories, established on other data in other classrooms, and it follows that it has less to do with the uniqueness of the particular observation. Nunan (1989: 16) demonstrates, using a transcript of a lesson excerpt, how three different ways of representing and analysing the data give quite different insights into the progress of that lesson, which is in fact the opening sequence of greeting and warm-up. He uses an adaptation of the Flanders FIAC, another system for categorizing verbal behaviour developed by Bowers for English for Specific Purposes classes; and a narrative description. They also differ in 'user-friendliness'. The reduction of the data for the FIAC abstracts and highlights certain processes characteristic of the opening of a lesson; the labelled transcript using the Bowers descriptors presents a ready-made interpretation, but the narrative casts the data with all its human signals, messages and nuances as the author (perhaps only the author) saw it. This version is, Nunan tells us, perceived as the most user-friendly by teachers. It describes the teacher not just as coming in and sitting down but 'slumping in his chair'; student talk is described as 'muttering', 'echoing', 'interjecting', 'suggesting' and 'venturing': a rich vocabulary for a rich set of nuances of interpretation. How accurate such a narrative can be is open to evaluation.

Recordings and field notes

Earlier, we discussed the use of recordings for the purpose of running a check on coding accuracy. An extension of the practice of recording, bearing in mind of course the caveats about recording and data selectivity, is to record a lesson or part of a lesson and then transcribe it using field notes taken at the time of the recording. Putting the two sources of data together represents a move away from reductionist observation methods towards something one might usefully call elaborative description.

Text analysis

Allwright, in his influential paper 'Turns, topics and tasks' (1980), presents a method of analysis that invoked both a (tentative) coding framework at each of three levels and a line-by-line commentary on the coded transcript of the lesson. The commentary acted as an immediate interpretation of the flow of negotiations that constituted the management of the interaction by all the participants in the lesson. This paper is also discussed in Allwright's book (1988), which describes the developments in observational research in language classrooms over the previous decade or so. An interesting theme drawn out by Allwright is the extent to which observation can in principle reveal a complete picture of the classroom dynamic.

Stimulated recall

Another technique which researchers have used with teachers but teachers could use with their colleagues and students is known as 'stimulated recall'. Here, a recording is made of the lesson or class to be observed, but interpretation of the observation is made with the collaboration of the participating teacher or students, the researcher stopping or freezing the recording at points of interest and asking the participant to think back to the lesson and reveal what had been going on, their perceptions at that point, and their decision processes. This technique has been used in published work by Nunan, working on lesson recordings with a teacher, but also for example by Poulisse *et al.* (1987) working on native-speaker/learner dialogues with learners of English. Taking the example narrative of a class given at the beginning of this chapter, this technique allows a researcher to ask why, for example, the teacher nominated students to say what they had done the previous evening but allowed the students to self-select who was going to read in the class, on the face of it a curious discrepancy the motivation of which is unrecoverable from the narrative.

The work of Peck

An example of language-teaching research on quite a large scale, which does not use a systematic observation schedule but at the same time does not espouse a full naturalistic enquiry philosophy, is given by the work of Peck

(1988). Peck's methodology was developed to enable him to compare the realities of language classrooms devoted to several different foreign languages in five countries (Britain, France, Germany, Norway and the USA; English, French and German) and yet it is readily adaptable for use by individual teacher researchers investigating lessons in their own schools. Peck intended to provide a workable scheme for describing language teaching: 'categories for the interpretation of current practice, and [to] make available a number of useful comparisons between lessons and teachers' (1988: 4).

Tellingly, his introduction contains the statement: 'I could not observe, or describe, language teaching from the point of view of an outsider, like for instance a Martian observing a cricket match; I tried to bring to observation and explanation all the knowledge and experience which I have acquired myself over a number of years as a language teacher, textbook author, and teacher trainer' (1988: 4).

Peck observes and describes a fair number of lessons and teachers using his 'insider' approach, without placing strict and difficult restrictions on himself as to his choice of unit of analysis or his observational techniques. His objects of study were normal categories of teaching, like presenting a text, new grammar, free expression, narrative, pronunciation, oral practice, teacher support. His unit of analysis was the 'part' of a lesson. His categories for observation are often expressed as comparisons or tradeoffs, plotting them on coordinates to show how a particular lesson or teacher rated:

Range of linguistic structures	versus	Pace of oral practice
Technical variety	versus	Intensity of language
Teacher intervention	versus	Student participation
Fluency	versus	Preparation for oral work

In many instances he plots a category over the time course of a lesson (see Fig. 7.1).

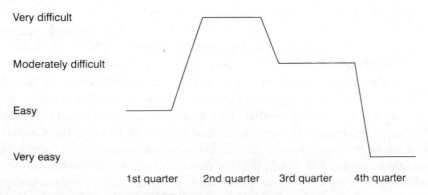

Fig. 7.1 Lesson difficulty (Peck, 1988: 69, Fig. 1.20, adapted)

A very useful feature of his book is that many of the suggestions for analysis are deliberately free of copyright so that any teacher can use them in examining their own or a colleague's teaching style.

Discussion of these approaches to interpretation of the process of language classes using semicontrolled but rich data serves as a bridge between the quasi-scientific reductionist paradigms of the systematic observation schedules and full naturalistic observation, to which attention now turns.

Naturalistic observation

Some definitions and implications

At the simplest and most general level, 'naturalistic' is to be taken in contrast to contrived, manipulated or experimental: it refers, in other words, to a concern with the understanding of natural settings and the representation of the meanings of the actors within that setting. In the case of EFL, a naturalistic observation would need as its database the everyday lesson with its usual participants in real time, rather than, say, a class constructed to try out a particular pedagogic method, or a 'one-off' with volunteers not normally together, or a teacher not known to the students, any of which – whatever their other research merits – would constitute inherent distortions of naturally occurring phenomena. (In passing it is worth noting Nunan's (1992b) somewhat surprising statistic that of 50 well-known classroom research studies only 15 were carried out in 'genuine' language classrooms.) Lincoln and Guba (1985) further remind us that naturalistic enquiry is itself defined at the paradigm and not necessarily at the methodological level, though clearly the tendency of such research would be weighted towards a preference for qualitative method. There are implications, therefore, not just for goal and setting, but also for the relative roles of participants and for the nature, collection and analysis of data.

In principle, then, in terms of the logic of the paradigm, there are at least two important corollaries. First of all, the notion of context becomes crucial, because it sites the phenomenon of study in space and time, and can therefore tap into the constantly fluctuating interactions and relationship patterns in a group of people working together. (This is the holistic, 'emic' world of Van Lier, 1988, where the setting speaks for itself.) As we saw in the short example in Chapter 3, a 'classroom culture' is usually built up over quite a long period of time, so even a short interaction may contain some complex verbal and behavioural presuppositions. The teacher in the lesson segment in the first section of this chapter may have 'insider knowledge' reasons for choosing not to nominate certain individuals to answer (which an outside observer might well misinterpret); a reference by a learner to 'that preposition problem' could be retrospective by several weeks. Walker and Adelman's (1976) example of the class who laughed when a new teacher talked about 'strawberries' is much cited. A researcher using a prespecified coding scheme could adequately describe neither the students' unexpected laughter response except weakly as a 'reaction' nor the teacher's bafflement at that reaction. (The students were, it transpired, amused because a previous teacher had often talked about bad strawberries when returning weak marked work.) All teachers would be able to think of a host of such examples, only apparently commonplace.

Second, the naturalistic observer will take as given the existence of the multiple perspectives of those observed, and will positively seek to interpret rather than avoid them. The observer as a 'human instrument' also has a perspective, of course. As Schwartz and Ogilvy (quoted in Lincoln and Guba, 1985: 55) put it: 'Perspective connotes a view at a distance from a particular focus. Where we look from affects what we see ... A whole picture is an image created from multiple perspectives.' As a direct consequence, in this view it is accepted that an understanding of bias and subjectivity is the norm, and notions of objectivity and neutrality become spurious: the famous 'observer's paradox' is elevated to the status of a principle. This view of the mutual interdependence between social settings and the accounts given of them is often referred to as 'reflexivity' (Hammersley and Atkinson, 1983), where everyone involved is part of the construction. A brief, observable illustration of perspective:

> The teacher hands out a summary in table form of the verb system of English, including a list of irregular verbs, the intention being to review ground already covered. Learners react in different ways. Some ask questions:
>
> *What's an imperative?*
> *What does (X) mean?*
> *Is (X) the same as (Y)?*
> *Why can't I use the same ending?*
> *How do you spell ...?*
>
> Others are silent: some are confused (and may or may not be prepared to say so); some know it already (and may be bored, or pleased to go through it).

There is clearly a range of different learning paths, and the lesson has different 'meanings' for the individuals participating in it.

Dealing with data

In our discussion of 'coding' models, we have already commented on the place that systematic observation can play in a teacher-designed research project. On the whole, however, to capture the natural setting, the techniques used will be at the open, less structured end of the methodological spectrum.

Describing settings

Description is a key technique in ethnography and anthropology: the researcher usually becomes immersed in the setting as a 'participant observer', a term which captures the role duality. Ethnographers and anthropologists are of course professional researchers who will spend long periods of time intensively studying their chosen environment. Furthermore, their studies will be 'macro-ethnographic', concerned with such large-scale settings as whole schools, or even whole cultures. As we have noted, practising teachers (unless taking time out for research) are very unlikely to become full-scale ethnographers, and a micro-ethnographic approach that focuses on the more manageable entity of a class, or relationships and events within that, is more realistic. Observer roles, too, then become more variable. Here are just two possible scales:

- active participant
- privileged observer
- limited observer

- complete participant
- participant as observer
- observer as participant
- complete observer

(Wolcott, cited in Johnson, 1992)   (Hammersley and Atkinson, 1983)

Teachers have a built-in advantage: when observing either their own class or that of a colleague they are always in a sense 'participant' or at least 'privileged' observers because they are an organic part of the institutional environment.

Whatever the detailed arrangements, the principal data-gathering instrument for naturalistic observation will be description, with the aim of producing 'thick' rather than 'thin' (i.e. restricted) data (Geertz, 1973), in other words a multilayered package that is as comprehensive as possible in terms of individuals, interactions and behaviours, as well as all facets of the physical setting. Description of a real-time process is an intensive undertaking. It may be a full text, attainable in the observation of others; or it may take the form of field notes written up later, as when observing one's own classroom in action.

Analysing data

There are two main approaches to the analysis of data derived from descriptive observation which essentially come at it from different directions.

First, we need to start with another example. For simplicity let us suppose this is the written outcome from an observation of another lesson with the same class as in the first section above – details of the physical setting will have to be assumed.

The teacher arrives early and changes the seating arrangements so that the class can work together in groups of four. Students gradually drift in, some talking to their compatriots in their L1. When most Ss are there, T returns corrected homework, which not everyone has done, and puts recurring errors on the board. There is some restlessness until he calls for attention and explains the task. It is a word-building exercise where one form of a word is given and Ss have to write down the adjective, noun, verb and so on. It is competitive in time between groups. After some initial confusion Ss get on with the task, those with the same L1 referring to their dictionaries and each other to clarify meanings. T does a mix of desk work and walking round to listen, spending differential amounts of time with each group and requesting 'English only'. One group finishes and 'wins', though their answers may not be correct. Others seem to be some way behind, poring silently over their dictionaries.

This is clearly a very broad description: space constraints preclude greater amounts of detail. From the observer's point of view, issues of potential interest are as yet unformulated, and it is the data itself that will suggest productive lines of enquiry. Even our rather minimal data would show a few themes hidden in these routine classroom events, such as:

- the frequency of certain behaviours
- L1/L2 use including patterns of dictionary reference
- individual styles and preferences in working patterns
- T's methodological preferences and their execution
- variable time-on-task
- contextualized/decontextualized language practice

and so on. Essentially the data examined and re-examined until recurrent patterns begin to be foregrounded. (More detailed data would show linguistic patterning as well, perhaps students' questioning style, or a teacher's classroom management phrases.) Walker discusses pattern analysis as a formal technique, based on audio recording and transcription, then 'looking for patterns ... regularities of behaviour, forms of interaction which occur over and over again' (1985: 140). Once foregrounded, such patterns are then open to structured scrutiny. It should be noted that this kind of observation is in tune with the 'emergent design' dictum of naturalistic research, where any one theme can be successively reformulated and focused, often by using different kinds of research tools once observation has elicited the area of interest. This kind of descriptive observation in a qualitative tradition is discussed by Day (1990), who also provides a lengthy descriptive segment of a class.

We have had to limit ourselves here to the one-off kind of observation, but regular observations over a longer period of time would arguably be more useful, partly because they would allow the researcher to build a picture of the developing classroom culture and its insider-knowledge and pre-suppositions, and partly because change over time – in learning patterns, or interactions, for example – can emerge more clearly. The 'thick descriptions' from this kind of observation are, in Lincoln and Guba's (1985) terms (a) inductive, (b) generative and (c) constructive. For all data analysis of this kind, Miles and Huberman's (1994) sourcebook is a key reference work. They collate in fascinating detail the methods available to date for looking at qualitative data starting from the three interrelated key principles:

- data reduction: coding, clustering, writing 'stories'
- data display: networks, structured summaries, synopses
- conclusion drawing and verification: triangulation, comparison/ contrast.

Second, descriptive observation and a data-first approach do not necessarily go hand in hand. Description can also be selective and focused after a particular issue has been chosen for further investigation. For example, a teacher researcher may have already decided that a particular learner exhibits problematic characteristics in uptake of instruction and materials, apparently following his own agenda (looking up words in the dictionary rather than following the flow of the lesson, and so on): he or she takes descriptive notes in class over time and charts the key patterns, perhaps going on later to look at success rates in tests as compared to others. Again, another teacher might invite a colleague to examine descriptively how he or she sets up pair work, because he or she is uneasy about its efficacy. Mention must be made here of the techniques of 'clinical observation' (or supervision, in teacher training: see Chapter 2), a cyclical process with three recurrent phases of planning, the observation, and a feedback meeting (which could lead to further observation). (For more detailed discussion, see Hopkins, 1993; Gaies and Bowers, 1990; Fitzpatrick, 1995.) This procedure belongs firmly in the tradition of research for action and change.

Seliger and Shohamy (1989) point out that description starting with an already narrowed-down scope and preconceived topic shares some of the features of the deductive approach, even if the 'hypothesis' to be 'tested' is a more diffuse sense that something is worth looking at. Descriptive research may also have features of quantitative analysis, for example by providing measures of frequency.

Conclusion

This chapter has surveyed systematic, focused and naturalistic, rich methods of classroom observation from the point of view of a teacher who wishes to use some of them. It began by considering how a 'window on the classroom' can be opened and how observation can be used for research purposes. The use of systematic observation schedules, both general and published, and invented for a specific local purpose was then discussed. Ways of analysing coding schemes that have been used in the past in language classrooms were then explored. A bridging section then gave a number of approaches which have been successfully used already, and which incorporate more data than was available from the more mechanical coding scheme approach. These methods combined different kinds of data in order to achieve a fuller interpretation and a more complete description of the language teaching classroom. The final major section described in some depth the naturalistic and ethnographic approaches to interpreting classroom events. It showed how the 'rich' description takes into account the context, the physical constraints, the individuals, and the interaction, to produce an interpretation. Analysis of such data concentrates on establishing patterns of various kinds and on scrutinizing them for evidence either for a general description or for the solution of focused detailed questions, which may have been flagged beforehand, or which emerge as crucial issues from the inspection of the data.

Discussion notes

1. Are there any aspects of the life of your own classroom that you think could be usefully investigated by devising a systematic observation scheme? For example, are there features that you think it would be helpful to quantify? How would you interpret the outcome in the context of your classes as a whole?

2. If possible, find an opportunity to sit in on a class together with another observer. Write as full a description as you can of what went on. Look at your description to identify the most frequent/significant events, and then compare your analysis with the other observer. Did you 'see' the class in the same way? (If you do not have access to a class, use video data, or even Day's, 1990, transcript.)

3. Do you think that being a participant observer in your own class would help you to observe accurately or make it more difficult to perceive what is going on? Can 'insider knowledge' aid interpretation and can observation challenge pre-existing assumptions?

8

Diaries and diary studies

Introduction

Diary-writing is a pervasive narrative form. It has, of course, always played an important role in many people's private reflections, and has had many famous exponents (Anne Frank, Samuel Pepys, Malinowski, Katherine Mansfield and many more). It is widely used in specialized and non-specialized ways in such diverse fields as history, literature, anthropology, autobiography, sociology, health studies, clinical psychology and psychotherapy. In education and in English language teaching, the diary has become increasingly significant both as a reflective genre in itself, and as one of a battery of interpretive micro-ethnographic research techniques. In Van Lier's (1988) terms, most diary-writing clearly belongs in the categories of least control and selection of data (see Chapter 3).

After running through some standard definitions of diaries, we go on to discuss the nature of the data that they generate. The next section looks at ways of analysing that data and at the place of analysis in the whole research process: it also invokes the important distinction between diaries and diary studies. We then set out and exemplify the main uses of diaries in research on language teaching and learning, including a short section on the 'reflective' ethos in teacher training and its research underpinnings. The final discussion section is concerned with both the benefits and problematic aspects of diary-keeping as a research method.

Some definitions

Most people who have kept a personal diary would recognize the following way of looking at it: 'It is such a rough, impulsive study of life itself, it will prove perhaps ... that life is not one thing but changes constantly, that character has not one face but a thousand, changing as these pages change' (Anais Nin, quoted in *The Guardian*, 4th January, 1996, p. 6). Indeed, the theme of change over time and the sense of writing about a process is one that resonates directly with the use of diaries in educational research. This is echoed in Elliott's prescription that a diary should contain 'anecdotes; ... accounts of conversations ...; introspective accounts of one's feelings, attitudes, motives, understandings in relation to things, events, circum-stances' and should be kept on a continuous basis (1991: 77). Bailey's well-known definition is more formalized: 'A diary [study] is a first-person account of a language learning or teaching experience, documented through regular, candid entries in a personal journal [and then analysed for recurring patterns or salient events]' (1990: 215; we comment on the significance of the quotes in square brackets a little later in this chapter). A diary, then, is personal, with oneself as addressee, long-term, and may also be relatively unbounded in the kinds of facets it records, at least within the broad area with which it is concerned. At the same time, a diary is not only a re-creation of immediate experience but is also a written record: the act of writing itself is a way of structuring, formulating and reacting to that experience, which is then available for reflection and analysis.

The diary as an open-ended narrative genre, which is the principal type that we shall be discussing in this chapter because of its relative frequency, is, however, not the only possible format. First of all, a number of writers (for example Holly, 1984; Hopkins, 1993) make a distinction between *logs*, *journals* and *diaries*. Holly regards (a) logs as a record of factual informa-tion, (b) diaries as the kind of subjective text described in the previous paragraph, and (c) journals as an amalgam of the two, containing both 'subjective' and 'objective' data. In practice the distinction is somewhat blurred: a conventional ship's logbook, for instance, will often contain a narrative section as well as essential details of course steered, distance run and weather conditions. In this chapter, we shall for convenience simply refer to 'diaries' and shall assume that any kind of information – factual, feelings, attitudes, reactions – may in principle be included. Second, a somewhat different perspective is offered in many areas of social research, where it is common for diaries to be commissioned for research purposes, as opposed to the non-reactive format kept of one's own accord. In such cases, although the diary remains a personal account, the domain is quite tightly specified by the researcher and the record kept is often behavioural, oriented to facts about activities rather than being evaluative and affective. Examples of this kind of research application include the investigation of patterns of consumer expenditure, how people spend their time or travel, diet and nutrition, alcohol and drug consumption (see Corti, 1993, for an overview). Clearly, as we shall see, there are implications here for the ways in which data are analysed. This kind of precoded diary is to date less common in reports of diary-writing in language teaching and learning contexts, though there are some instances of its use.

Diary data

One of the problems in reproducing diary material as *raw* data is the virtual impossibility of providing long enough samples. Diaries are best written over an extended period, and 'snapshot' extracts cannot capture changes over time which can often be very marked, so any one segment belongs organically in a broader temporal and contextual picture. Nevertheless, we begin with two short diary extracts which must suffice to give at least a stylistic flavour of a narrative diary entry. (There is more detailed discussion of thematic content in the next main section of this chapter.) The first extract is from a teacher's diary, the second by an elementary learner of modern Greek. Both diaries were kept by one of the present authors. A further problem in publishing diary data is of course the issue of confidentiality and ethics, and no material should be reproduced without the writer's permission, and indeed approval of the whole text in which it appears, if necessary with due regard to anonymity. That said, some published data is generally available (see, for example, Nunan, 1992b, and the individual sources cited in the later review of teacher and learner diaries).

Extract A: Teacher's diary

Am looking forward to having more students next term, particularly in this group which seems to operate so much from shifting balances of personalities and others' reactions to them. Like introducing new ingredients and seeing what happens ... Worried today about not 'teaching' enough, at best giving them opportunities to explore in English. Not that the class went badly, but I felt I did rather little of the work. Maybe I should volunteer to teach grammar or something next term ...

I wonder why X often doesn't understand the simplest classroom instructions and exercises, and why he refers to himself in the 3rd person? He seems to want to 'explore' a lot in English, but reverts constantly to the electronic dictionary ...

Extract B: Learner's diary

Chatting before the beginning of the class, some people said they felt they weren't making any progress. Personally I feel on a bit of an upward swing at the moment, though it will no doubt change. The language feels like a constant discovery process as things gradually fit together – am more confident about talking, and I catch myself at odd moments trying to work out what I might want to say in Greek, though I still have to work it out in English first. I'm pleased that things that seemed to 'crowd in' too much at the beginning of the course are now becoming more routine, though of course there are new 'blocks' to fill their place. This time it's the future of the passive verbs, which I've decided not to learn till later ...

Let us first review the kind of data that in principle becomes available from a diary.

The nature of data

There are at least four features that can be identified as characteristic of diary-generated text, apart from the fact that it is rather casual and unpolished. We refer particularly to the more prevalent open-ended narrative type, though we also comment on more prespecified kinds of data.

First of all, the textual material (like ethnographic-style interviews or descriptive observation, for example) is very 'rich' both quantitatively – there is a great deal of it – and qualitatively, in that more than one theme is addressed. This is evident even in these short extracts: the teacher's diary talks about an individual, the whole group, her own methodology; the language learner talks about learning curves, other people's patterns of learning, cognitive overload, specific strategies. Second, the diary is self-evidently subjective and introspective where the perspective of the 'I' dominates, and this includes filtering the assumed and reported attitudes of others. However, the nature and focus of this introspection may well differ depending on whether the self is the sole intended addressee as in the most free styles of diary-keeping, or alternatively a researcher (who might be a teacher or colleague) who has provided some guidelines for writing with a specific line of investigation in mind. Open-ended diaries too can subsequently be made available to others for analysis.

Third, diaries are necessarily written retrospectively, even if the timelag between the event and the recording is very short – just after a lesson, same day. As with any kind of autobiographical memory, there is likely to be some decay in accuracy over time, at least as far as factual logging of activities is concerned. However, few people would claim that a diary is a 'true record' (a notion which our earlier discussion of objectivity and bias has anyway called into question), rather that, in Elliott's words, it can 'convey a feeling of what it was like to be there participating in it' (1991: 77). Finally, the minimal data in the above extracts is still able to demonstrate that diaries can record what happened, what the writer felt about it, what might or should have happened, what could change, opinions, anticipation and immediate reactions, as well as a more reflective tone. These characteristics of the raw data have implications for the procedures that an analyst can use to deal with it.

Analysing diary data

Particularly with the more open-ended styles of diary writing, there is obviously a problem of seeing the wood for the trees. So 'thick' is the data that its density does not allow immediately transparent results. However, as we saw in Part 1, many researchers see this as positive: Saville-Troike, writing about the ethnography of communication, comments that 'one kills something thin only to discover that it is fat' (1989: 129), a backhanded critique of overly normative analysis. Themes must be 'teased out' from the mass of data.

In terms of research methodology, diary material of this kind fits naturally into the classic data-first procedures. Scrutiny of the text may lead to a self-contained analysis – of behaviour, interaction, learning processes, and so on – as a diary study in its own right, or alternatively may be, in Nunan's (1992b) terms, a 'ground-clearing' preliminary, generating topics worth pursuing with other research tools both qualitative and numerical. To take just one possible example, studying one teacher's diary could lead to a set of interviews with that teacher, to observation of his or her classes, to the distribution of a larger-scale questionnaire, or to the collection of comparative diary data. Whatever the objective, the approach to analysis, as Seliger and Shohamy (1989) remind us, is essentially heuristic and one of discovery, not deductive and hypothesis-driven.

The most commonly reported procedure for analysis is a very simple one, consisting of reading and re-reading the text to allow significant themes to become gradually foregrounded. The reader (of one's own diary, or those of others) may notice, say, that certain uses of language recur, perhaps style features, semantic grouping of lexis, tense usage, and so on. Or a particular focus may emerge – on individuals, or aspects of methodology, or preoccupations with learning specific aspects of a language. Allwright and Bailey (1991: 193) have proposed that three key features need to be taken into account:

1. *frequency* of mention
2. *distribution* of mention (across writers, when several diaries are being examined)
3. *saliency*: the strength of the expression with which a topic is recorded.

Mention of frequency and distribution, as Allwright and Bailey point out, implies that content analysis is likely to be quantitative: they even suggest this as a possibility for 'salient' items as long as analysts can agree on a 'strength scale' for language used. Computer packages for the analysis of qualitative data including diary text are also now available (Corti, 1993; Weitzman and Miles, 1995). It is important to remember, however, that a counting approach will be necessary but not always sufficient, because an interpretive analysis will need to take full account of the whole context in which the diary-writing took place – features of the setting, assumptions and intentions, the specific classroom culture. It is also important not to start the analysis too soon, because early identification of themes may lead to an involuntary precoding that shapes subsequent entries in a restrictive way.

The above comments notwithstanding, we noted earlier that diaries as a more closed genre are common in some fields of research. With some degree of pre-specification a diary can become at least an interim research outcome as much as a trigger, a kind of 'soft' version of an inductive approach where analytic categories precede data. As we shall see, in language teaching and learning this is not particularly unusual in teacher training, or where diaries are collected from learners in classrooms, because trainers and and teachers are of course in a position to be directive if they so choose. More generally, Richards and Lockhart have suggested a large number of 'reflection questions' that any teacher could address in a diary format. The list is too long to reproduce in full here, but includes questions about what happened during a lesson, looking at teaching style, planning, actual events, what students did, and 'questions to ask yourself as a language teacher' (1994: 16–17).

Diaries and diary studies

A major function that a diary fulfils is to offer what Holly (1984) simply calls 'private space', a forum for reflection. This may be extended into collaborative journals, shared with colleagues, or into dialogue journals (Peyton and Stanton, 1991), where teachers and learners respond in writing to each other through the diary medium. These can all play a central role in many aspects of professional development. It is, however, only when they have been processed analytically that they start to become instruments for research. This point has been made particularly strongly by Bailey (1983; 1990). Her argument, briefly, is that, while a diary is private, a diary *study* means going public, contributing to a growing body of 'different insights into the largely unobservable processes of second language learning and teaching' (Bailey and Ochsner, 1983: 191). The addressee is then not only the self but a wider professional audience, whether reached through conferences, journals, newsletters or local teachers' groups. The goal of the research may be an enhancement of our knowledge in a particular area, or an action research one of change and innovation.

Bailey (for example, 1990: 219) diagrammatizes the production of a diary study into five steps:

1. account of diarist's professional background
2. confidential diary
3. revision of entries for public version
4. analysis
5. interpretation and discussion.

The unpolished diary is thus embedded in a broader more formal and analytic text, and research becomes a public activity within a critical professional community.

We now turn to an examination of ways in which diaries have been used in language teaching and learning research, with examples from a number of published studies.

Diaries in language learning and language teaching

Along with the growth of interest in naturalistic modes of enquiry, so the use of diaries to investigate a variety of aspects of teaching and learning has likewise burgeoned, with a concomitant more widespread availability of reported diary studies. In this section we look first at different types of learner diaries, then at diaries written by teachers in the context of their regular teaching. We conclude with a comment on the use of diaries in teacher training. We are principally concerned here with diary *studies*, or at least with diaries that have been used as a platform for research.

Language learner diaries

There are two rather distinct uses of diaries written by learners of a language.

Pedagogic use

In many teaching programmes, it is now quite common practice for class teachers to ask their students to keep a journal. Occasionally this is unfortunately a course requirement which may meet with some resistance from individuals in the 'captive audience' environment: data from such conscripts is anyway likely to be unhelpful because it will probably be skewed merely towards expressing their unwillingness to keep a diary at all. Where participation is voluntary, the usual procedure is as follows:

- The diary is confidential between teacher and individual learner.
- It is usually written in the target language except at elementary level. It is interesting in passing to speculate that, while L1 data will probably be more sophisticated in expressing feelings and opinions about the language-learning experience, it will of course not provide any material to investigate actual L2 language development.
- It is not normally used as a vehicle for error correction, its overt purpose being expressive rather than formal.
- Any subsequent write-up as a diary study requires permission and a reading of the research report by writers of any diary cited substantially.

It is characteristic of pedagogic diaries that students are given some guidelines before they start writing. These may be in the form of quite detailed points to address, for instance (McDonough and Shaw, 1993):

- lessons followed
- what you found most/least useful and enjoyable
- what you found easiest/hardest
- reactions to your teacher
- reactions to other learners
- comments on specific lessons

or they may be designed to constitute a loose framework around which the writer has more space to choose topics (Parkinson and Howell-Richardson, 1989):

- in-class activities
- out-of-class activities
- my problems
- what I have learnt.

This kind of pre-categorization has the advantage of giving learners (who are rarely specialists in language-learning theory) a kind of 'metalanguage' with which to talk about their experience. Parkinson and Howell-Richardson report two different diary studies, both intended explicitly as research instruments *ab initio*. One study analysed informativity, use of English outside class, and anxiety levels; the other also looked at out-of-class use, and added a category of learning strategies.

Clearly the initial specification will determine to some degree the themes that emerge from these kinds of diaries. Furthermore, the process and outcome of analysis will depend on whether the teacher researcher chooses to look at a broad spectrum of the whole class, or particular individuals: an in-depth examination of learning styles and strategies can be more fruitfully carried out by selecting individuals, whereas the diaries of the larger group will more readily show patterns of reaction to the lessons and the teacher. A further dimension is whether the investigation is intended as a form of action research, carried out in order to make changes to aspects of one's practice. Finally, even though error correction is rarely the goal of a learner diary, there may well be an interesting spin-off for an individual's language development through the process of regular diary entries. (See, for example, Jones', 1994, experience of writing his diary in Hungarian, or the learner reported in McDonough and McDonough, 1993, who moved from simple sentence reporting of daily activities to more complex exploration of his whole language learning experience and the context in which it was taking place.)

Expert diaries

By 'expert' here we refer to language learning diaries kept by language specialists who may be teachers, applied linguists, or second language acquisition researchers, and all of whom are used to dealing with language as a central part of their professional lives. Their diaries, even if not consciously crafted artifacts, are typically written from their inception with the intention of completing a diary study of their own language-learning processes. Quite an early form of this kind of self-report can be found in Pickett (1978) who, using a detailed set of prompts, invited successful adult language learners to write to him about their learning experience in a diary-letter format: the data, which was principally concerned with learning processes, was clearly (very) retrospective. In most cases, however, the 'expert' writer is his/her own initial addressee.

There are a number of published examples of language-learning diary studies of this kind. The most quoted is Bailey's (1983) work on competitiveness and anxiety as evidenced in the journal she kept while learning French. Other well-known studies are those of Schumann and Schumann (1977), who reported on learning Farsi and Arabic; and Schmidt and Frota (1986), who documented the experience of one of them of learning Portuguese in Brazil. Jones (1994) analysed his own self-study of Hungarian using teach-yourself materials.

As might be expected, second language researchers in particular are interested in exploring their own language-learning processes and thus making links with the research field more generally. Their raw diary data is itself quite revealing (the short quotations are taken from Bailey [B], Jones [J], and Schmidt and Frota [SF], and where unacknowledged from the language learning diary of one of the present authors):

Fantastic feeling: I can read my magazine articles without a dictionary ... [J]

... in the beginning I was very shy, I didn't even dare open my mouth ... [J]

I was really up, self-confident, feeling fluent ... [SF]

I feel very anxious about this class. I know I am (or can be) a good language learner, but I hate being lost in class. I feel like I'm behind the others and slowing down the pace ... [B]

I really like doing verbs and guessing the 2nd stem – more like a logic game ...

... his face showed complete non-comprehension. I grabbed my dictionary ... [SF]

Some people said they felt they were getting worse and I didn't like to say I don't!

I hate the feeling of being unable to talk to people around me ... I don't like the silence ... [SF]

It seems that it's easier to learn sentences or expressions instead of lone words ... [J]

My grammar background is probably stronger than most of the students'. I'm just having trouble in recognizing and producing the spoken language ... [B]

The remainder of the class was choral repetition ... I didn't like that much either ... what a sour start! But I think I'll stick with it ... [SF].

Today I decided to speak to the man who is so uptight about his ... test. I was sad that he didn't come to class. I hope he doesn't drop the course. I said hello to another student in the hall ... but he just nodded. I would have liked to have someone to commiserate with ... I am absolutely worn out ... [B]

Certainly these diaries turn out to have a great deal to reveal about language-learning strategies and processes: indeed, most of Jones' formal analysis is concerned with these factors, being divided into categories he calls thresholds/grammar/writing/reading/pronunciation/speaking/listening, with just a short section at the end attending to motivation. However, it is clear that expert writers are also preoccupied with affective, social, interpersonal and classroom-methodological influences and reactions. Allwright and Bailey (1991: 38) make the following point, which is worth quoting in full, about Bailey's French class diary. Bailey, as a researcher, was particularly interested in error treatment. However:

> error treatment apparently had not been important enough to her as a language learner to be recorded in the journal entries. What she found instead were numerous references to competitiveness and anxiety ..., a topic that arose from the data rather than from any preconceived hypothesis or theory of classroom language learning. This topic turned out to be a productive focus in itself, but a certain amount of frustration arose and time was lost in the search for the learner's reactions to error treatment – a topic for which there were no pertinent data in the journal.

Rather curiously, Allwright and Bailey regard this as a reason for at least novice researchers not to collect data first: in fact it is fascinating evidence of a tension between a theory- versus data-first paradigm, and between a learner (or pedagogic) versus researcher role.

Teachers' diaries

In comparison to learner diaries, particularly the second type, there are rather fewer published accounts in EFL to date of diaries kept by teachers during their everyday work in Schön's (1983) 'swampy lowlands' – another kind of 'expert' diary. The genre is somewhat more endemic in teacher research in school-based education (see, for instance, Hitchcock and Hughes, 1995, who discuss the use of diaries in this context in their book on qualitative research; also Enright, 1981, and Tranter, 1986). The relative lack of teacher diaries in EFL may be due in part to the historic dominance of the applied linguistic tradition and the 'scientific' paradigm, or perhaps to the timelag between learning about diaries and related methods on teacher-training programmes and actual uptake in practice. Whatever the reasons, diary-keeping is arguably one of the ways in which teachers can get closest to their own work and hence, via critical reflection, to researching it.

Potentially there are many and varied themes that could emerge *post hoc* from a teacher's diary, and which tap directly into the researchable issues that we discussed in Part 1. As Holly (1984) puts it, what to write about is 'limited only by your imagination'. She lists three areas:

1. teaching: what you do and why
2. students: what they do, circumstances, descriptions of behaviours
3. collegial interactions.

To this we could add a further category:

4. metacomment: thoughts about the process of diary-writing, and reactions to one's readings and the research of others.

Each of these can be broken down to become much more specific, so the very general label of 'teaching' might include (to nominate just a few):

- planning the lesson and selecting material
- dealing with different types of learner in the class (mother tongue, learning styles, attitudes, pacing, proficiency ...)
- whether the plan matched the reality; why some things worked, others not
- coping with the unexpected; changing direction
- using available resources and technology
- speculation (about learning; behaviour ...).

Turned on its head, Richards and Lockhart's (1994) list of prewriting prompts referred to earlier provides a useful checklist of themes to look for when diary data have already been produced.

The potential range of topics is reflected in the diary studies publicly reported. Bailey (1990) has a useful survey of a number of these (Telatnik; Butler-Wall; Deen; Ho), which cover such diverse areas as the relationship between a teacher's ideas on teaching and those of experts and theorists; teacher power; teacher's choice of classroom language. McDonough and McDonough (1993) report on a teacher's diary that both reflected the gathering and interpretation of qualitative data and, by focusing on an individual learner, turned into a case study subsequently invoking other methods. Llewelyn (1995), working in the context of a collaborative action research project on the Australian Adult Migrant English Program (AMEP), charted her course design processes and her developing understanding of functional grammar through the medium of a teaching journal. Burns (1995) in her introduction to the collection of papers in which Llewelyn's is included, situates journals in the framework of all the action research methods used in the AMEP project. McDonough (1994) examined the diaries of four teachers (including herself) on the same language programme, and found that the analysis yielded themes to do with individuals; the whole group; methodology; teacher roles; style and language of diary entries; and metacomment on the value (or otherwise) of writing a diary.

The most extensive report of a teacher's diary is to be found in Appel (1995) who looks back over and comments on the diaries he kept during his first six years of teaching English at secondary school level in Germany. The book is divided into three sections, entitled 'Survival', 'Change' and 'Routine', charting Appel's own 'journey' as a language teacher. He writes: 'I was sifting my personal and subjective evidence with certain guiding questions and concepts at the back of my mind. At the same time the concepts themselves were sifted and modified as they were confronted with the evidence' (1995: xiii). Each section is preceded by the diary entries, and is followed by analysis. The presentation is a little crafted, and on occasions the diary entries do not so much generate analysis as support the author's broader line of pedagogic argument, and the juxtaposition of individual entries with generalizations about teaching sometimes stretches credibility a little. Nevertheless, the record of Appel's experience gives a powerful sense 'of what is was like to be there participating in it', and his accumulation of experience over time offers a fascinating thematic transition from 'novice' to 'expert' concerns. He moves, for instance, from a preoccupation with discipline and control to a position where language learning and methodology become more centre-stage.

Teacher training

Diaries kept by trainee teachers have several obvious parallels with what we have termed 'pedagogic' learners' diaries (Bailey, 1990, chooses to use the term 'academic journals'). In particular, they are usually in some sense a requirement of the training programme, and they almost invariably have prespecified categories as a framework for writing. It is also unlikely that the trainees themselves, even on INSET courses, will carry out a research-oriented analysis that will eventually go public: rather, they are exploring in the foothills of that research, being sensitized to the valuable role of critical reflection on practice at the same time as learning about at least one research tool. Porter *et al.* (1990: 240) make the further point that 'The journal encourages students to go beyond learning course content in isolation and to strive to link this information to theories and knowledge beyond the particular assignment and the particular course ... In sum, it teaches them to do what we do as professionals – to work to integrate new ideas with what we already know and to talk with each other as we do so', a perspective that makes a direct link with Ramani's (1987; Chapter 5 of this book) 'theorizing from the classroom'. There would, incidentally, be much scope for comparing the kinds of topics addressed by experienced teachers, on the one hand, and 'novice' trainees, on the other.

As with the teacher who carries out a diary study based on his/her learners' writing, so of course a teacher trainer's analysis and write-up of trainees' logs and journals is a research offering to the wider professional community. Murphy O'Dwyer (1985) looked at the attitudes to learning reflected by participants' diaries on a short training course, and in her analysis identified the four categories of group dynamic, general administrative constraints, personal variables and presentation/content. Thornbury (1991) used teaching practice logs for trainee self-assessment, and found that they talked about perception of self, subject-matter, tasks and learners/learning, and also about the development of their own 'craft knowledge'. Other reports of trainee diaries, and general discussion, can be found in Jarvis (1992), Bailey (1990), and Porter *et al.* (1990). Finally, Richards (1992) proposes an interesting variant where he asked trainees to learn a foreign language and keep a written log of their experiences. Major themes recorded were the teacher; the learning experience; motivation; authenticity of materials; vocabulary; cultural factors; phonology.

In this section, we have considered the following types of diary writing in language learning and teaching (see Fig. 8.1).

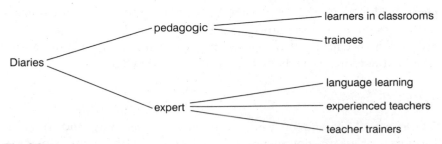

Fig. 8.1

134 RESEARCH METHODS FOR ENGLISH LANGUAGE TEACHERS

We conclude this chapter with a brief overview of practical procedures for diary keeping, and a short discussion of some of the broader issues.

Keeping a diary

Methodology

Reference was made earlier in this chapter to Bailey's (1990) five-stage procedure for carrying out a full-scale diary study. On a practical level, keeping the diary itself is in principle straightforward. No special arrangements are required, just pen and paper (or a wordprocessor) and a modest amount of time that is anyway organically related to the teaching or learning activity that it records.

With precoded diaries, particularly where the writer (or 'respondent' in this case) is writing under the guidance of a researcher, advice on the 'how' is likely to be quite detailed, perhaps including the type of notebook, a model entry, standardization of the time period allocated to particular pages, and a checklist of items to jog the writer's memory (Corti, 1993). This kind of systematization is clearly helpful to the researcher in sifting through a large amount of data collected with specific research questions and hypotheses in mind. With all kinds of diaries, whether open-ended narrative or with prespecified categories, the standard advice is in line with that given by Bailey (1990), and Allwright and Bailey (1991):

- set aside a time each day (or each lesson if it is less frequent) to write the diary
- tape-recording is an option, but may be more time-consuming if it requires transcription
- allot roughly the same amount of time to the diary as spent in class (less feasible if one is teaching/learning on an intensive programme)
- concentrate on recording data, not on style, grammar or organization
- record facts and events as well as reflections.

Richards and Lockhart (1994) also suggest reviewing entries 'regularly', but do not specify what this might mean: we have noted the possible danger of inadvertently restricting subsequent writing by doing a preliminary analysis too soon into the process, especially with self-driven diaries. It is also worth speculating that diarists may use a different style of writing whether the addressee is the self or a teacher/researcher.

Discussion

Those who keep and/or work with language teaching and language learning diaries are, not surprisingly, advocates of the genre, linking it particularly to naturalistic paradigms: 'The journal holds experiences as a puzzle frame holds together its integral pieces ... clues lead to new clues, partial perspectives to holistic perspectives' (Holly, 1984: 8). In the course of this chapter we have already identified a number of salient issues to do with diaries in research, including the quantity of data, the benefits of sharing interpretations in a public domain, and the nature of exploratory process writing itself (see Raimes, 1983; White and Arndt, 1991). Here we briefly add to these, noting that a counter can be found to most pros and cons depending on one's beliefs and assumptions.

In terms of research method, teaching and research, teacher researchers and professional researchers are in particularly close approximation in the diary mode, whether researchers are keeping language-learning journals or teachers are critically reflecting via their diaries on the many facets of their role. This is, then, one significant instance where everyone is engaged in a comparable process and working within a comparable paradigm. The perceived advantages of the technique are also shared: the diary, it is argued, is a primary vehicle for process research, for getting 'under the skin' of the psychological, social and affective factors involved in teaching or in language development in ways that cannot readily be reached by staff meetings or tests or population sampling or experiments. Progoff, who pioneered the use of journals in psychotherapy and whose work has also been influential in education, writes of 'experiential feedback', and puts the point thus: 'The journal enables our subjective experiences to become tangible to us. Experiences that would otherwise be intangible and therefore too elusive to grasp thus become accessible to us so that we can work with them' (1975: 37). We still, however, need to add a cautionary reminder that introspection of the kind recorded in diaries is not universally suitable and not everyone finds such self-scrutiny illuminating.

With diary studies, as with much interpretive research, there are inevitable charges that they lack reliability and validity. Some researchers attempt to deal with this on its own terms by using parallel diaries or other forms of triangulation, such as data gathered from other sources or other kinds of documents as part of a single study. Others reject the concepts themselves: Lincoln and Guba (1985), arguing that 'bias' and perspective' are of central importance in social and human research, prefer, as we have seen in Chapter 4, to think in terms of dependability and credibility. Jones (1994: 444) asks: 'But is subjectivity forever wicked? If the object of a study is to discover individuals' reactions to the learning process ... then one might argue that "subjectivity" (how one perceives the processes, what one chooses to record, etc.) is a prime research aim. More good fairy than bad, in other words'.

These questions, and the crucial one of generalization, will resurface in the later chapter on case studies, to which diaries are conceptually closely related.

Conclusion

This chapter has shown how important diaries can be as a research tool. There are a number of different formats for diaries, all sorts of categories of information can be included, and there can be varying degrees of advance specification of what is to be included and how often they should be written up, depending on the research purpose. However, the nature of all diary data is that it is 'rich' and 'thick' and retrospective. Some methods of analysis of this kind of data were explained in the chapter. We also highlighted the difference between a private diary and a public diary study of one or more diaries.

A major section of the chapter then reviewed extant samples of diary material in language learning and teaching and their use in research, making a distinction between 'pedagogic' diaries, written to aid reflective language learning and teacher education, and 'expert' diaries, in which the writer records language-learning experiences or incidents in professional life. A further section highlighted the necessity for method and indeed personal discipline in keeping a diary to be analysed for a research purpose, to protect the quality of the data.

Finally, the chapter commented on the value of diary information and diary studies, on some reasons for their popularity and perceived utility in teacher research, and on some counter-arguments to the inevitable accusations of unreliability and invalidity. Many of these arguments link directly also to the issues of participant observation and case study research discussed in Chapters 4 and 13 respectively.

Discussion notes

1. To what extent do you think that a diary kept as a teacher about one's own language-learning experiences can shed light on the ways in which our learners learn?
2. If you have not kept a teaching diary, try to set aside some specific times each week to record fairly freely your experiences with a particular class. After a few weeks you will have some useful data which can then be compared with the outcomes of other studies such as those reported here.
3. What, if any, are some of the specific ways in which diary data might be able to deal with particular preselected issues in language teaching?

9

Using numbers

Introduction

This chapter looks at the use that can be made of more or less simple counting techniques by language teachers doing research. It also gives some background to those techniques to harness the considerable power of numerical analysis in describing and interpreting many kinds of data. It also attempts to uncover some of the assumptions of numerical methods, which, as we saw in Chapter 4, are not shared by all the approaches to research covered in this book. The chapter that follows then takes a brief look at the notion of experimentation to establish what might be useful to the readers of this book from that approach to research. Neither chapter can act as a comprehensive manual for numerical techniques; for that the reader is referred to books such as Hatch and Farhady (1982), or Woods *et al.* (1986).

Numerical methods are only of use to the researcher whose data can be expressed as numbers. A first question, therefore, is to ask:

- What advantages are there in obtaining numerical data in the first place?

There are also several kinds of numbers, each having different assumptions and associated permitted operations. A second question, then, is:

- What can be done with the kinds of numbers obtained?

Numbers may be obtained from one respondent (for example, a learner) or from a class, a cohort, a year group, a school region, a county, a host – in other words the third question is:

- How can numbers cope with the scale of the data?

The use of numerical methods in large-scale research highlights the primacy of reductionism: the reduction of large amounts of data to one or two figures, commonly known as *descriptive statistics*. The issue of scale also highlights the distinction between 'insider' and 'outsider' research: a teacher wanting to know about activities in other school contexts might be able to send a questionnaire to colleagues and count up the answers (as an 'outsider') where doing observations or case studies would be impossible. Numerical data is usually associated with a positivist, normative approach as discussed in Chapter 3, but numerical methods also have their place in qualitative research.

Why count, and what to count

In a learning context, there are many kinds of data that can profitably be counted. A teacher might wish (for example):

- to look at students' scores on a test or examination
- to evaluate the responses to a questionnaire
- to estimate the relative importance of items in a needs analysis
- to compare the frequencies of different teaching/learning exchanges in a classroom observation
- to investigate the frequency of mention of different themes in a study of learners' or teachers' diaries.

Counting may be the first step in a purely normative kind of study, or it may be only one way of analysing data which may be looked at in a number of different ways. Counting may therefore be useful also in qualitative and interpretive research approaches.

Different kinds of counting

The teacher looking at the coded exchanges in the classroom is most probably counting frequencies only. Frequencies are usually called 'nominal' data – often in fact only counting names or labels. The teacher looking at examination or test scores will be looking at some kind of scale, in which a lower figure usually means worse performance than a higher figure. Sometimes all such a scale means is a rank order: A is better than B who is better than C who is better than D who is equal to E and F, etc. These are 'ordinal' scales, and in many circumstances are the most appropriate and fairest statement of learner differences on some criterion.

Mostly, however, people dealing with scores of various sorts want to be able to distinguish levels of achievement or proficiency with greater precision, and specify by how much A is better than B and if B is better than C by the same or different amount. Examination and test scores usually aim at this kind of statement, which is normally called an 'interval' or 'equal-interval' scale. The assumption is that the differences between any two scale points are equal. Thus the difference between someone scoring 60 and someone scoring 65 is larger than the differences between the first and a classmate who scored 58. However, as can readily be seen, when dealing with most kinds of knowledge, and language in particular, this does not seem to mean very much. What the 60-scorer must do to emulate the 65-

scorer is in no realistic sense two and a half times what the 58-scorer has to do to emulate the 60-scorer.

This equal-interval scale is therefore some way short of the 'highest' level of numerical measurement, the 'ratio' scale, which has a zero and permits multiplication and division, although it may look like one.

Consider the ESU Framework (Carroll and West, 1989) or the BC/UCLES IELTS Band scores:[1] the difference between levels 3 and 4 may be, conceptually, much the same in size as that between levels 5 and 6, and might be translatable into roughly equal numbers of hours of instruction needed to move from one level to another. However, the actual skills and language items required, range of text types in reading and listening to be mastered, interactional demands required will differ, as defined by the framework scale. Alderson (1991) gives a lucid account of the notions of scores and levels in ELT professional measurement, remarking that language test scores and bands are not even really interval scales, although they are often so treated.

The ratio scale is rarely relevant for the kinds of research discussed here. Obvious examples are weights and measures, or money, where there is a meaningful equality of unit and a meaningful zero: but virtually no data collected in educational settings can make the assumption, for example, of 'no knowledge at all'.

This section has introduced, rather quickly, four levels of measurement: nominal, ordinal, interval and ratio scales. It is, of course, highly debatable whether the kinds of data collected in language-teaching research are 'measurement' in any useful sense anyway. After all, most of the discussion in the present volume has been in terms of description and interpretation, not measurement. Certainly some of the research approaches make that assumption, but not all.

Describing the numbers with other numbers

When dealing with reasonably large amounts of data, like scores from a whole class, or the results from a questionnaire returned by 20 people, or much larger-scale results from some experimental investigation, there is a need to find some way of summarizing the data to reduce the mass of figures to an easily understood general picture, perhaps to find the typical value that more or less characterizes the whole.

In fact there are two arguments here:

- first, the practical one that finding some kind of 'typical value' enables the researcher to think about the group who produced the

---

[1] BC : The British Council; UCLES: University of Cambridge Local Examinations Syndicate; IELTS: International English Language Testing Service.

data as a group rather than as a collection of independent individuals
- second, the more abstract argument that no one case can be taken as characteristic of a group, but that the truth of the matter is in the distillation of information from many observations.

The classic example of the second is the distribution of height among humans: the answer is not any one person's height, but an average which lumps together differences of ethnicity, nutrition, age, diurnal variation, posture, and so on. This normative belief in the nature of truth as lying in a statistical reduction of data from many observations, whether of different people or of the same person at different times, is clearly important for many kinds of knowledge but is the subject of reasoned attack in educational and sociological research, in particular where the effect of educational variables on individuals' learning is the subject of study.

Central tendency

Having thus rather loosely introduced the concept of an average or mean, we should now look more closely at ways of representing the typical value or 'central tendency' of a mass of data.

With frequency data, the simplest statement is the most frequent value. Thus, in a questionnaire, one of the questions might be agreed with by most people (see Fig. 9.1).

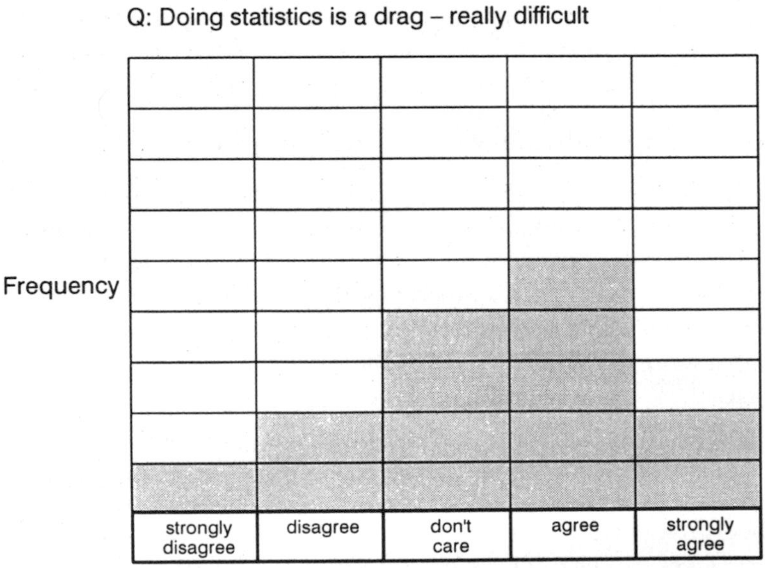

Q: Doing statistics is a drag – really difficult

Fig. 9.1

This would be the 'mode' or 'modal' answer, the most popular. It is readily obvious that more than one outcome is possible – this degree of homogeneity in a group answering a questionnaire would be rare. In fact there might be two most popular answers (see Fig. 9.2).

Q: Doing numbers is a breeze – really easy

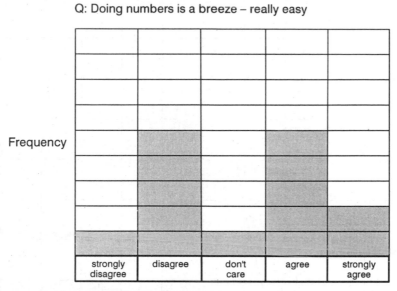

Frequency

| strongly disagree | disagree | don't care | agree | strongly agree |

Fig. 9.2

This would be a 'bimodal' distribution, indicating that the group returning the questionnaire fell into two distinct camps on this issue.

With rank-ordered or 'ordinal' data, the normal way of choosing a typical value or of representing the midpoint around which all the other values cluster is the 50 per cent point: the score with half the data points above and half below. This is called the 'median'.

With interval data the midpoint is determined by using the familiar average or mean: the sum of all the values divided by the number of values. A moment's reflection will confirm the equally familiar fact that median and mean are not always the same, and that often the cruder measure is actually a better figure to work with simply because it is not affected by extreme values which may distort or 'skew' a mean.

Dispersion

Simply finding a 'typical value' or a 'midpoint' is often not a sufficient statistical description of a group or distribution of scores or results: it is usually important to know how typical it is or how closely the other results cluster around the midpoint. In other words, the researcher will be looking for a measure of 'dispersion' around the midpoint, or the typical range of scores – in a sense, the degree to which, on average, the results disagree with the typical value, midpoint, or mean. This measure gives an indication of the homogeneity of the group (see Fig. 9.3).

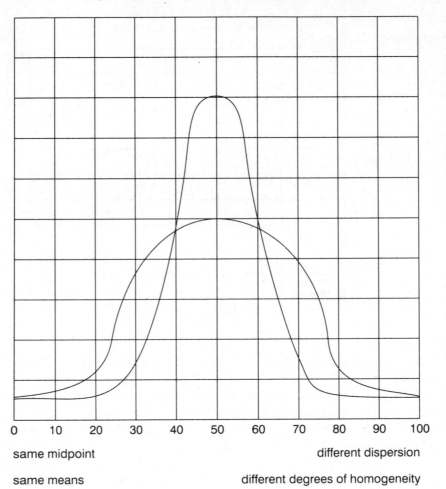

| 0 | 10 | 20 | 30 | 40 | 50 | 60 | 70 | 80 | 90 | 100 |

same midpoint   different dispersion

same means   different degrees of homogeneity

Fig. 9.3

The usual statistic for this purpose borrows a useful principle from probability theory that teachers familiar with interpreting test and examination results will also be familiar with: the idea of expressing a score in terms of its distance from the midpoint, of its deviation from the norm, or the 'standard score'. A standard score is a score expressed as the difference between the raw score and the mean, in terms of the general shape of the distribution of scores around that mean, which is given by the 'standard deviation'. The useful side of this borrowing is that according to probability theory, one standard deviation either side of the mean encompasses approximately 68 per cent of all the scores, two either side 95 per cent, three either side 99 per cent. This is illustrated in Fig. 9.4.

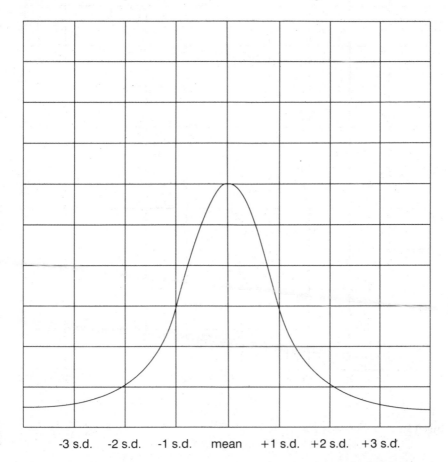

-3 s.d.   -2 s.d.   -1 s.d.   mean   +1 s.d.   +2 s.d.   +3 s.d.

Fig. 9.4

Thus the most useful descriptive statistics for any group of scores are the arithmetic mean and the standard deviation (within certain restrictions); and any individual score can be interpreted in terms of the performance of the group by reference to these two descriptors.

For example, the group mean of a certain test might have been 50; one student scored 65. Was that exceptional or fairly ordinary? If the standard deviation of the group had been 20 points, indicating that nearly 70 per cent of the students scored between 30 and 70, then clearly it was on the good side of ordinary (see Fig. 9.5).

But, if the standard deviation had been only 5 points, indicating that nearly 70 per cent of his classmates scored between 45 and 55, very much level-pegging in a very homogeneous group, then clearly it was an exceptional performance (see Fig. 9.6).

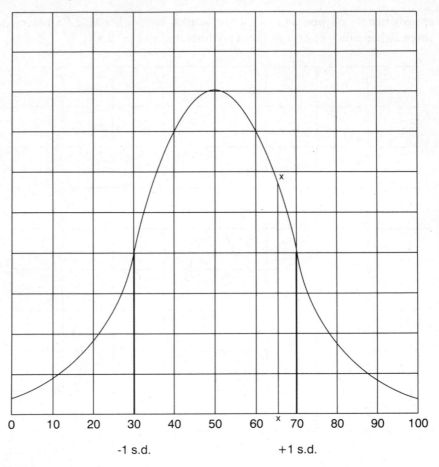

Fig. 9.5

Notice how these normative methods allow one to interpret individuals in comparison to groups, and certain aspects of group behaviour. They do not allow interpretation of an individual's learning experience, nor of the relationship between the individual and his or her own goals, except as they are measured against some group score, or reference norm.

Correlation

Another kind of descriptive statistic that is both very familiar to people by name and also very useful is a measure of how well a certain characteristic or property goes with another – measure of association or correlation. There are two kinds of question here:

- how to establish an association or correlation
- what it might mean.

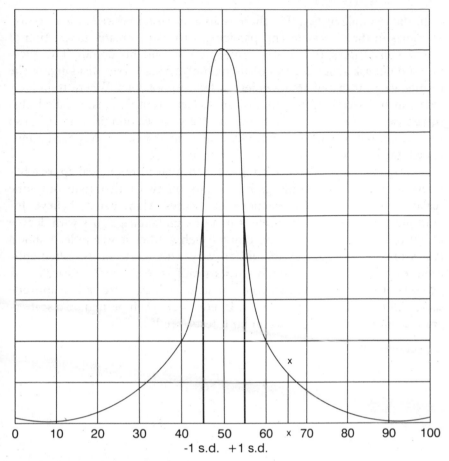

Fig. 9.6

It is here that we introduce two of the most widely used and familiar statistics of all. The first is a measure of *association*. For the purpose of example, it is a frequent observation that teachers like games in the classroom more than students (cf. EFL Services, 1992; Nunan, 1988): a questionnaire study could perhaps settle the matter. Imagine a questionnaire about using games in the classroom given to a group of students and a group of teachers. One of the questions might be a simple one of liking. The responses could be set out simply as a 2 × 2 table, with liking and disliking in the columns and teachers and students in the rows (see Fig. 9.7).

	like games	dislike games
teachers	*lots*	*few*
students	*few*	*lots*

Fig. 9.7

In the example in Fig. 9.7, there is an association between the question of games in the classroom and participant role: the greater proportion of teachers like games, the greater proportion of students do not. The question did not ask about degrees of liking, only liking versus disliking, so the results are in terms of frequencies, in fact proportions. Where frequency data can be assembled in this fashion, a very useful statistic called chi-square can be used to test the strength of any association present. It is also simple, but tedious to work out. Once such an association has been established, the real work begins – interpreting it.

A *correlation* is another widely used term that in numerical approaches refers to a group of people giving results on two rather than only one scalar variable – i.e. not frequencies but scores. Many people believe, for example, that learning achievement in a foreign language goes with degree of aptitude or talent. In the heyday of such studies it was indeed shown that scores on language exams did co-vary with scores on so-called aptitude tests, but not very strongly. In its simplest form, such research took two sets of scores from each learner: an achievement score and an aptitude score. All the people (here called A, B, etc.) were then plotted on a scatter-gram according to their marks on both tests (see Fig. 9.8).

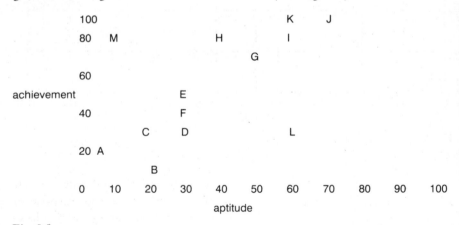

Fig. 9.8

In the example in Fig. 9.8, one can readily see that most of the people, but not all, have scores on the two tests that roughly tally. There is a 'positive' correlation. It is not perfect: it is not true of either M or L. It is possible to work out a figure, called a 'correlation coefficient' which gives a description of the overall degree of agreement between the two measures or sets of scores. It is worth pointing out that correlations can be positive or negative. If it were true, which it does not appear to be, that achievement in learning a foreign language diminishes with advancing age, it would be an example of a negative correlation. They can also be calculated for all kinds of data, except frequencies.

However, interpreting both associations and correlations can be difficult, since one always wants to know what the two features actually have to do with each other and whether one causes the other. In the case of the association between participant role and game preference, one could not argue, for example, that the students' reaction was directly to do with the teachers' predilection, because in that example nobody suggested the teachers and students had ever met. Even if the students were being taught by the teachers, the reasons each group had for their preference might be quite unrelated: the teachers might have thought in terms of participation, distribution and control of interaction and lightheartedness, whereas the students might have thought primarily about boredom with long setting-up times, constraints on their freedom of expression, or lack of learning pay-off. In the case of the correlation between achievement and aptitude one might want to assume that aptitude 'caused' the achievement. There would be no justification for this because with two measures taken at the same time there is no indication of what the actual relationship might be: being better at the language might as well be helping with the aptitude scores as vice versa. Mostly, interpretation of correlations means looking for other factors which might be influencing both sets of results. Causal arguments, if appropriate at all in language learning, can properly only be made on the basis of experimental, not co-variance, data.

This is because the nature and purpose of experiments are to reduce all possible extraneous influences on the results to the particular treatment or treatments being manipulated, i.e. to the effect of one action on another (in the simplest case). In a correlational study, however, it is usually not the case that all the other possible influences on the results, the rival explanations, can have been isolated, and it is also usually not the case that either one of the measures taken can be considered to be affecting the other one, because they are taken contemporaneously.

An interesting issue arises when scores are taken from the same people at different times. An example of this is the use of correlation to establish predictive validity of proficiency tests. A major use of tests such as TOEFL[2] and IELTS is to estimate the chances of non-native speakers of English with certain language levels succeeding in academic study in North American and British and Australian Higher Education. Typically, validation studies take a large sample of applicants and compare their test scores at the beginning of their course or before the course begins with their academic results at some point during or at the end of their course of study. The interpretation of such 'predictive validity' is that performance in the academic study, if in general it co-varies with initial language proficiency, is because of that proficiency. Academic qualifications of new

[2] TOEFL: Test of English as a Foreign Language (Educational Testing Service, Princeton, New Jersey, USA).

entrants are in this instance held to be equal. Such tests are used by receiving institutions as part of their selection process. A great deal is at stake: accepting a student who is likely to fail because of language problems is against various codes of practice (such as that of the Committee of Vice-Chancellors and Principals); it will cost the sponsor or possibly the student a great deal of money for nothing, for fees, living expenses, and travel, and the unhappy experience of failing to cope in an alien environment could cause long-term psychological difficulties; the waste of time and effort might cost the individual a start in an alternative career. While it is undoubtedly sensible to use tests to safeguard against these consequences, it is illogical to interpret the correlation to mean that language levels 'cause' academic success or failure, since variation in academic success occurs, obviously, with native speakers anyway, in the absence of the foreign-language problem. It is, however, reasonable to suggest that the correlation reflects some kind of real relationship, the nature of that relationship being quite complicated and tenuous. This is an instance of Van Lier's (1989) argument that there are principled differences between causes and reasons. On the specific point of predictive validity of test scores, studies have shown (Criper and Davies, 1988) that in fact it is difficult to establish good correlational data on this point, and that statistical evidence for using particular scale points as decision points for acceptance or rejection or for recommendations for extra language courses of different lengths is often unreliable.

Groups and individuals

This example highlights also a general point about numerical data and correlation in particular: such data can tell us quite a lot about groups, but rather less about individuals. Teachers of English for academic purposes and English for specific purposes probably have as many stories about students who seemed unlikely to succeed at the language going on to be academically successful as they do about linguistic high-fliers failing their first-year examinations. Statistics can tell us important information about general trends which may feed properly into institutional plans and resource allocation, but they cannot be held responsible for decisions about the proper treatment of individuals.

Bivariate and multivariate research

In each of the above examples of association and correlation, there were two variables: we discussed a hypothetical association between participant role and game preference in the classroom, a correlation between aptitude and achievement, and a correlation between language entry level and academic success. In many, perhaps most, situations, life is more complicated than that, and there are more than two relevant and interacting variables. More complex numerical methods involving correlations are available for analysing more complex sets of data. Inevitably, such studies tend to demand data on a larger scale than is available to most individual teachers working in one context, so here a few examples will be given, only to give the flavour of such research.

Multiple regression and partial correlation can analyse several sets of scores to determine the strength of the effect of one on the others, or the strength of the prediction from each to a final score. A frequent example is the tester trying to determine which of a battery of tests – of grammar, pronunciation, listening comprehension, cloze reading, stress perception, sound-symbol correspondence, vocabulary, oral production, etc. – is having the strongest influence of the final discrimination between the test-takers.

Factor analysis and cluster analysis, which can handle very large amounts of data, are used to reduce the scores from large numbers of measures to a few underlying influences or 'factors', and indicate how strong the influence or loading is from any one of the factors on the individual scales used to derive the analysis from. In language learning research, perhaps the most widely known use of factor analysis is the work of Gardner and his many associates on motivation in language learning (Gardner and MacIntyre, 1993) which has investigated the relationship of many issues such as orientation to language learning, anxiety, strength of motivation, aptitude to learning achievement in a foreign language. Gardner's research over the years since 1959 has involved thousands of students in many contexts, but not all multivariate studies are mega-scale. Johnson (1992) cites the interesting study by Ely in her chapter on correlational approaches, which used a sophisticated correlational method to try to tease out the strength and direction of influence of emotional concerns, such as discomfort, risktaking, sociability and motivation, on classroom participation and proficiency in the language in one institution. Ely's study did, however, use 75 college-level learners of Spanish in six classes, so it might not be fair to claim it was small-scale.

Condition-seeking research

In general, the kind of research described above usually involves looking for the interaction between some particular learner trait, like motivation, willingness to participate, extroversion, willingness to take risks, and so on, and some treatment or instructional approach. In other words the research looks for the conditions under which certain influences are important or certain approaches succeed. For these reasons both Skehan (1989: 134) and McLaughlin (1987: 162) equate 'condition-seeking' research with research based on 'aptitude-treatment interaction'. Most teachers would readily accept that some students respond to certain ways of teaching and others to different ones, and vary within themselves from time to time. Condition-seeking research attempts to clarify and systematize these interactions between variables. Skehan comments: 'The three major conclusions we can draw from this chapter [1989: Chapter 7, Interactions] are first, that the completed condition-seeking research has been some of the most fascinating in applied linguistics; second, that there are many studies whose interpretation is not clear for research design reasons; and third, that abysmally little research of this sort has actually been done' (Skehan, 1989: 134).

He goes on to call for more, better-designed research in this vein. However, it is instructive to note that, outside the numerical or normative approaches to research, condition-seeking research is regarded in a much less favourable light. There are basically two reasons for this:

- it presents group results which cannot easily be applied to individual learners
- it fragments the participants and the situation rather than providing an elaborated description of the learning situation.

Inference from chance – 'significance'

So far in this chapter we have considered various uses of counting and ways of using powerful numerical techniques to make sense of what has been counted. A core concept in statistical techniques goes beyond description into the nature of what constitutes a fact in such approaches: the significance of the result. Significance in this sense does not necessarily equal meaning – that is a question of the importance of the fact discovered for the researcher's interpretation, hypothesis, theory or whatever. Significance here refers to the likelihood of obtaining the given result by chance as opposed to the operation of some effect, presumably the one being manipulated in the research. If, after all, it were possible to show that the correlation between aptitude and achievement referred to above was just chance, it could not be considered a fact at all: in normative approaches facts are contrasted with chance occurrences. But how can one tell them apart? For this, we can use *inferential statistics*.

Perhaps it helps to imagine a situation in ordinary life outside the discussion of research matters. Consider jaywalking: it would be unfortunate if a bus hit one of us when we attempted to cross the road. If we counted how often it happened to everyone else – say we found it was 1 in 20 times on average on walking out to cross the road we might compare that to our own experience. How would we feel if it happened to us every 2nd time, or every 5th time, every 20th time, or every 100 times? If 1 in 2, in 5, or in 10 times, we might think we were jinxed; 1 in 20 times would be par for the course; but 1 in 100 times we would think we led a charmed life. In other words, we would define ourselves by reference to chance levels. Conventionally, normative methods start taking events seriously – calling them facts – if they actually occur in the investigation when the chances of them happening are 1 in 20 or less, and see them as established facts if the chances of them happening are 100 to 1 against, *all other things being equal*.

But we do not have infinite time in which to determine chances of survival of jaywalking in this way, so we have to turn to mathematics to determine how many accidents indicated a deviation from normality: whether we were jinxed or charmed. The mathematicians would look at the accident figures for a 'sample' of the general population with which to compare our particular case. The larger the sample, the more accurate the estimate.

To return again to the correlation example, the same logic shows that the significance of the correlation is dependent on the size of the sample from which it is obtained. The more people contributed data, the greater the likelihood that the resulting correlation coefficient was a real phenomenon and not just an effect of chance. In the case of the association, the data was in terms of frequencies, that is to say what proportion of teachers liked or disliked games and ditto for the students. Chi-square evaluates the significance of these proportions by comparing them with the distribution one would expect if there was no association (i.e. equal proportions of teachers and students liking and disliking). It then evaluates the size of the difference between the observed and the expected results taking into account the total sample size: the number of people polled. As one might expect, the larger the sample size the smaller the difference need be to prove to be significant, and the smaller the sample size the larger and more extreme the observed proportions have to be to be distinguished from chance and thus be significant.

Interpretation

Having established whether a result is significant, the researcher has to go back to the design and purpose of the research to decide what the result actually means. Depending on that purpose, both significant and non-significant results might mean important things. A teacher might be interested in the use of particular kinds of tasks in the classroom, and obtain students' popularity ratings on these and on alternative task types. If a significant difference was found between the ratings on the two types of tasks, the teacher might be encouraged to continue developing whichever set was favoured. If no significant difference appeared, the teacher would be faced with a very interesting situation, because it would probably mean that the principled difference he or she perceived between the two types of tasks just was not relevant to the tastes or experience of the students. That discrepancy of perception between teacher and student might be valuable to do some more research on.

Computational aids

When one of the authors was taking basic statistical training several decades ago, it was typical to teach shortcuts to number-crunching along-side the standard statistical techniques. Large data sets were reduced to small ones by grouping – counting numbers of groups rather than indi-viduals – to save on manual computation or card-punching time for the computer, the slight loss in accuracy more than compensated for by the time saved. Nowadays the widespread availability of PCs means that pow-erful statistical analysis programmes like the Statistical Package for the Social Sciences (SPSS) or Minitabs are available (at a price in both money and memory terms) on domestic machines. In some cases those who can access a large mainframe computer from their own machine do not even need a copy of the programme. The sophistication of such programmes has increased dramatically even in the last few years. Data entry and exec-utive commands look increasingly like ordinary paper layouts and natural language rather than special formats governed by computing and pro-gramming language constraints, reducing the user's fear of complex statis-tical operations by making it apparently easy. Naturally this can only be welcomed. However, there are still some dangers:

1. using tests of greater power and sophistication than one needs because they are easy to execute, but then finding they are less easy to interpret
2. being presented by the machine with impressive and complex results which the user cannot understand.

This second danger is even more to be guarded against when someone else actually runs the data through the statistical programme. It is better to use a less powerful test which the user can interpret than a more powerful one which only an expert can interpret.

The important principle is that the researcher needs to be in control of the interpretation and can only accept the statistical advice that he or she can use in that interpretation. It is a trap which postgraduate students fall into regularly – taking sophisticated statistical advice and entrusting their precious data to an expert consultant, only to find that they cannot under-stand either the advice or the expert's interpretation at the end of the day. The outcome is that they cannot then defend their conclusions to their colleagues, supervisor or examiners. However, such disasters are easy to forestall with planning and preparation.

Conclusion

In this chapter we have introduced the most frequently used techniques of numerical analysis, and have tried to show that they, too, can form part of the teacher researcher's available approaches to investigating their classrooms and other aspects of their professional work. Specifically, the chapter has looked at the different perspectives on the notion of 'counting' and at a variety of standard ways of analysing numerical data depending on the nature and goal of the research. These include the concept of 'mean' and how it can be interpreted, the correlation of individual factors with each other, and the complexity of our field such that multivariate analysis is often more suitable than bivariate.

Throughout the chapter, a background ('paradigm') question has been the extent to which the complexity of human behaviour in an area such as language teaching can in fact be reduced to statements concerning 'means' and the like, balanced against the equally problematic issues of generalizability and so on that are raised by more individualized and interpretive research modes. Finally, it is worth emphasizing – with the crucial proviso that the research question and purpose must be clearly formulated – that the researcher himself or herself does not have to take training in statistics, which are a tool like any other: specialist support is available to handle the data, whether from statisticians or computer packages.

Discussion notes

1. In your everyday life as a teacher, what 'level' of measurement are the numbers you use, such as marks, roll-calls, costs, and so on?
2. What kinds of events could you count to investigate some of your students' learning problems, such as errors, turn-taking, strategy use, marks, and so on, and how could you describe them numerically?
3. Try to think of your own examples of situations where we distinguish fact from chance in both professional and private life.
4. How could multivariate analysis help in analysing the influences on students' learning achievement in your particular teaching situation?

10

Doing experiments

Introduction

It is not at all self-evident that the experimental method as practised, for example, in the psychology laboratory or in psycholinguistic research is at all relevant for the conduct of research in language education, whether by teacher researchers or anybody else. There are several reasons for this, but there are also reasons to consider the experimental paradigm and some relevant examples to see what utility it might have. This chapter will concentrate first on the positive benefits of the experimental paradigm and later on some of the problems it poses for research on language learning inside and outside of classrooms, and for the teacher researcher who is the probable user of this book. It will not attempt to give a detailed step-by-step guide to experimental design, since there are many texts which discuss such matters to whatever degree of sophistication is required (Brown, 1988; Hatch and Farhady, 1982; Guilford and Fruchter, 1973); but it will discuss several of the most important principles, review the arguments about establishment of causality from Chapter 3, discuss features of design such as controls and counterbalances, and briefly analyse some published examples of experiments on classroom learning issues.

Why experiments?

Conducting an experiment

An experiment is 'a controlled look at nature. The experimenter sets up a task in which the structure of the task is explicit, the nature of the performance being studied is explicit, and the question that is being asked is precise' (Paivio and Begg, quoted by Cook, 1986: 13). These themes of control, explicitness and precision mean that in certain circumstances an experiment is an attractive option. Data-gathering itself need not involve a long, protracted period of time; the relationship between the data sets gathered, their numerical analysis, and the research question is decided in advance; the interpretation of the results depends on features of the experiment which are also decided in advance. So, if a teacher wants answers to precise-enough questions and has the power to manipulate the learning context to design an appropriate experiment, there is sense in doing so. Later in the chapter we shall look at two examples of classroom experiment, one on the distribution of question types in teacher-fronted and pair-work modes of class interaction, and the other on the effects of different kinds of feedback on writing in a second language. Of course, in practice it is rare for teachers to have the power to manipulate the contexts and the tasks to the extent that true experimentation demands. Outside researchers may be given such power if the need for the research is perceived as great enough by those in authority; but usually a teacher must live in the context after the research is done and classes are returned to normal, whereas an outside researcher does not. Hitchcock and Hughes' (1995: 40) remarks about 'smash and grab ethnography' apply even more strongly to experimental approaches, where the 'smash' element – disruption of normal classes, regrouping, matching of students by extra testing, and so on – is probably more thoroughgoing than in ethnography. A teacher considering experimentation would be wise to ponder the longer-term wisdom that 'you can't make an omelette without breaking eggs'. These issues were laid out for educational researchers in the first *Handbook of Research on Teaching* (Gage, 1963) by Campbell and Stanley, who introduced the distinction between true experiments and quasi-experiments. It is probably true to say that most studies claiming the rigour of experimentation in language learning are in fact quasi-experiments. There are usually too many variables for them all to be effectively controlled. The same is also often true of apparently well-controlled psycholinguistic experiments in second language acquisition (see Gass and Schachter, 1989) where task performance is often determined very precisely by sophisticated theoretical linguistic considerations, but the actual exposure to the second language of the participants or subjects cannot be known more than impressionistically or in terms of length. However, a quasi-experiment, relaxing some aspects of control, may still yield valuable information and enable a teacher to answer some specific question arising from his or her experience.

Understanding other research

Brown (1988), in particular, has argued that, while it is unlikely that teachers will want or be able to get involved in experimentation (except as subjects themselves), a knowledge of how experiments are designed and conducted gives them access to valuable literature which is difficult without such prior knowledge. Whether they want to have such access depends on deeper considerations of the validity and utility of knowledge gained through the approach. Accordingly, an acquaintance with the procedures and design features of experiments, and of the usual format of experimental reports, arms the teacher with some critical faculties for evaluating such research and empowers them to go beyond an uncritical acceptance of the conclusions, or more likely to take the conclusion seriously because the steps in the argumentation are clearer.

A language for talking about design

Experimental method has evolved a jargon of its own, which can be used outside its strict boundaries. The different kinds of variable considered, the abstractions of canonical versions of different designs, the terms for different aspects of control, have their uses in many other kinds of research and may serve to clarify the research question and the means of conducting the research in other traditions as well. The literature on experimental design deals mainly in abstract principles and offers a way of looking at research design at one remove from the details of particular projects, allowing strengths and weaknesses to be spotted.

Causality and the method of detail

By and large, experimental method searches for effects of certain treatments on given measures. Van Lier's (1989) criticisms of this model for research on language learning and teaching were given in Chapter 3: that (a) teaching does not cause learning and (b) any causal chain in language learning is inevitably long and complex, involving many conditions. Second language learning is not the only field where such arguments are increasingly held to be valid: other areas of education have moved away from simplistic accounts of achievement being influenced directly by treatments, and linguistics has never embraced the experimental method despite being an empirical science. In some areas, for example, computer modelling has been found to be a more powerful tool for analysis, and this is perhaps true in our own field, though it has yet to be demonstrated.

However, any teacher who notices that certain consequences follow from certain ways of dealing with a class is entitled to consider doing an experiment to investigate it. An example is the suggestion that certain question types stimulate and others depress levels of student participation in the lesson. A teacher noticed (in another teacher's class) that open questions directed at the whole class seemed to produce less discussion than closed questions directed at specific groups of students – this in a class with several groups of students sitting around tables. Whole-class questions appeared to undermine the purpose of the groupings, and the class did not respond, whereas questions to a subgroup seemed to have the effect of getting each subgroup to work together. This observation stimulated a hunch that there was a researchable issue here, and it could be one which a fairly simple experiment could answer. In this case, Van Lier's general criticism is irrelevant, because the teacher concerned wanted to research the effect of two kinds of procedural signals from the teacher on the level of interaction. It would be a further, and difficult, step to argue that level of interaction affected individual learning outcomes. Nevertheless, this would be an interesting and topical question.

It follows that, in order to find precise questions to answer and construct explicit tasks and explicit controls to make sure that the answer is correctly related to the question, the issue has to be decomposed into small parts. This is sometimes called 'the method of detail'. To follow up the question discussed above, a teacher researcher could wait a long time for other instances of the discrepancy she noticed to arise naturally. An experimental approach would seek to establish under precisely what conditions the phenomenon occurred, and set up a classroom situation to compare various question types, intended audiences and named addressees, group sizes, language learning tasks, perhaps proficiency levels, group composition, and so on. In a (somewhat far-fetched) sense, the experiment attempts to recreate in a controlled and reliable way an interesting phenomenon which was observed by chance in the natural classroom, in order to study the effects more closely. The issue and the situation which give rise to it would be decomposed to find the crucial variables in play and how they interacted. To do this, the researcher would have to look at all the features of the situation and decide if they were relevant, that is if they could plausibly explain the observation and therefore be a rival for the original idea that question type was the determining factor. Perhaps the content of the questions directed at the whole class and at the groups differed; perhaps the way in which the students sat gave them no sense of interaction across groups; perhaps the co-acting group allowed individuals to hide and reduced their anxiety levels but whole-class discussion was perceived as too risky; perhaps the phenomenon was real but restricted to one cultural group. Decomposition of a problem into details is thus the basis for manipulating comparisons which isolate cause-and-effect relationships and remove, as far as possible, rival interpretations of the results.

Isolation of such details and reduction of the research question to one crucial issue which this 'controlled look at nature' exposes are also designed to remove the issue from the immediate context and investigate it as a general problem. Experimentation therefore uses tight controls to establish 'external validity' or more simply generalizability. Other means of establishing this include replication and testing in other contexts.

Experiments and quasi-experiments

Basic features of experiments

Experiments are designed to answer precise questions. An experiment therefore needs:

1. a precise question
2. an explicit set of variables
3. an explicit task which can be measured (at whatever level of measurement)

4. sufficient participants to enable statistical inferences to be made
5. controls and counterbalances to eliminate rival interpretations
6. a means of ensuring the relevance of the results to the question.

Let us look briefly at these six features.

1. The precise question is usually in the form of a prediction. For our putative example above it might be: 'Whole-class questions will stimulate less interaction than questions addressed to subgroups with students of x proficiency doing y type of language learning task in monolingual classrooms.'

In reality, given the requirement of falsifiability associated with much positivistic research, the hypothesis is more likely to be phrased in 'null' form, which the experiment tries to reject: 'There will be no difference in interaction levels following whole-class questions and questions addressed to groups, with students of x proficiency doing y type of language learning task in monolingual classrooms.'

If the experiment found there was a difference, this hypothesis would be rejected. The direction of the difference (favouring one or other of the treatments) would then be evaluated.

2. Variables usually come in four kinds:

a. Moderator variables (MV): usually a difference between the participants which may systematically or unsystematically affect the results. In a questionnaire study, interest might focus on the way two different kinds of pupil, e.g. girls and boys, answered the questions. Here, sex would be a moderator variable.

b. Independent variables (IV): the crucial variable being manipulated which the hypothesis concerns. Argument about experimental techniques often concerns the validity of the relationship between the IV and the hypothesis.

c. Dependent variables (DV): these are the measures of the effect of the manipulation of the IV. In our example, the interaction level – presumably some measure of amount of talk, number of student turns of speech, and so on.

d. Confounding variables (CV): often it is difficult to separate out variables from one another satisfactorily. In the present case, the researcher would have a difficult time sorting out the difference between a groupwork task and a groupwork seating position. These two variables, which might be important, are so far confounded. Of course, confounding variables are undesirable features of experiments.

3. The measurable task performance refers to both independent and dependent variables: both have to be precisely defined and clearly identifiable.

4. Sufficient participants. In the case which is serving here as an example, there would have to be sufficient participants to ensure a meaningful difference between the whole class and the subgroups: three or four subgroups of four each, giving 12, 16 or 20 students in the class. A further consideration would be if the comparison was going to be between the same students at different times (a correlated sample design) or between two different groups (an independent groups design). The former would require fewer people and be more sensitive, but might be subject to problems of order, because the order in which the different kinds of questions were asked might be significant; and the latter would require more people and be less sensitive, but not be subject to order effects. Yet another consideration affecting numbers and sample size might be the representativeness of the people involved of some larger grouping that was thought to be significant. The participants in experimentation are usually called 'subjects'.

5. Controls and counterbalances. We have already seen some of these in the discussion so far. One popular way of controlling for systematic biases among the people participating is to assign them to the different treatment groups at random. Thus, in our experiment on teachers' questioning behaviour, we might have chosen to set up two independent groups and make up the groups from the available subjects randomly, in order to have an equal chance in each group of people who were, for example, good and bad talkers, friends with the others, skilled or unskilled in social interaction, favourably or unfavourably disposed to interaction, extrovert or introvert, or any of a whole host of possible variables. Another form of control would involve matching the students as closely as possible by having them do tests of proficiency level, attitude, personality type, aptitude and so forth. Effects of order of presentation of the experimental treatments would have to be counterbalanced as discussed above.

The consequence of such measures is to reduce possible rival interpretations by controlling their effects, and, manifestly, to increase the artificiality of the situation at least as compared to the normal context of the learners' and teachers' everyday experience. The greater the influence of such design measures, the nearer the research is to a true experiment; quasi-experiments, which are more usual in real-world situations outside a psycholinguistic laboratory, have to sacrifice some controls because of real-world constraints.

6. Since experiments aim to answer specific questions by rejecting specific hypotheses, anything that compromises the relationship between question and conclusion is a threat to internal validity. Internal validity may be seen in terms of several links:

    a. between specific hypothesis and research question (is the prediction justified?)

b. between the measurements produced by the data-collection instruments and the hypothesis (are they really the right measures?)
c. between the result and confounding variables (can rival interpretations be eliminated?)
d. between the result and the original hypothesis (does the result make sense in terms of the hypothesis?).

Some examples

In this section, we shall briefly review three studies of aspects of English-language classrooms in the experimental tradition, to illustrate the kind of questions attacked and the methods used. None of these studies was carried out by the teachers responsible for the classes; they are therefore not to be seen as direct models for teacher-led research. They are mentioned here to demonstrate the nature and problems of doing experiments in this field, as discussed earlier in more abstract terms. Because the degree of control over extraneous variables is very different in all of them (only one used a randomization procedure) they should be classed as quasi-experiments rather than true ones.

They are instructive examples, and some lessons to be learned from them for the nature of successful experimentation are drawn from them in the following section. They may also serve as pointers for how teachers might go about designing experiments for their own research questions. Experimentation could be used, for example, for the teacher questioning issue mentioned above; for investigation of the motivating effects of authentic and contrived material; for a study of the teacher's optimum handling of latecomers in the class; and a whole host of manageable questions. These particular examples were among those suggested by a group of EFL teachers in a research methods class.

An experiment on methodology for teaching reading

Carrell *et al.* (1989) conducted a study comparing the effectiveness of two kinds of reading strategy training. Independent variables were a technique called 'semantic mapping', in which students learned to draw and then re-draw diagrams based on their knowledge of the topic and what is said about the topic in the text, and another called 'experience-text-relationship' (E-T-R) which involved structured discussion sessions with the teacher. The control group took the regular classes in the programme. The dependent variables were gain scores, that is the difference between scores on a specially designed reading comprehension test before and after the strategy training. The moderator variables included a questionnaire giving a picture of the individual differences among the students, including strategy preference and cognitive processing. The students were adult ESL students in regular classes at approximately the same proficiency level in a university ESL centre in the USA, and were of mixed national and linguistic backgrounds and ages. The experimenter did not randomly assign students to treatments. The timescale of the experiment was nine days: a day for pre-testing, four days of strategy training, and later a final day of post-testing.

The structure of the experiment was as follows:

Group 1	n = 9 pre-test	semantic mapping	post-test
Group 2	n = 9 pre-test	E-T-R	post-test
Group 3	n = 3 pre-test	control	post-test
Group 4	n = 5 pre-test	control	post-test

Both types of strategy were taught by the same teacher and another teacher taught the control groups. Unfortunately the semantic mapping group was disrupted on their fourth training day by having to evacuate the building because of a bomb scare.

The results showed that there were statistically significant advantages for the strategy training treatments over the controls on open-ended comprehension questions but not on multiple-choice questions, and that these differences were strongly influenced by individual student differences. When the results were analysed using the moderator variables, they found that 'deep' cognitive processors in the control groups did make significant gains on the tests, whereas the strategy training worked for both 'shallow' and 'deep' cognitive processors among the students. Presumably deep processors can make these gains independently, without strategy training.

This relatively simple and timebound quasi-experimental study showed that such issues are amenable to experimental attack, but the results demonstrate a typical feature of all research: a number of tantalizing questions are raised which can only be answered by further research with modifications to the design. For example, why did the advantages only show up on some measures? Why did the 'deep' processors apparently not need the special training? If they could do without the training, why did they not perform much better on the first test and not make a gain?

A classroom interaction experiment

In the late 1980s there was a flurry of activity, sparked off by the increasing popularity of communicative methodology, which was directed at the advantages of group and pair work over traditional teacher-fronted 'lockstep' teaching. One quasi-experimental study was conducted by Doughty and Pica (1986) to investigate the nature of classroom interaction in the new language using an information gap task in three kinds of organization. In this study, the IV was class organization: teacher-fronted, groups (of four students), and pairs. Students attending regular classes in a university ESL programme were assigned randomly to the three classes. In the teacher-fronted class, the teacher read out the instructions and stayed to run the class and complete the task; in the group and pair-work classes, the teachers gave out written instructions and left. The DVs were amount of interaction (measured by the number of turns taken by all the participants) and quality of interaction (the proportions of interactional modification such as comprehension and clarification checks and confirmations) and accuracy on task. No MVs were measured, it being considered that random assignment would adequately counterbalance the inevitable differences in attitudes, experience of the treatments, friendship groupings to be found in a group of students. Proficiency was counterbalanced by drawing the sample of learners from regular classes at one particular level. There was no control group as such. The task set all the classes was to plant a garden using a feltboard and a number of icons of garden features such as flowers, flower beds, lawn, patio and garden equipment, according to some instructions which required some interactional decision-making. The hypothesis was that interaction would differ in amount and quality according to the class organization adopted.

The results showed that both amount and quality of interaction did indeed differ between the three treatment groups. Briefly, there was more interaction in the teacher-fronted class than in the pairs, and more in the pairs than in the groups. The reasons for this were open to speculation: perhaps the teachers' directive function stimulated more interaction through nomination and invitation, whereas in the groups it is possible that some students were able to 'hide' and leave it to the others. There was, however, more modification through comprehension and clarification checks in the groups and pairs than in the teacher-fronted class. Perhaps the students did not want to challenge the teacher by frequent checking, or perhaps they did not feel they needed to because the teacher's input was anyway clearer and more grammatical. Oddly, the accuracy of the task of planting the garden was lower in the teacher-fronted classroom compared to the others: perhaps the students only pretended to understand!

This study illustrates the neatness of an experimental approach, but its inability to support a clear interpretation shows that there are too many issues, too many confounding variables, which remained uncontrolled. Perhaps more kinds of data would have helped, for example lesson transcripts or interviews with the participants. This study was, however, only one in a series by these authors and other co-workers on related problems. This question perhaps affords an opportunity to combine experimental measurement with naturalistic description in the interests of greater precision. (This is discussed further in Chapter 14.)

Feedback on writing

The third example to be discussed is a quasi-experimental study of the effects of different kinds of feedback on teacher comments on EAP students' writing. In this study by Fathman and Whalley (1990), the IV was type of feedback: no feedback, feedback on grammar (locating an error by underlining), on content (minimal and rather unspecific encouraging remarks and generalized criticism) and both. The DVs were numbers of grammatical errors and holistic content rating. The learners were in a selection of six intermediate college composition classes, 72 students in all, from two similar colleges, from mixed language backgrounds. The task, presented to the learners in the same way by their own class teachers, consisted of a set of eight pictures which represented a narrative, which was talked through by the teachers. The hypothesis was that writing should improve according to the kinds of feedback received. The students were given 30 minutes to write the narrative individually.

The scripts were collected and assigned at random to one of the four treatment groups; the feedback was written on the scripts. The scripts were returned a few days later and the students required to rewrite the composition. Both originals and rewrites were then graded for grammar errors and quality of content by two independent raters. The report does not mention if the raters knew whether they were rating originals or rewrites or had sight of the feedback comments; one presumes not.

The results of this study were analysed in two ways: by averaging the scores within the feedback treatment groups, and by counting the numbers of students improving between original and rewrite. The first analysis showed that significant improvement in grammatical accuracy occurred with grammatical feedback (with and without content feedback), but content improvement occurred in all the treatments, including the no-feedback group, although at a slightly higher level when content feedback was given. The second analysis showed that the grammar feedback had a more powerful effect on accuracy than content feedback had on content. The hypothesis was, then, only partially confirmed.

As with the other examples, this study is subject to a number of methodological criticisms. It is a relatively small-scale quasi-experiment, despite involving six classes in two colleges, because:

- only one composition topic was used, so there is no way of knowing if topic or type of writing assignment might affect the issue
- only one rewrite, or 'fair copy' was required, so there is no information on the persistence of the improvements claimed
- only one form of feedback in each area was tried.

Reflections on the experimental approach

This last section will recap on a number of issues concerning doing experiments in general and the use of experimentation in teacher-led research on language learning in particular.

Reporting experiments

One advantage of this approach is its history and conventions of reporting. Since it has been used for a long time in many contexts, a great deal is known and published about the power and shortcomings of different designs. One result of this has been the almost universal adoption of a convention of reporting designed to ensure that all the features of the experiment necessary for replication are mentioned:

- research question
- literature review
- hypothesis
- experimental task
- design and method
- controls and counterbalances
- subjects
- method of analysis
- results and statistical analysis
- discussion and interpretation.

We have already discussed, in Chapter 4, the problems of replication in language learning research. However, the frequency of the format (for some journals it is a condition of acceptance) means that for the initiated it is relatively comprehensible; but like all such conventions, it is not easy to learn.

External validity

The feature of generalizability, or external validity, referred to in Chapter 4 is a prized attribute of good experimentation. The fact that this method can attack issues isolated from other effects and contaminations from contextual details enables conclusions about those issues to be made in the form of general statements. As we have seen, however, such general statements lose their force when there are problems in interpreting exactly what the experimental data mean and how strong the support for those statements really is from the data.

Decontextualization

Much of the apparatus of experimental controls and counterbalances is directed at the isolation of issues from context, for reasons of specificity, generalization and precision. However, it is obvious from the three illustrations given that decontextualization also leads to disruption of normal patterns of class timetables, activities and teaching patterns. The 'experimental' treatments discussed also were by definition different from what the classes were normally receiving as tuition: in these examples no attempt was made, or at least reported, to integrate the methods under study into normal classes. It is reasonable to ask, first, if there is any effect resulting from a student knowing they are doing something out of the ordinary or special (usually known as the 'Hawthorne' effect) and, second, if the results of such experiments so carefully decontextualized can be generalized to learning in 'normal' classes or tell us very much about the fate of the innovations proposed when they enter regular teaching programmes. The artificiality of this 'controlled look at nature' may in the end be self-defeating.

Time

It will be evident that the experimental method cannot seriously be used as a relatively quick, albeit well-prepared, economical approach, since in each of the illustrations the results only partially confirmed or rejected the hypotheses. The issues addressed therefore required second and third attempts with design and materials modifications to actually be settled: any research is an ongoing process. It is probably not fair, therefore, to contrast the time economy of experiments favourably with the fairly lengthy process of review, replan, reconnaissance and recycle of action research: the advantage is illusory.

Randomization

It is worth noting that random assignment of subjects to treatments, one of the biggest difficulties in using an experimental approach in a regular educational context, does not actually have to disrupt normal classes in all cases. Fathman and Whalley's experiment (1990) preserved the integrity of regular classes in two colleges but randomized the assignment of the written products to the markers, the postage but not the people, as it were. Normally, random distribution implies fairly massive interruption to normal timetables and programme arrangements which itself may bring serious educational disadvantages and prove a costly item in relation to the benefit to the profession of the results. Any administrator or gatekeeper responsible for allowing access to the learners for the researcher(s) may well say 'It had better be worth it'. However, it is clear that for some purposes, with ingenuity, disruption can be minimized. An alternative strategy, frequently used in quasi-experiments, is to use existing classes anyway, and attempt to control the various confounding variables by measurement. This is the strategy used by Carrell *et al.* (1989), and in that example it is defensible. It is remarkable, however, that although the regular class composition was not rearranged, the normal pattern of teaching was, with one teacher doing both experimental treatments and another the normal programme.

Scale

Clearly all three of these illustrative experiments concerned larger numbers of students than an individual teacher in a class has responsibility for. The scale of a conventional notion of experiment is usually larger than individual teacher researchers can manage. As experiments, these illustrations could in fact be criticized for not being on a large-enough scale to incorporate all the design features which control and objectivity might lead us to desire (we have already seen that, in all three cases, the conclusions would have been stronger if more time had been given, further comparisons made, or larger numbers had been available in one or other treatment groups). However, by chance all these illustrations used independent group designs, which is expensive on numbers because there are different people in each group. It is also possible to give the students the different treatments at different times, and use a correlated groups design. In this kind of design, learners act as their own controls because their performance is measured under the two (or more) treatments. Such a design might in some cases be more suitable, especially where scale is a major factor. It is also possible to solve the scale question by using collaborative methods, where a group of teachers work on the same problem at the same time.

Numerical analysis

In each of these examples, the results were expressed as numbers: scores on reading tests, frequencies of interaction and linguistic features, numbers of errors or scale of quality, and the figures were analysed statistically in more or less sophisticated ways. The Carrell et al. (1989) study looked at the significance of the size of the differences between pre- and post-tests in each treatment group, and then used a more powerful technique, analysis of variance, to look at the differences taking into account the various individual differences they had measured. No account was taken, in these examples, of qualitative data such as learner or teacher reflection, diary notes, observations or interviews.

Disclosure and ethics

In none of the articles which report the above examples is there any mention of whether the learners who provided the data were given explanations of what the experiments were about. This is a somewhat difficult ethical question, since, on the one hand, learners may be considered to have a right to know what a researcher is doing with them for the sake of research and the advancement of knowledge, but, on the other, knowing what the purpose of the experiment they are subjects in, not obviously by their own volition, could bias the results. It would have been difficult for the subjects in the three illustrations not to know they were in experiments, since unusual things were happening: assignment to new groupings, extra tests, a special form of feedback or none at all.

Consider in particular the control groups in Carrell *et al.*'s (1989) study. Their only participation in the study was to have to take the same tests twice, the content of which bore no resemblance to the 'normal' teaching they were receiving. No wonder they did not improve – it is interesting to speculate what their attitude to the extra testing might have been. Erickson's remark (1986) that a billiard ball cannot make sense of its surroundings but a person can is relevant here: the 'subjects' in an experiment are trying to make sense of this slightly odd temporary world, and it is probable that they will come to quite different conclusions, which may affect the results. That is the meaning of the 'Hawthorne' effect, which basically tells us that experiments in schools tend to confirm their hypotheses because the learners given the new experimental treatments become more interested than those given the traditional treatments and work harder to justify their special status. Of course, it is perfectly possible to obtain agreement and voluntary participation on the basis that the full story will be revealed afterwards, but cannot be beforehand precisely because of the danger of bias.

Third-person research

Kemmis (1991) draws an interesting distinction between third-person research, which is 'positivistic' and strives for objectivity, second-person research, which is 'interpretive' and acknowledges subjectivity, and first-person research, which is 'critical' and identifies the researcher with the respondents and the providers of the data. He is very scathing about third-person research based on statistical measurements and the use of learning achievement outcomes. Clearly, most experimental approaches in language learning fall into this category, and any intending researcher will want to decide what the purpose of doing research is and what kind of research they want to do before opting for any particular approach. Experimentation is primarily about objectivity, the suppression of researcher and other personal bias, the isolation of issues, precision and measurement. If these are needed or considered desirable, then there are many well-worked-out designs available.

Conclusion

The term 'experiment' is sometimes used rather loosely, with a meaning approximating to 'trying out' – whether that be an innovation, a different teaching method or technique, a new coursebook and the like. We might talk, say, of 'experimenting' with a different kind of grouping in the class, to see whether we get different learning outcomes.

This chapter has set out the most important characteristics for the more rigorous design of true experiments. It has also pointed up the distinction between experiments and quasi-experiments, suggesting that the latter are more appropriate for language teaching and learning research – or indeed in any field of social life where variables cannot so readily be isolated, and where behaviour and outcomes are relatively unpredictable. Beyond the actual details of design, the chapter has also commented on the advantages and disadvantages of experimental method for use in the language class-room, relating them to such broader issues as validity, generalizability, context and ethics that underpin much of the present book.

Discussion notes

1. Bearing in mind the discussion of design features of experiments, take the issue of teacher questioning behaviour and sketch out a plan for an experiment to investigate it.
2. Can you imagine ways of controlling (in the sense of the word in this chapter) the variety of influences on the learners in your classroom so that you could isolate one variable and experiment with it?
3. Do you consider that any of the examples of experiments mentioned produced knowledge that you could use as relevant for your own learners?

11

Asking questions

Introduction

This chapter is devoted to the central topic of asking people questions in order to obtain research data. Although there are very obvious differences between the two general categories – questionnaires are associated with survey work and interviews with individual respondents – there are also many points of congruence which derive from the simple fact that both are rather specialized forms of conversation. In what follows we shall look at questionnaires and interviews in turn, bearing in mind that much of the discussion of one is applicable to both. Taking questionnaires first, we shall explore Low's (1991) illuminating distinction between questionnaires as conversation and as tests; look at the range of types of questionnaire use in ELT research; explain some general guidelines for constructing questions; discuss some popular methods for analysis and give some recent examples. Moving on to interviews, we investigate the main kinds of research interview and their different characteristics, and then draw out some general points.

Popularity of questionnaires

Questionnaire research seems to be very popular among educational researchers in general (especially in the survey context – see Cohen and Manion, 1989: 97) and ELT research in particular. This is because, although it is quite labour-intensive in construction and analysis, the researcher can benefit from several advantages.

- The knowledge needed is controlled by the questions, therefore it affords a good deal of precision and clarity.
- Questionnaires can be used on a small scale, in-house, and on a large scale, requiring little more extra effort than photocopying and postage (though for large-scale survey work this can consume a significant budget, especially when using stamped self-addressed envelopes for returns).

- Data can be gathered in several different time slots: all at once in a class, in the respondents' own time as long as it is easy to return, at convenience when a suitable respondent happens to come along, and in different locations at different times; but in all of these the data is comparable, the questions are the same and the format is identical.
- Self-completion questionnaires allow access to outside contexts so information can be gathered from colleagues in other schools and even other countries.

Sensitivity of interviews

Interviewing is also a popular technique but for different reasons. It lacks, obviously, the administrative conveniences and in many forms the standardization of questionnaire work. It features as the preferred research tool in many investigations because (depending on the format):

- it is (usually) one-to-one, and therefore sensitive to individual differences and nuances of emphasis and tone even if a standardized structured list of questions is the content
- it has a potential for openness and allows control of what is revealed to remain more or less with the respondent, giving room for individual expression and broaching of new topics
- it is more like ordinary conversation and therefore to some extent a more personal context for information exchange
- comprehension checks, hedges, and assurances of confidentiality can be requested and given at any point during the interview in order to maximize the usefulness of the data
- the form of the answer is not (usually) constrained to ticks and circles, but is ordinary language with all its freedom and sensitivity.

Questionnaires

Questionnaires as a genre

Low (1991) compares questionnaires to two other human activities, conversations and tests, pointing out that each analogy explains some part of the way people react to questionnaires and holds some lessons for the questionnaire constructor.

As conversations

One of the most frequent acts in conversation is asking and answering questions, but in conversation there is a dynamic of power and trust which concerns the acceptability of certain kinds of questions, the right to ask them, the pressure to provide an answer, and the right to conceal the answer. Since interviews are also conversations of a kind, using language to negotiate such tensions is part of the interviewer's skill, but respondents often have difficulty with questionnaires precisely because there is no, or only inadequate, protection of their rights. A questionnaire must solicit the respondent's cooperation or it is valueless.

Low (1991) continues by discussing the parallel between conversations with strangers and eliciting information from strangers via questionnaires. Such conversations, he points out, involve a great deal of hard work, with wary self-revelation on both sides, before important information is entrusted to the other person: no wonder that impersonal questionnaires, often through the post box, with little explanation or personal appeal, are often not returned. Low further discusses the 'human-sized' nature of conversation involving frequent topic and key term repetition, stories, social talk, tailoring requests to the conversation partner, and redundancy. Questionnaires rarely show these features and suffer a reduction in their power to elicit good data as a result. A large amount of questioning also features in another specialized form of conversation: 'People do not like being interrogated' (Low, 1991: 124). Interrogations feature traps, repetitions, consistency checks and hints of punishment; questionnaires can as well, but the respondent is in the privileged position of choosing not to return the paper if it is perceived as threatening.

As tests

Low (1991) argues that tests are constructed according to particular canons of validity, reliability, lack of redundancy and repetition, and independence of items. Designing a questionnaire along those lines produces indeed a familiar kind of document with short and simple questions, no irrelevant information, as little as possible interaction on paper with the researcher, or often little explanation for the presence of certain questions, few verbal links, and little structure even in terms of divisions into thematic sections. It should not be possible for the answer to one question to be dependent on the respondent being able to answer another question, nor for one question to suggest the answer to another. Questionnaires are often evaluated like tests – the same technology for automatic score reading can be used, the same statistical methods may be invoked.

The central issue explored by Low, and the reason it has been examined in some detail here, is the question of the relevant and proper criteria for good quality data out of a questionnaire. There are choices, sometimes quite difficult ones, to be made between what the designer may ask with a reasonable hope of a true and cooperative response, and what might be most valid and reliable but so off-putting that few responses are yielded; between user-friendliness and accuracy; between revelation and explanation and minimizing hints about preferred answers and response bias; between length and conciseness.

Types of questionnaire

Questionnaires come in all shapes and sizes. The optimum length of a questionnaire is governed by the expected yield: the more work respondents have to do the less likely, given a free choice, they are to return it. However, if the topic (or the researcher!) is important to them, long questionnaires may be completed and returned without complaint. There is a rule of thumb, with no theoretical research backing, that a questionnaire extending over two sheets of paper may be too long. However, there is great variability depending on purpose and expected yield. Student course-evaluation questionnaires at the authors' institution are one page including invitation, explanation, questions and machine-readable answer blocks; a recent international survey by the British Council for their e2000 project was in booklet form.

Questionnaires may contain only one kind of question or a mix. It is usual for the majority of questions to be answered by ticking a box or circling an alternative to enable easier counting. For very large samples, machine-reading facilities may be required. In any case, respondents have to be given clear instructions on how to answer. If this is not done, either they will not answer, or the researcher cannot believe the answers given.

What to include will depend on:

- the kind of information needed
- the kind of analysis proposed.

In general, the question will be of the following types.

Factual questions

These are often used for 'moderator' variables to tap divisions in the population being polled. These are usually multiple-choice, but not exclusively, such as

Age   under 15
15–19
20–24
25 and over etc.

Proficiency level
Beginner
Post-beginner
Pre-intermediate
Intermediate etc.

Sex

Male
Female

Yes/no

These are often informative but blunt. Very often a respondent will be uncomfortable when unable to hedge with 'it depends' or 'sometimes'.

Multiple-choice

These are the usual way of asking questions which in an interview or conversation would be prefaced by Who?, What?, Which?, Where?, Why?, How?, and so on – the Wh-questions. Given a set of choices, the respondent can indicate more divisions in the information: but the questionnaire designer should consider if only one response is allowed or several. For example:

Which teaching mode did you like?

>   small group
>   pairs
>   whole class
>   discussion
>   lecture
>   video presentation
>   language laboratory

Patently, these alternatives are not mutually exclusive, so several self-consistent response patterns are possible. The assumption that respondents only liked one is anyway probably unwarranted; the question could be re-phrased as:

Which teaching mode did you like best?

or

Which teaching modes did you like (choose 4)?

In either case, the question is constraining the choices of the respondents and possibly compromising the quality of the data. The similarity of both yes/no and multiple-choice questions to test items is also obvious.

Ranked questions

Another way of asking Wh-questions is to ask respondents to rank the alternatives with an instruction like:

Please indicate your order of preference with a number between 1 and 7 where 1 = most favoured and 7 = least favoured.

A frequent pitfall with such instructions is that some respondents seem to do it the other way round, thus again compromising the data. *Prima facie*, there is no way of choosing between counting up and counting down. If several ranked questions are used, they should be consistent in rubric, otherwise the question type will confuse the respondent.

Open-ended questions

Many questionnaires include open-ended questions to allow the respondents to feel that they can contribute more individual points of view and more detailed information than is elicited in closed questions. To have a majority of such questions looks like an invitation to write a number of essays, and is likely to reduce yield. However, in certain circumstances, this may not be a disadvantage. Powell (1992) reports a study (to be discussed briefly below) in which language teachers were polled by a series of open-ended questions on their involvement in a curriculum development project. Open-ended questions do present data-analysis problems which may require more sophisticated treatment than counting yes answers and no answers: content analysis, for example, as discussed at the end of this chapter.

Scaled questions

One familiar type, the Likert scale, presents not questions but statements and asks for degrees of agreement. These are often used to elicit opinions rather than facts and are sometimes called 'opinionaires'. For example:

> A teacher should wait longer for an answer from a poor student than from a good student.

> strongly disagree   disagree   no opinion   agree   strongly agree

Likert scales may have three, five or more choices. Their advantage is that shades of opinion may be given numerical values: it might be significant if large numbers of respondents could only bring themselves to agree with a particular statement, showing weak support, but strongly agreed with others. Unfortunately they also have two disadvantages. First, the midpoint is often difficult to interpret (no opinion because the question is not relevant or because the respondent is not interested?) and second, people vary in degrees of caution, and one person's agreement may be another person's strong agreement. In quantitative analysis, the five alternatives may be reduced to three anyway in order to have enough people in all the cells for the expected values.

Guttman scaling

Another kind of scaling is often used to gauge the strength of feeling on some issue. Here, each question is related to the others rather than being essentially independent information, and the answers from individuals can be summed over the whole questionnaire to give a measure of strength. This technique has been used, for example, to measure strength of motivation in language learning. It has also been used extensively in personality studies, which in their turn have been used by language learning researchers to investigate various questions concerning the relationship between personality types and language learning.

Constructing questionnaires

It is evident from the above discussion that a good questionnaire is one which is relatively easy to answer, easy to record and evaluate, user-friendly and unambiguous. The designer has to choose a mix of question types that will maximize the range and detail of the information elicited. However, there are some fairly obvious difficulties in constructing questions which Cohen and Manion (1989: 108–9) succinctly describe (in the context of survey research) as a list of outcomes to avoid. They are summarized here:

- *leading* questions which suggest there is one desirable or desired answer
- *highbrow* questions, using portentous long words which are liable to be misunderstood
- *complex* questions with many subparts
- *irritating* questions or instructions, asking for example for responses in several category boxes at once
- *negative* questions, especially double negatives.

Cohen and Manion do warn against open-ended questions or self-completion questionnaires since they may make too great a demand on the respondents' time or goodwill, and are possibly difficult to interpret. To this list one need hardly add:

- *ambiguous* questions.

Questionnaire designers try therefore to avoid poor types of question, but often the difficulties with individual questions do not become apparent until a version of the questionnaire has been piloted. A kind of item analysis can be performed, looking at:

- the consistency of answers, which might indicate a lack of discrimination in the questions

- the yield on individual questions, since a question attracting a large number of 'don't knows' may indicate too difficult a choice or an ambiguity
- any other comments available from the respondents.

Giving questionnaires in a second language might prove less useful than translating the questions into the respondents' mother tongue(s); if this is done, however, it is usual to have an independent person translate back into the original language as a check on the comparability of the translated version.

Methods of analysis

Most questionnaires are designed to be evaluated numerically, and are amenable to fairly simple counting techniques. These can be done by hand for relatively small runs and can be performed by computer when the numbers grow large. The first step is to draw up a table with all the questions down the left-hand side and all the respondents along the top:

	A	B	C	D	E	F	G	H	I	J	K
Q1											
Q2											
Q3											
Q4											
Q5											
Q6											
Q7											
Q8											
Q9											
Q10											

Each person's response can then be plotted, giving an overview of all the data. Each data field will have values corresponding to the mode of response demanded in the question: yes/no; never/sometimes/often; rank 1–10; and so on. Exactly the same procedure is required for entering the data into a computer using for example the Statistical Package for the Social Science (SPSS). For each individual question, frequencies and therefore proportions can be easily calculated, and it is often clearer to translate these into percentages. Occasionally, the researcher will want to test the significance of the proportions compared with chance, in which case chi-square as discussed in Chapter 9 is appropriate.

Interpreting a questionnaire numerically normally means evaluating each question separately. However, a further and very useful level of analysis is 'cross-tabulation', in which the responses of subgroups can be blocked together. It is usual to do this with the moderator variables. For example, one of the authors recently polled a class consisting of members of two different courses. Cross-tabulation revealed the differences between them on several questions, to do with the feasibility of doing research in their normal teaching situations. Cross-tabulation plots one question against another:

Q10 Would teacher research be feasible in your situation?

	Yes	No
Q3 Course A		
Course B		

By this means, different kinds of divisions and splits in the block of responses can be analysed. It does not have to involve only moderator variables, as there may be significant divisions by other answers. The power of cross-tabulation is that it can be used (by hand or more easily in the computer) to look at more complicated divisions, for example at three or four questions at once, so extending the above example, there might be some interest in seeing if course choice (Q3) interacted with perceptions of feasibility (Q10) for those teachers involved in evaluation (Q13). In principle, cross-tabulation can cut swathes through a mass of responses looking at intersections of any number of questions, but in practice it becomes impossible to represent satisfactorily on paper after four levels (Q by Q by Q by Q) and exceedingly taxing to conceptualize.

Finally, a recurring worry about questionnaire-based research is the validity of the instruments: do they really describe or measure what they are believed to? The only way to decide the issue is to compare the results with similar information obtained by other methods, through interviews, diaries, case studies, verbal reports or tests. A recent large-scale example of such validation is by Gardner and MacIntyre (1993) who attempted to cross-validate their 'Attitude Motivation Inventory', a collection of 13 questionnaires with two alternative ways of eliciting comparable information.

Questionnaire-based research in language teaching

There have been many examples reported in the literature. Here is a small sample for illustrative purposes.

Study skills

Jordan (1993) presents the results of questionnaire surveys on study skills among overseas non-native speaker students at Manchester University over a three-year period.

Needs analysis

Weir (1988) investigated the linguistic demands of work in different university departments as part of a needs analysis. The purpose was to determine the kind and range of English-language skills required of new entrants and therefore derive a specification for a new task-authentic test. In ESP there are many further examples of needs-analysis questionnaires: see, for example, Mackay and Mountford (1978).

Assessment

Brindley (1991) discussed the problems of assessing achievement in the learner-centred curriculum of the Australian Migrant English Programme. He used a ranking method and compared the perceptions of teachers, programme administrators and learners of the various possible reasons for testing achievement and ways of doing so.

Involvement in curriculum development

Powell (1992) used open-ended questionnaires combined with diary entries to study the perceptions and emotions of 15 teachers involved in a regional modern language curriculum development project. The teachers were participants in an in-service professional development programme, and were also writing language teaching materials. The responses reveal fascinating variety of detail about the way the teachers reacted to the project, to the problems they encountered in writing materials, and to the various extra activities set up in the programme.

Writing skills

Casanave and Hubbard (1992) used a questionnaire (adapted from one published in a TOEFL research report on the Test of Written English) to investigate writing skills and writing requirements of first-year doctoral research students (both native and non-native speakers) in a large university in the USA. The questionnaire consisted mainly of Likert-type questions, ranking questions and open-ended questions, and was six pages long. The paper analysed the yield of 85 questionnaires, a respectable number, but it is worth noting that they sent out 563, a yield of only 15 per cent. The survey investigated a wide range of issues: writing tasks, the importance of writing skills, evaluation criteria, writing problems of native and non-native English speakers, explicitness of assignments, and a bunch of open-ended questions.

Metacognitive strategies

Carrell (1989) decided to use a questionnaire to investigate learners' strategies in reading a text in a foreign language for an interesting reason. Previous research had used sensitive 'think-aloud' methods, essentially asking people to talk about what they were thinking while they read specific texts. Carrell wanted to free her data from the constraints of reading specific texts and look at more general issues, to tap into the beliefs, intentions and preferred modes of learning of her respondents. She elicited data from Spanish-speaking learners of English and English-speaking learners of Spanish, and requested responses to the questionnaire under two headings: reading in the first and reading in the second language. The results were then evaluated by quite a powerful statistical technique to separate out the various preferences operating in the different situations.

Programme evaluation

Questionnaires are often used as a means of data collection in the evaluation of language teaching programmes. They may be given to students requesting feedback on course delivery, to institutions as a means of quality audit, and to staff in pursuit of information about course development and staff involvement. Many examples are given in Weir and Roberts (1994).

Interviews

Interviews may be used as the primary research tool, or alternatively in an ancillary role, perhaps as a checking mechanism to triangulate data gathered from other sources. In education, uses include large-scale surveys, ethnographic studies, 'micro' research on individuals, and the kind of action-research perspective explicitly favoured by Hopkins, who lists three applications of interviews in classroom research (1993: 125 and 127):

- to focus on a specific aspect of classroom life in detail
- teacher-pupil discussion → diagnostic information
- to improve the classroom climate.

For applied linguistics, Nunan's list (1992b) covers SLA research, language testing of oral proficiency, conversational analysis, linguistic variation and so on. Teachers may well share some of these goals, though to these uses we could also add (for example):

- needs analysis
- programme evaluation
- individual case studies
- mini-surveys (within institution).

Interviews, of course, are just another way of asking questions, this time in face-to-face interaction, rather than the questionnaire format discussed above. In fact the label subsumes a number of diverse modes that roughly parallel the different orientations to research discussed in this book. In this section of the chapter we look at the main types of interview available to suit different purposes, the kinds of data they generate, and some of the issues associated with using the technique.

Types of interview

Interviewing is a very basic research tool in social science, from which the conventional classification largely derives. Most commonly, interviews are divided into (a) *structured*, (b) *semi-structured* and (c) *unstructured*, and these are the terms we shall adopt here. (Terminology is, however, varied: Cohen and Manion, 1989, for instance, use (a) and (c) alongside the two further categories of '*non-directive*' and '*focused*'.) What is essentially being represented is a spectrum, not hard-and-fast self-contained categories, from formal and controlled at one end to more open and less predictable at the other. Lincoln and Guba see this as a normative/non-normative continuum: they gloss the structured interview as when the interviewer 'knows what he or she does not know', and the unstructured interview when the interviewer 'does not know what he or she doesn't know' (1985: 269). It is important to remember that the categories merge, and can also be combined in the same research 'event'.

Structured interviews

These are closest to the standard questionnaire both in their format and the assumptions on which they are based. In other words, using questions tightly specified in advance, they aim to survey relatively large populations by asking the same questions in the same order. Many people will have had the experience of being approached in the street to answer market-research questions, for example, and on this very large scale it is necessary to use cohorts of trained interviewers. As we write, the *Guardian* (6 March 1996) has just reported on the interviewing by telephone of 1200 people concerning the future of the British monarchy. Data analysis, seeking representativeness and an overall picture of trends, is predominantly quantitative and often tabular and diagrammatic.

Such interviews do have some advantages over the questionnaire. They allow the interviewer to seek clarification in limited ways, and to disambiguate questions if necessary, and they normally yield a better response rate (I can throw a piece of paper into the bin because I feel too busy to deal with it, but it is more difficult to send someone away in a face-to-face situation). On the other hand, the anonymity of the questionnaire may mean that more honest responses are given.

Cohen and Manion (1989: 312ff) set out the three main types of item used in structured interviews (and here there are clear parallels with questionnaires):

- fixed alternative: i.e. dichotomous yes/no
- open-ended: some response flexibility possible (e.g. 'What TV programmes do you watch?')
- scale: usually degrees of agreement–disagreement.

Structured interviews have been widely used in research on language learning, for example in data collection on attitudes or proficiency, and often on a large scale. In more localized contexts, they offer practitioners a very useful tool in a number of areas, particularly when the population is small enough to make personal interviewing realistic, rather than requiring a questionnaire format. For instance, a profile of institutional English-language proficiency requirements can be gathered relatively quickly with such standardized questions as:

How many non-native speakers are there in your department?

What proportion of the total student population do they represent?

Do you ask for a score on a standard test such as TOEFL or IELTS?

How do you deal with language problems?

Further typical applications are in the analysis of learner needs, methodological learning preferences, evaluation, and so on; indeed any aspect of school and classroom life where the teacher researcher is interested in gaining an overview.

Semi-structured interviews

Interviews in this category have a structured overall framework but allow for greater flexibility within that, for example in changing the order of questions and for more extensive follow-up of responses. So, for instance, answers to the fourth question above could be probed further:

How do you usually deal with language problems?
I usually try to correct the grammar myself
Do you think that is an appropriate role for you?

(and so on).

The interviewer, then, remains in control of the direction of the interview but with much more leeway. Although this format has characteristics of both other types, it is usually regarded as being closer to the qualitative paradigm because it allows for richer interactions and more personalized responses than the quasi-automaton interviewer armed with entirely pre-coded questions.

Unstructured interviews

This style of interviewing still has to start with some kind of agenda, but it is usually a loose one, a rough checklist built around issues formulated in outline only. The direction of the interview intentionally follows inter-viewee responses, with some of the characteristics of natural conversation: 'The qualitative interviewer should arrive with a short list of issue-oriented questions ... The purpose for the most part is not to get simple yes and no answers but descriptions of an episode, a linkage, an explana-tion. Formulating the questions and anticipating probes that evoke good responses is a special art' (Stake, 1995: 65).

In the sense that less structured interviews are more in touch with the social world, being able to tap into everyday reality, they are clearly quite well suited to teacher research and to the ways in which teachers interact with learners, colleagues and others in their working environment. The interviewer needs a well-developed feeling for context and some under-standing of the concerns of interviewees as a starting point. For instance, one of the present authors is currently investigating patterns of change in the experiences of overseas students in Britain by means of interviews with a small number of people, using issues as 'triggers' (e.g. 'Tell me some-thing about the people you interact with' and 'Have there been any import-ant turning points for you since you arrived?'). Open-ended questioning is also particularly appropriate in interpretive case study research and, perhaps cross-referred to other data sources such as diaries, can contribute to a rounded portrayal of individuals.

Qualitative interviewing and ethnographic research methodology are clearly closely related. From a language teaching perspective, studies in the ethnography of language and communication are of particular interest. Saville-Troike's survey book explains that ethnographic interviews do not on the whole have predetermined response alternatives because of the need to be 'open to new meanings and unforeseen patterns of behaviour'

(1989: 124). She makes the important point that many concepts are not universal but language- and culture-specific ('friendly' is one of her examples) that have to be explored in the context in which they are used. Although most teachers are instinctively sensitive to such differentiation in language use, there is rich research ground here for someone interested in cross-cultural factors of language use and ways in which they affect classroom interaction.

One further format of interest here is the group interview, usually with three or four participants rather than a whole class. Hopkins (1993) finds this the most productive because, he claims, individuals can 'spark' each other into perceptive lines of discussion. The most obvious, though by no means the only, use is in formative evaluation. An example of this is EFL Services' exploration of student attitudes in courses in British private language schools (EFL Services, 1992), using the 'focus group' method.

Finally, we reiterate that, at least methodologically, 'structured' and 'less structured' interviews are not mutually exclusive. Qualitative interviewing may lead to more structured questions at later stages, for example when checking details with respondents; conversely, precoding may help with initial 'ground-clearing', or may be the first stage in opening up key issues.

Issues in interviewing

The interview as a research instrument raises a number of issues of both principle and practice. Here we comment on just three areas that seem particularly to impinge on language teacher research.

1. Interviewing, like any activity that deals with personal data, raises obvious questions of access, confidentiality and privacy. More specifically – and depending on the type of interview – there is a further ethical dimension that requires us to take into account the role relationship of interviewer-interviewee. Borrowing the terminology of social psychology, this relationship may be symmetrical, as between peers, or asymmetrical, as between (say) teacher and headmaster, or teacher and student. A probing, interpretive interview 'invades' the interviewees' private space: especially in the teacher → student interview an element of power is introduced. This is even more salient when teachers/researchers are dealing with non-native speakers: not only is the question-and-answer technique itself a control device (as so much of the research on teachers' classroom language shows), but there is, automatically, another layer of control, this time by the teacher of the medium itself. This will therefore have implications for the formulation of questions as well as for their content, and will require a good deal of linguistic sensitivity and adaptability by the researcher. (For a particularly negative instance see Nunan, 1992b: 151, quoting Van Lier.)

2. In EFL methodology generally, there has been considerable discussion of the parallels between teaching and therapy or counselling (see for example Stevick's discussion, 1980, of Curran's model of Counselling-Learning). A similar parallel has been drawn with unstructured interviewing, likening the researcher-interviewer's role to that of the therapist. Cohen and Manion (1989) discuss in particular Carl Rogers' advocacy of the non-directive interview, at the same time shedding doubt on its usefulness in educational contexts, where the objective is not to 'cure' by changing behaviour but 'to leave a residue of results rather than a posse of cured souls' (p. 326, quoting Madge).

3. In the social science and educational research literature, the best method to record interview data has been much debated. There are three main possibilities.

- *Write-up after the interview*. Despite obvious problems of memory, this method is favoured by Stake (1995) among others. He calls it a 'written facsimile', claiming that data written up within a few hours can best capture the meaning and innuendo of ongoing conversation. It also enables annotation as to para- and non-linguistic aspects of the encounter.
- *Audio recording*. A tape/cassette-recorder may be intrusive (and will require permission from the interviewee). Data will have to be transcribed, a very time-consuming undertaking. However, when language learners are being interviewed there is a clear advantage in this technique because it ensures an accurate and detailed record of actual language data which may not just be the *vehicle* for the interview, but its *object* as well. (For an interesting variation on qualitative data analysis, see Hycner's 'phenomenological' model, quoted in Cohen and Manion, 1989. It begins with transcription and proceeds through 15 steps which cluster segments of meaning and include member checking and re-interviewing.)
- *Note-taking*. There may be problems with the sheer quantity of ephemeral data, and the activity itself may distract the attention of both interviewer and interviewee.

Walker makes the point that these are not just technical nuances but represent 'different ways of going about doing research ... They each imply a different kind of relationship between the researcher and the task and between the researcher and the subject, and a different conception of the nature of the task' (1985: 109).

4. The analysis of structured and semi-structured interview data can follow some of the same numerical lines as that of questionnaires. The more open-ended, exploratory and ethnographic interviews referred to above may be analysed qualitatively by searching for themes, by looking for patterns, by looking for interpretations which are consistent with all

the information revealed in the interview. The criterion of validity of such interpretations has to be their plausibility and the sense of accounting for all that the interviewee has revealed. This process has been likened to writing fiction, where the criterion is also its plausibility and convincingness to other people; but in this case the research is discovering someone else's truth, not inventing an imaginary world.

There are also methods of 'content analysis' (Cohen and Manion, 1989: 62–4, and Chapter 8, for example) for naturally occurring texts which can be extended to interview data. Content analysis is essentially a way of taking verbal documents, not necessarily elicited for research purposes, and codifying them for quantitative analysis. A content analysis sets up a number of categories which are appropriate to the specified text type and content, and creates units of analysis – words, phrases, themes, and so on. Ways of systematically identifying these are set up and the resulting tallies can be grouped, nested, ordered with respect to each other, counted and otherwise displayed. A language learning example is given by Wenden's paper on 'How to be a successful language learner' (1987). In this, she used content analysis of semi-structured interviews lasting about 90 minutes each with 25 learners of English (nearly 40 hours of tape!). The topic was their beliefs of how best to learn English. Wenden set up a number of criteria to identify statements about her respondents' beliefs about language learning. These systematically defined the 'themes' in the data by focusing in various ways described in her Appendix 3 (1987: 116). Essentially, this involved finding generalizations, characteristic approaches, justifications, certain verbal contexts or linguistic frames (like 'I think ...'), repeated phrases and topics, and lengthy explanations. From the mass of data this procedure allowed Wenden to distil the learners' beliefs into 12 statements, most of which most of the group had contributed to.

Conclusion

This chapter has discussed two closely related ways of obtaining data. Both questionnaires and interviews require care and subtlety in questioning techniques, but in different ways. Their use ranges widely across the spectrum from normative to non-normative, and also in terms of scale. Questionnaires and certain forms of interview can be used in large-scale and small-scale contexts, by individual researchers or groups working in collaboration, and in different sites. Data-analysis techniques also may range from simple numerical ones to subtle and sensitive interpretive methods. Both kinds of research can be seen as somewhat specialized forms of conversation, and the parallel with conversation reminds us of the many interesting features of such information exchange: power and status distribution, risk of giving and taking offence, loss of face, properly formulated requests, self-revelation and disclosure to strangers, rights of refusal, and so on. Both questionnaires and interviews are very popular forms of research tool and may be used in conjunction with each other and other forms of data.

Discussion notes

1. Have you ever had the experience of writing a questionnaire – whether for course evaluation or any other purpose? If so, were there any aspects of the design that in retrospect did not yield the kind of data you wanted? Try to enumerate some of the reasons for this. You may also like to consider your own attitude to responding to questionnaires designed by other people. Do you usually complete them?
2. Suppose you are conducting a needs analysis or a programme evaluation within your own institution. To what extent would (a) questionnaires and (b) interviews be appropriate methods? Might you use both, for different reasons?
3. What kind of teacher-research project might best be served by the use of naturalistic, unstructured interview techniques?

12

Looking inside: methods for introspection

Introduction

Many interesting questions can be answered by considering what a person is thinking about while they perform some task. It is a commonplace of skill theory that skilled performance of tasks requires varying degrees of conscious attention: some aspects of tasks are virtually automatic, others require close concentration and the conscious integration of many different kinds of information. Similarly, the same task for an unskilled person may require more conscious attention than for a skilled person. To the extent that language learning and indeed language teaching may be regarded as skills, the same points apply: attention is needed for any language learning, using and teaching processes. Therefore, asking someone what they are thinking about when they perform some more or less skilled activity can reveal the content of those attention processes. People may report on the points at which they make decisions and their sequence, their strategies, their perceptions, their means of monitoring and controlling what they do, their frustration at memory loss or cognitive overload, or sometimes nothing at all – the mind goes blank. This internal aspect of the active participant in language learning and teaching may be partial, since there may be automatic and autonomous processes running as well, but it is crucial, since so often decisions about future action are made on the basis of the perceptions expressed in those reports.

This chapter will first look at some of the ways in which this kind of research has been characterized, roughly how it is conducted, and what some of the major problems are. Then it will turn the discussion round to look at doing research on oneself by observing oneself rigorously in various situations and what might be learned from that. From there the discussion proceeds to outline introspective research methods for other people, mainly, but not exclusively, learners. The final section will give the flavour of this kind of work in a couple of brief accounts of research work.

Introspection

There has been a long history of introspective research on learners extending back more than 20 years. Techniques have been developed for getting learners to reveal their own thought processes while or shortly after performing some kind of language activity. One of the earliest researchers in this field, Hosenfeld (1976), commented that, after conducting a lengthy series of individual interviews with members of a class learning intermediate French, the class teacher expressed surprise at how much more the researcher knew about her students than she did. In the light of subsequent developments, this remark can be seen as a justification, not merely for research, but for teachers doing research. In fact in the case of Hosenfeld's work the distinction between teaching and research becomes blurred, since she went on to develop remedial teaching methods for L2 reading based on think-aloud revelations by students of what strategies they typically adopted. There has not been the same history of research on teaching using verbal reports either by teachers or anybody else: the equivalent is probably the teacher's diary and diary studies, which began seriously at much the same time, and which were described in detail in Chapter 8. Second language acquisition studies have pursued lines of research about autonomous acquisition processes and voluntary learning processes for some years. Ellis (1994) presents a comprehensive overview; McDonough (1995) explores the many interesting studies in strategy use and skilled language learning. This area of research has also spawned a number of evaluation studies of the effects of teaching strategy use to language learners, with mixed results.

Studying language learning, or anything else, by using verbal report methods sits fairly firmly in a long tradition of individual psychology studies. Typically numbers of participating learners are few, because of the amount of data that any one learner produces for analysis in a couple of sessions. It is for this reason not usually bracketed with the study of social contexts; however, context of learning will manifestly affect what learners will report. Where verbal report is used for analysing classroom behaviour or in combination with classroom observation, it could be argued that the individual study interacts with the social study. However, just as other techniques can be used in several research traditions, so can verbal report protocols be analysed either quantitatively or qualitatively, and often both kinds of analysis are used to support an interpretation. Verbal report methods have allowed learners as individuals to take centre stage in investigations of language teaching and learning, rather than language acquisition theories, teaching techniques, or materials development.

Although the methods developed for introspective research are neither purely experimental nor naturalistic (but they can be used in both kinds of research), nor do they fit into the elaborate action research cycle, teachers will find that they produce fascinating data. This often gives quite unexpected insights into how a learner is processing the material, why a persistent error will not go away, what kind of contribution particular text types, activities, classroom tasks and writing demands make to the learner's growing competence in the language, and it also enables teachers to assess the challenge they set for their learners in the light of their own experience as foreign language learners and users.

Verbal report and think-aloud

It is obvious that not all our mental activity is available for our conscious inspection. In many areas of our lives, especially in using our native language, we are only aware of a proportion of the decision processes that we go through. However, both in using and learning language, we are aware of some of them, and we often pay close attention to them, for example in how we speak or how we phrase messages, and in how we try to notice what seems to be important in our learning and how we try to ensure we remember something. Verbal reporting methods are premised on the idea that these insights are not just 'epiphenomena', that is imperfect reflections of the real but invisible decision processes in our minds, but real phenomena in their own right. Furthermore, we tend to place some reliance on the ways in which we believe we operate, to the extent that we base future actions, tolerance of failure, expectations of success and more generally our hopes and fears in learning achievement on these cognitive insights. Verbal reporting methods are designed to help us reveal these so a fuller picture of learning processes can be constructed. Obviously, also, people do not necessarily want to have all their thoughts revealed to others, so there is a strong ethical dimension to this kind of research, in terms of confidentiality, publication, protection of contributions, as discussed in Chapter 4 and elsewhere.

There is a chain of events involved in this kind of research, and there are important decisions to be taken for each link in the chain. It runs roughly as follows.

Thoughts
Does directing attention to one's thoughts spoil the flow of thought?
Does introspection require any kind of training?
Is attention divided between doing the task and looking at oneself doing it?

Think-aloud
Is the reporting immediate, say within 20 seconds of the mental event (introspection) or later (retrospection)?
Does reporting or giving a verbal report itself benefit from training?
When is verbal report requested and how often?

Recording
Is the report spoken directly into a recorder, or written down?
Is the report in the form of a checklist or structured questionnaire?
Is it recorded by an external observer using field notes?
How closely can what the reporter says be related to what they are doing?
Is time information available?

Analysis
Can the events being reported be related to an existing set of categories, e.g. an inventory of strategies or a coding scheme?
Can they be described qualitatively?
Can a content analysis be developed?

Comparison
How does one report compare with others?
Are there differences according to moderator variables such as proficiency level, activity type, text difficulty, topic familiarity, task importance?

Interpretation
How can the reports be best described?

Verbal reporting has had a chequered history. Suspicions about the relevance, usefulness and indeed acceptability of such data were elaborated into strong criticisms by Nisbett and Wilson (1977), who argued that our reports of our own mental life are too flawed and, among other things, too influenced by what we believe we want others to think to be used as data. According to them, our own reports are too unreliable, since we are not necessarily good observers, and also because our explanations of our ourselves to ourselves may be complex and spurious, not admitting simple but unprestigious explanations. There are, as mentioned already, limits on the depth of process to which we can have conscious access. Lastly, the act of reporting may alter the event compared to doing the same thing when not required to report. On the other hand, Ericsson and Simon (1987; 1993) have argued (particularly in the first edition, in 1984, of their 1993 book, on which much verbal report methodology has been based) that such data is admissible, interesting and usable. They introduced a number of sensible constraints. First, they emphasized the limitations set by human attention. Verbal reports can only be expected to yield data on 'heeded' processes. Second, some processes may be easy to put into language (called Level 1 reporting) and some may be difficult (Level 2 reporting). Third, they pointed out that some reporting involves going back some way in time, called 'retrospective' reporting, while some is concurrent, reporting as closely as possible to the actual performance of the task. Concurrent verbal reporting is the normal kind of data used nowadays in this method. The report is usually called a 'protocol', and the method, 'protocol analysis'. Cohen (1992) has summarized these various differences in this tripartite distinction, which he glossed as follows in a later a paper (1995):

Self-report
Generalized statements about learning behaviour, descriptions of what learners believe about themselves, e.g. 'I tend to be a speed listener'.

Self-observation
The inspection of specific language behaviour, e.g. 'What I did was to skim through the incoming oral text as I listened, picking out key words and phrases'.

Self-revelation
'Think-aloud', stream-of-consciousness disclosure of thought processes while the information is being attended to, e.g. 'Who does the "they" refer to here?'

There are many problems with this kind of data, but the interest inherent in discovering what learners actually do in their classrooms and places where they learn and use the language makes it worthwhile. Often it can be surprising to a teacher to discover, as Hosenfeld (1979) did with Cora, that the student is actually subverting the instructions for a particular exercise but, in the process, making it her own contribution to her own learning. Disobedience to instructions was revealed as normal and understandable in the testing situation, where test-takers often report refusing to read a text through first but going straight to the questions, because (a) maximum time is needed for the questions, which is where the reward is, and (b) the testers' contention that the tests assess ability to comprehend the overall meaning of the passage is dubious and the testees know it (Cohen, 1984) .

The problems particularly concern reliability, timelag, yield, reactive effects and fullness of reporting. Unreliability is inherent in the data, as we have seen, and is also inherent in using coding systems and categorization systems for analysis of observational data for classrooms (Chapter 7). The usual answer is in terms of triangulation, here the use of multiple raters or categorizers. Timelag between mental event and verbal report may simply mean that useful data is lost, just forgotten, and the premium is on immediacy, hence the accent on concurrent verbal reporting.

However, it has been suggested that a comparison between concurrent and retrospective verbal reports is needed to get a more balanced picture. Low yield can be a problem if the reporter does not want to say much, is confused about the task, or has linguistic difficulties when reporting in L2; high yield can also be a problem because many human beings become particularly loquacious when talking about themselves. Reactive effects refer to the effects of performing verbal reporting on the task being observed. These may, as claimed by Ericsson (1988) referring to reading studies, merely slow down but not change the quality of the task performance, but Cohen (1995) documents a number of reports where people have said that doing verbal reporting has changed what they normally do, both detrimentally and also beneficially, by drawing their own attention to habits of theirs that they can modify with advantage. Fullness of reporting (by the researcher) can be a problem if insufficient detail is given about the reporters, such as their proficiency level, known languages, experience in doing verbal report, and other significant pointers, since such research deals with individuals rather than groups.

Research on oneself

Most of the considerations above have arisen in the context of developing methods of investigating other people's introspections. They are also relevant when considering how to reveal and capitalize on one's own observations as a language learner, user and teacher, for the potential benefit of one's own teaching. Observing oneself may seem to be a strange kind of research to be advocating here, but it can be a serious factor in understanding what might be happening to learners and how they might be reacting to the language and language tasks with which they are faced. Of course, one should not commit the 'egocentric error', that is assuming that, because we act the way we do, everybody else does the same. Such insights into oneself need to be tested out on others – but therefore they form a rich source of research questions. The discipline implied in the previous section about decisions to be made concerning the immediacy of recording the observation, method of recording and analysis apply equally to observing oneself. They are obviously and closely related to the discipline and rigour described in Chapter 8 about diary-keeping, and fit neatly with the idea of the self-reflective teacher.

However, what can one observe? Relevant areas for self-observation and self-revelation will include one's own experiences of language learning and foreign language use, of language teaching, and of working in institutions and interacting with students, colleagues and persons in authority. Under the heading of language learning and language use, two autobiographical examples which one of the present authors has noticed but never seriously researched while operating in a foreign language are the use of mental translation in talking and writing and the complete failure to use the strategy of skim-reading. With regard to translation, the present author has noticed many times clear auditory images of the L1 sentences being used as the basis for L2 production even when that has been fairly fluent. In fact the only times he was fairly happy that he was not translating was when the audience pressure was very strong: in particular, when talking to a class of schoolchildren in their language, when any hesitation or lack of accuracy was swiftly penalized by loss of authority. This may serve as a very obvious example of an area in which individual experience contrasts with received wisdom. It is possibly an example of accepted knowledge being defined by researchers (here, old work dating back to the behaviourist tradition of research on 'transfer') and enshrined unchallenged in methodology texts long after the original research is forgotten or discredited. The other autobiographical example is skim-reading, often advocated in textbooks as a useful learner's strategy, but which this author has always found extremely difficult in the few foreign languages available to him and also difficult in his native English. Attempts to skim-read usually result in fast reading and the realization that good chunks of the meaning have been missed. Of course, the personal examples do not matter: what matters is the availability of evidence from one's own processing to check against received wisdom, other learners' experience and one's students' own preferred processing strategies.

There may well be instructive experiences in teachers' interaction as learners with other teachers, as commented on in Chapter 8. While the majority of these are probably best captured by using a diary method, there are some situations where the teacher-learner might consider using a more immediate or concurrent verbal report method. The most obvious opportunities for observing one's own reactions to another teacher's methods are when doing a listening exercise, when concurrent written notes or interrupting the tape for spoken verbal report are feasible; carrying out a reading assignment, using a version of protocol analysis, or when attempting to write in the new language, again using a concurrent verbal report.

Using concurrent verbal reporting in the activity of language teaching presents obvious problems; however, the more immediately a note of the thoughts in the teacher's mind can be made after conducting some teaching procedure, trying out something new, using various new strategies for classroom management or for maximizing work involvement, the more accurate and detailed the evidence for later reflection and incorporation into a diary can be. One private area in which a full-scale protocol analysis would be feasible, and which to this author's knowledge has not yet been performed, is in marking and giving feedback on students' writing. Given the topicality and popularity of studies of students' writing processes and strategies for interpreting and using teachers' feedback, it is curious gap in the ELT literature.

A third opportunity for research on oneself as a teacher concerns interaction within one's own teaching context. Time management, staffroom interaction, assembling resources, preparing material, attending meetings and many other activities are the normal scene of a teacher's professional life: here there is scope for introspection both for one's own purposes of reflection and in order to complement 'outsider' research on these kinds of activities. Dadds (1995) has argued for the importance of such detailed reflection under the heading of 'first person research'.

Research on learners

The suggestion of teachers' self-observation in the previous section may appear unrealistic and even quirky to some; to others it will not even count as research. It is, however, in the spirit of 'teacher development' and consistent with the aims of the more familiar methods of diary research. The main thrust of verbal report methods has, however, been in trying to elucidate what learners are actually doing while they perform activities and tasks that are considered to be relevant for language learning. This section outlines the main steps in eliciting and analysing verbal reports of introspective data. For the purposes of clarity, the research process can be divided into six steps: any actual investigation will make different choices at each step consistent with the research purpose or the particular question being investigated.

1. Training

It is usual, in this kind of research, to give some demonstration of what is meant by giving a concurrent verbal report to the reporters. This varies from simply doing the task in front of the learners to setting up a number of activities for them to do to give them a sense of what is involved. The usual method is to ask the reporters to perform some simple task which has nothing directly to do with the task to be investigated. The reason for that stipulation is that it is important not to suggest to the reporters what the researcher wants them to say. The usual tasks used for training in verbal reporting are solving anagrams aloud, doing simple letter puzzles, and doing simple mental arithmetic aloud.

2. Elicitation

The chosen method of elicitation will depend largely on the particular task being investigated but an important general distinction is between a 'planned' reporting point and a 'free' one. Examples of 'free' reporting points are:

- asking for a response whenever the reporter thinks he or she has something to say
- asking for a concurrent verbal report while writing an assignment
- asking the respondent to pause a tape or video in a listening task at will
- asking for a report on reading when something occurs to the person.

Free reporting points may be 'democratic' but they also involve a judgement on the part of the respondent as to when they have something relevant to say: this may conceal some useful information.

Examples of 'planned' reporting points would be:

- asking a reader to report at the ends of sentences, lines, clauses, or where a marker is inserted into the text
- pausing a tape at pre-determined intervals for reporting
- asking for a report after each item in a test
- stopping a class and asking for a report on what people were attending to at that point.

Planned reporting points are a way of ensuring quantity and to some extent quality of data: however, they may break up the flow of the activity in question in uncomfortable ways, even to the extent of altering its nature significantly.

When working with language learners, it is important to give them the opportunity to report in whatever language comes to them naturally. It is not always their native language. Even when they choose, or are instructed to use the L2 as the language of report, they should be allowed to use L1 for phrases and words, and code-switch freely. A subsequent interview can be used to discover what was meant. The importance of making reporting easy cannot be over-emphasized.

It is normal to request people to report on what they are thinking at the time of doing the task, not how they think they are performing it. Questions that require interpretation of mental activity are usually 'level 2' and involve more than just reporting: in particular, self-monitoring and interpretation.

3. Recording

Almost universally, verbal reports are recorded on to audio- or video-tape. It is important to ensure, either by a time code or by field notes by the observing researcher, or by some other mechanical means, a clear link-up between the tape of the verbal report and the progress of the activity being reported on. In a writing task, for example, there must be some way of tying the verbal report directly to the text as it is being written. One of the frequent activities noticed in this situation is 'self-dictation', i.e. speaking while writing, and this can only be recorded if there is some means of establishing exactly what the writer was writing when he or she said the comments. Sometimes the link-up can be established naturally from the contents of the verbal report; the method of 'planned' reporting points allows more accuracy than a free method.

4. Analysis

Introspective methods produce messy and obviously qualitative data. They can be analysed both qualitatively and quantitatively, as with other data forms discussed elsewhere. Coding systems can be used; large amounts of work on the writing process have used versions of the coding system for written protocols set up by Perl (1981) for studying written composition by native writers. In many cases the coding categories have been elevated from the status of data-analysis categories to mental events themselves, under the general heading of 'strategies'. The status of the idea of mental strategy has been discussed by Bialystok (1990) and McDonough (1995), and placed within cognitive theory by O'Malley and Chamot (1990). The products of such classification systems can be counted, and frequency distributions compared for various purposes. Alternatively, or by way of complement, qualitative analysis may be performed, in which the verbal report is interpreted to show the flow and development of, for example, a student's comprehension of a text, or to compare writing performed for different purposes or in different genres (narrative versus expository; paraphrase versus summary). A qualitative analysis is usually elaborative: the researcher attempts to interpret the learner's protocol.

5. Reliability

The reliability of the data analysis is normally checked by having two or three independent judges operate the classification system and compute their levels of agreement. In addition, a 'within-judge' check can be performed in which one judge (usually the researcher) reworks part of the data again and compares the original classification or interpretation with the second time around.

6. Triangulation

Already mentioned often elsewhere in this book, triangulation is a frequent technique in introspective methods too. The first and most important triangulation is between the verbal report and the product of the activity (for example, evidence of the actual comprehension of the passage, the written composition, residual memory of the vocabulary items tackled) both to establish the link-ups referred to under 3 above, but also to act as a first step in interpretation of how the learner performed the task. Another important triangulation is between the verbal report and field notes by the observer, to supplement the respondent's account with other observations. Further opportunities for triangulation may arise from using other performance data such as success or failure in tests, independent judgements of quality of written work, other indices of task performance such as comprehension questions, and so on, depending on the task being investigated. Verbal report data may be used in triangulation of other kinds of data, such as lesson observation transcripts (Cohen and Aphek, 1981) or in studies of 'uptake' of lesson contents (Slimani, 1989).

This brief six-stage outline of the methodology is intended to facilitate undertaking this kind of research by any teacher who has the opportunity to investigate individual learners, or in some cases groups of learners, and find out how they are solving their language-learning and language-using problems. The methodology has already been used for some time to establish strategies for learning and use (see McDonough, 1995, for a comprehensive survey) and has been closely associated with the notion of 'learner training': the suggestion that one function of language teaching is to give learners certain kinds of instruction in how to learn. Thus teachers can use this kind of research method for a variety of projects that may be close to home in their own teaching, and find out more about how their own students react to the language and to language instruction, particularly, perhaps, in remedial situations. It is noticeable that a good proportion of the published 'think-aloud' literature has in fact been concerned with remedial situations. A teacher wanting to find out why a particular student does not seem to be able to cope in certain circumstances, for example in expanding vocabulary, can use the method to find out what the student normally does and perhaps make suggestions on that basis for remedial strategies. The methodology is suitable for small-scale individual studies and for large-scale survey work; for qualitative description and for precise experimental work involving comparison of groups and treatments. Perhaps the most tedious aspect, certainly the most time-consuming, is the transcription of the reports from the immediate taped record; but, on the other hand, this necessary process can be used for a preliminary impressionistic analysis of the kind of information to be found in the data and some indications of the most appropriate analysis categories or analysis method for that data. The versatility of the method allows projects on a whole range of problems, for example:

- students processing in reading comprehension
- listening comprehension

- writing compositions and other tasks
- the processing of feedback
- learning the organization of talk and pragmatic strategies
- vocabulary learning and recall
- the use of translation
- encounters with different kinds of materials and resources
- taking tests
- learner training
- evaluation of learning activities including learning strategies.

Some examples

There have been published studies in all of the above areas. Cohen's book (1992) uses predominantly verbal report data and strategy work and is addressed, interestingly, to three separate sets of people – researchers, teachers and learners – in the belief that talking about language learning in this way and doing this kind of research is equally interesting to all three groups of participants in the profession. Two mainstream examples of published work will be briefly described here.

Writing processes

Arndt (1987) used protocol analysis to study six Chinese writers writing first in their native Chinese and then in English. She performed a full analysis of the verbal report transcripts using an adaptation of Perl's (1981) scheme with full time-based linkage to the written products. She was interested mainly in the comparison between the writers' processing in their L1 and L2 (English) in which they were moderately proficient. The protocol analyses revealed that, perhaps surprisingly, the very different expression opportunities available to them in the two languages did not swamp their individuality. She found evidence that each writer operated in consistent ways in whichever language they were writing, and that each writer was very much an individual in their approach, to the extent that she was able to show how the ways in which each writer planned, rehearsed, reviewed, edited, commented and revised their texts fell into distinct and individual styles.

Reading comprehension

Block (1986; 1992) investigated first and second language readers in college who were at a low level of proficiency compared to the level demanded by their courses. She used a planned reporting method consisting of prepared texts with a red marker at the points where verbal reporting was requested: basically at the end of each sentence or clause. The readers also gave an immediate verbal summary or retelling of the text. On the basis of previous work and the categories that the data seemed to suggest, Block set up a category system of reading strategies, and proceeded to code each report for the use of these strategies. Thus, comparisons could be made between patterns of strategy use and learning outcome as indicated by grade-point average (the crucial measure of academic progress in the USA). However, the most interesting aspect of her analysis was the identification of two patterns of strategy use adopted by the students, which were connected to their empathy with the meaning of the texts. She called them 'integrators' and 'non-integrators'. The 'integrators' kept their comments fairly exactly to the actual text, and highlighted the main theme in their retellings, using self-monitoring moves and noticing the internal structure of the text. The 'non-integrators' talked a great deal about their own reactions to the text and their personal associations, reacted less to text structure, monitored themselves less, and reported more details and fewer main points in their verbal summaries. These two modes of responding to the text are derived from the patterns of strategy use as revealed by the protocols, and were also associated with academic progress. The integrators had higher grade-point averages at the end of the first semester. This research demonstrated differentiation among students working in English as a first and as a second language, but at an unsatisfactory level of achievement, on the basis of strategy use. It also demonstrated the depth of insight which this method can provide.

Conclusion

This chapter has taken the notion of 'introspection', which was the *de facto* framework for our earlier review of diaries and diary studies, and has more formally defined it as a procedure for research, particularly but not only in language learning. We looked at a number of the more problematic aspects involved in verbal reporting of internal cognitive processes, including the issue of how comprehensive, accurate and reliable such data can be. Comparisons were then drawn between research on others and research on oneself. The chapter also discussed the more pragmatic areas of think-aloud procedures and data analysis, noting particularly the appropriacy of interpretive method. This section included a discussion of the ways in which people might be trained to conduct research, and actually 'do' verbal reports themselves.

A number of examples from language learning and teaching have been included, both actual and potential; and we have tried to show that research based on introspection is appropriate as an approach for teachers and also viable in methodological terms.

Discussion notes

1. Reflect on some of your own experiences while using or learning a foreign language, and how you might investigate your own thoughts while performing these tasks.
2. Perhaps you have students in your class who need remedial teaching in some areas of language learning: observe how they tackle these different tasks, and try to work out a way of asking them what they are thinking about when they are working at them.
3. Do you think there are recommended learning practices in methodology textbooks which could bear re-examination by introspective methods?

13

Studying cases

Introduction

A case study, it must be said at the outset, is not itself a research method nor the equivalent of one: it employs methods and techniques in the investigation of an object of interest. Given that case studies typically offer instances of the use of several methods for one piece of research, they are discussed in this penultimate chapter which leads directly to a consideration of multimethod projects. As we shall see, the notion of a 'case' is in many ways quint-essentially naturalistic, though not exclusively so, notwithstanding Cohen and Manion's assertion that 'present antipathy towards the statistical-experimental paradigm has created something of a boom industry in case study research' (1989: 125). Case studies can range from large- to small-scale, though it is particularly at the more 'micro' end of the spectrum that they are arguably most appropriate for teacher-generated research. They have an important role to play in action research, whether for personal or whole-school development (Elliott, 1991). Closer to our own professional concerns here, they are a very suitable format for studies of language learning. In sum, case studies have a good deal of potential, but are also somewhat problematic in both principle and practice, especially from the point of view of the single case and the wider value of such a study.

The most explicit discussion of case studies as a research genre is to be found in education, and in social science more generally, rather than in language learning and TEFL, so we begin this chapter with a review of the key definitions of case study and its major characteristics and subdivisions. This is followed by a discussion of its methodological underpinnings, including the nature and analysis of data. The central section of the chapter is concerned with manifestations of case study research in language learning and teaching. We conclude with a look at some of the controversy surrounding the use of cases in research, a debate which focuses particularly on the requirement – or otherwise – for research to be valid, reliable and generalizable.

What is a case?

To most people, the term 'case' probably suggests much the same as the initial meaning in the *Concise Oxford Dictionary* – an 'instance of things occurring'. This is general to say the least, but it does carry the important implication of a focus on the singular, the individual. From a research perspective, the study of cases plays a role in many diverse disciplines, for example the following.

- Clinical uses/health studies: medical practitioners hold 'case conferences' to look at the symptoms and treatment of individual patients; these cases contribute to broader etiological study, and conversely, known phenomena are invoked for specific diagnoses.
- Law: 'case law', where individual cases are used in the interpretation of future cases, is an integral part of many legal systems.
- Sociology and anthropology: social scientists study whole cultures, particular subgroups (the elderly, drug addicts ...), or individuals, sometimes by constructing biographies and life histories (see, for example, Plummer, 1983).
- Education: practitioners study schools or groups of schools (see Cohen and Manion, 1989: 134ff); curricula; the effect of innovations; the implementation of materials; classrooms; teachers; students. Much of this work comes under the heading of 'evaluation', putting it firmly within definitions of research. We return to this topic when discussing case studies in EFL.
- Language learning: researchers often study mother tongue acquisition and L2 development by looking at individual learners, and at what they have in common.

Yet more examples could be drawn from psychology, history or business studies. Although there are obviously many differences in scale, purpose, focus, approach and method in these various orientations to case study research, we look now at some encompassing definitions and shared characteristics, based principally on educational research.

Definitions and characteristics

The study of cases is not only a qualitative undertaking, nor does it present an either/or perspective in quantitative/qualitative terms. Where, for example, researchers need to study large-scale trends, cases will usually be selected on the basis of random sampling and the data submitted to statistical analysis. The individual cases are important in terms of their representativeness and their ability to contribute to making predictions about whole populations – of patients, consumers, children, and so on: indeed, we shall see later that both this paradigm and methodology have a place in research on language learning. It is nevertheless true to say that the weight of current discussion on case study is on interpretive approaches and, since teachers have access to certain kinds of data, resources and timing, naturalistic case study is in tune with their reality for reasons of practicality as well as principle.

Leaving aside for the moment the considerable controversy surrounding the study of individual cases, let us now run through the key features of case study. An educational researcher who has written a great deal about it (especially in relation to evaluation) is Stake (1994; 1995), who offers a number of overlapping definitions: 'the epistemology of the particular', 'the study of the particularity and complexity of a single case' and 'an integrated ... working system'. These are echoed by other writers: Walker (1986) writes of 'an instance in action', and Nunan (1992b: 76–7) quotes six sources whose definitions cluster round the same perspective.

From this definitional starting point, there are a number of important corollaries: we should at this point recall that a case can be one of a number of different entities. First, and most important, a case is now conventionally referred to as a 'bounded system', a term originally coined by Louis Smith, an educational ethnographer (see Stake, 1995). Stake himself represents it with the Greek letter Θ (theta) to indicate that it has both boundaries and working parts. The notion of 'boundedness' is conceptually neat but operationally complex: a moment's reflection will show that actually delimiting a 'case' is no easy matter. If a teacher decides to study one of his or her learners, for example, he or she might well puzzle over what aspects of context and environment to include/exclude when considering influences on learning behaviour; a team evaluating a particular programme will need to decide on the extent to which they should take the institutional and social framework into account. Stake (quoted in Johnson, 1992: 76) proposes 'confining the attention to those aspects that are relevant to the research problem at the time', a useful if somewhat chicken-and-egg argument. Hitchcock and Hughes (1995: 319) are rather more specific, suggesting that a case can be looked at in terms of 'key players', 'key situations' and 'critical incidents' in the life of the case, and going on to refer to Miles and Huberman's (1994) boundary definitions related to:

- temporal characteristics
- geographical parameters
- inbuilt boundaries
- a particular context at a point in time
- group characteristics
- role/function
- organizational/institutional arrangements.

Second, a case study in a naturalistic setting will follow the central tenets of qualitative research by being emic (from within the case) and holistic (the whole system in its context). Third, although a case is to be thought of as an 'object', this is not an inert, reified concept, but is crucially concerned with an understanding of people's own meanings and perspectives. Fourth, as data from a case study are interpreted, research questions are 'emergent' rather than fixed *a priori*. Finally it is, perhaps surprisingly, still possible to invoke the notion of sampling where it is appropriate to compare or aggregate cases. However, this is done by what Stenhouse (1988) refers to as 'judgemental' (as opposed to random) sampling, with decisions taken about relevant characteristics: 'balance and variety are important; opportunity to learn is of primary importance' (Stake, 1995: 6).

Before leaving this section, we should note that some researchers, because of the elusiveness of the concept, define cases in terms of what they are not. Stake points out that a teacher may be a case, but not teach*ing*, nor policies, nor relationships among schools, because they are not sufficiently specific: 'the case to be studied probably has problems and relationships, and the report of the case is likely to have a theme, but the case is an entity' (1995: 133). This is, of course, to ignore the more general study of aspects of teaching (or policies and so on) that might be invest-igated via case sampling and aggregation, and we comment on the criti-cism levelled at this position in the final section of this chapter.

Classifying cases

Whatever the entity chosen for investigation, case studies can be classified in different ways, and the type preferred will depend on the objective of the research and probably on the paradigm underpinning it. A teacher or researcher may be interested in following the language development of one particular learner and the contextual influences on that; a public presenta-tion of this one case may stimulate others to examine individuals to com-pare and contrast with the original case; an aggregation of such cases may lead to a fresh perspective on learning strategies, or programme evalu-ation, or teaching styles; and this perspective may in turn generate further case studies. (This is, it should be stressed, a possible but not a necessary progression, and is merely intended to be illustrative of different orienta-tions to how cases are selected.)

A number of useful taxonomies are on offer. Yin (quoted in Hitchcock and Hughes, 1995) focuses on the outcome of the study and differentiates between case studies that are:

1. *exploratory*   (like a pilot study)
2. *descriptive*   (narrative)
3. *explanatory*   (testing or generating theory).

The same authors quote Merriam's three-way schema, divided into:

1. *descriptive*
2. *interpretative* (developing conceptual categories, supporting/chal
        lenging assumptions)
3. *evaluative*   (adding judgement to the first two).

Both of these classifications are concerned particularly with the way the research is conducted and its outcome in the final report.

Stake (1995) looks at case selection from the point of view of the purpose informing the initial choice, and distinguishes between:

1. the *intrinsic* case study, where the interest is in the case for its own sake (a teacher looking at a problematic student, or a single course)
2. the *instrumental* case study, selected to help in the understanding of something else (looking at a teacher to see how he or she marks student work, for example)
3. the *collective* case study (coordinating data from several teachers, or several schools).

The broadest taxonomy is put forward by Lincoln and Guba (1985: 361). They note that case studies:

1. may be written with different purposes (to chronicle; to 'render' = to describe; to teach; or a combination)
2. may be written at different analytic levels (cf. Merriam and Yin)
3. will demand different actions from the enquirer
4. will result in different products.

This variety of overlapping categorizations is set out here because it illustrates that case studies operate on different continua (such as singularity – aggregation – transferability), all of which can be usefully harnessed by the teacher researcher.

Methods in case study research

Cases, as we and many others have noted, are objects to be studied and are not themselves synonymous with any particular techniques. They are for this reason methodologically eclectic, with a number of different permutations and possibilities for choice. In this section we do not go into any detail about specific methods because they are covered in the relevant chapters elsewhere in this book. Instead we look at the main trends in methods selection and some of their implications. More detailed exemplification of case study research in language learning and teaching follows in the next section.

Where cases are sought out – sampled – primarily because of their typicality and/or their intended contribution to some more general pattern or theory, the research is clearly more likely to use techniques allowing for numerical analysis of elicited data, particularly questionnaires and structured interview schedules. Other instruments, such as coded observation and factual logs, will make use of prespecified categories of information. The goal of such research may be to examine large-scale trends, for example to make predictions, or to study correlational relationships between different factors. Qualitative methodology, as we know, does not stand in diametric opposition to quantitative, though it is driven by different aims and approaches to data collection, and techniques will usually sit at the more 'naturalistic' end of the spectrum. The battery of possibilities for interpretive case study – whether of single entities or groups of instances – typically includes:

- naturalistic and descriptive observation
- narrative diaries
- unstructured and ethnographic interviews
- verbal reports
- collection of existing information (students' written work or test data, for example: see Johnson, 1992).

Within these parameters there are priorities and preferences. Cohen and Manion see observational methods 'at the heart of every case study' (1989: 125), whereas Stake claims that 'qualitative researchers take pride in discovering and portraying the multiple views of the case. The interview is the main road to multiple realities' (1995: 64). Clearly his view is most relevant where the entity is a whole school, or a programme, with a number of different people involved. Whichever combination of techniques is considered appropriate for any particular case, it is as always important to remember that *structured* interviews, *coded* observations, *pre-specified* diary entries are in no way precluded. Just to invent a brief example: Irina Petrov (see Chapter 1) has decided to study the fate of a new-style ESP syllabus via questionnaires to colleagues backed up with selected ethnographic interviews; her own diary; student feedback and test results; and a structured interview with the Head of Faculty. (Cohen and Manion, 1989, have some interesting examples from mainstream education of mixed method case studies combining numerical and qualitative techniques.)

The wide range of ways of analysing data from these various sources include, as we saw in the chapters preceding this one, correlation, tabulation, tallying, coding, thematic frequency and saliency, quantitative content analysis, and so on. In the interpretive mode, Stake (1995) uses a modern idiom and talks of 'surfing through the data', and with specific application to case study research adds the two further categories of (1) categorical aggregation of instances within and across cases and (2) direct interpretation. Furthermore, in the process of analysis and interpretation, triangulation will obviously be an important feature, particularly of data sources (human and documentary) and methods. (We recall that Denzin, 1978, also refers to 'investigator' and 'theory' triangulation.) Other factors to be taken into account, especially with a longitudinal case study, are permissions and ethical considerations. This will include the technique of 'member checking', where research outcomes are taken back to the people in the context studies to be checked for accuracy and plausibility and also for further illumination (see Chapter 4 for a longer discussion of research ethics).

We leave this section with a further perspective offered by Stake (1995) that particularly addresses the emergent research design and ways in which it can become gradually more focused. It is useful to us in the context of the present book because it is an attempt to distinguish between the substantive content of research and its methodological procedures (a distinction, however, that Stake acknowledges to be a difficult one to explain). For Stake, case study research has two central elements, as follows.

- *Themes*. Subject-matter, information, topical content (e.g. 'What are the typical academic programmes taken by these students?'; 'What do the parents want from the music programme?'; or, from our own examples in Chapter 5, 'patterns of participation' or 'How do teachers deal with latecomers?'). To a degree these questions are amenable to descriptive data.
- *Issues*. These are not themes. Rather, they constitute the researcher's 'conceptual structure'. They are the problematic scaffolding on which research questions are built and which move them on to the next stage. (For example: 'Is [x] at risk? Why was she identified by teachers as a subject for study, and what is the institutional responsibility?' or 'What are the triggers for the varying learning styles exhibited by this student?')

We leave the final word here to Stake because he uses this notion to link different orientations to research: 'In a qualitative research project, issues emerge, grow, and die. In quantitative research, as an issue becomes more refined or important, a parallel or subsequent study is started; the present one keeps its issues intact' (1995: 21).

Case studies in language learning and teaching

This section comments on how case studies have been used by language learning researchers and by teachers, and on their potential for teacher research in particular. Both professional researchers and teachers are obviously interested in how learners learn, so in principle, and simply intuitively, learner case study is one area where their concerns should dovetail most closely, and indeed where there should be fertile ground for collaboration.

Research into second language acquisition

The present book is in no sense about SLA (second language acquisition) research *per se*: there are many sound works written by specialists on the subject (for example, Beebe, 1988; Chaudron, 1988; Ellis, 1985; 1990;

Sharwood Smith, 1994), some of which deal with the implications of this research for learning in formal classroom settings. SLA is something of a minefield, containing a very large body of often disparate microstudies. What is interesting from our point of view is how SLA researchers approach the notion of a learner as a 'case' in terms of what it reveals about research methodology. (Researchers also look at teachers, though the interest is usually in how teachers construct learning environments for their students.) There is some methodological discussion, though much is implicit.

It will come as no surprise that SLA is underpinned by the two major paradigms of hypothetico-deductive and inductive-interpretive research. Researchers of the first persuasion typically set up experimental situations to test hypotheses derived from theory, so an individual 'case' is a 'subject' serving the goals of the research design. Inductive researchers, on the other hand, first let the cases speak for themselves in advance of theory-building. So, for instance, a researcher may deliberately construct a set of interactions between a native and non-native speaker, hypothesizing that the non-native will pattern the discourse in certain anticipated ways: altern-atively, another researcher will observe naturally occurring classroom phe-nomena and then see how they fit into known patterns. Ellis has some very useful tabulations of the techniques used to investigate a variety of issues in SLA, including tests of different types, recordings of spontaneous speech, oral description of pictures, and written data based on stimuli (1990: 147–9).

Whichever perspective is taken – experimental, empirical, naturalistic – most mainstream SLA research is intended to contribute to building, and falsifying, specific hypotheses, such as:

- creative construction
- interlanguage
- collaborative discourse
- input
- interaction

(and so on: details can be found in the references given earlier). Both data- and theory-first approaches, then, relate case research to more general pat-terns of how people learn languages. Ellis is unequivocal: 'Classroom research should be directed at building a theory of language learning – a goal which both types of research can help to meet' (1990: 5). Furthermore, the role of contextual factors tends to be more restricted than in interpretive modes of educational or social science research. At the same time, Ellis writes, almost in passing, about 'the *differences* between classrooms – *which should never be underestimated*' (1990: 90, italics added), but it is not clear how this variability might be fully incorporated into the objective of building an overarching theory. He also (p. 48) quotes

Lightbown, who writes, in relation to a particular set of studies: 'This research has been very persuasive, *but* it can be shown to be *limited in generalizability*. For every one of the examples ... there are other studies which provide counter-evidence' (italics added). There is, then, some unease about the fit between hypothesis- and theory-building, on the one hand, and actual instances – cases – on the other, a point to which we return in the final section of this chapter. In this context it is particularly interesting to recall the 'expert' language learning diaries (Chapter 8) as individual case studies, because they sit firmly at the naturalistic and context-bound end of the spectrum. The same is true, for example, of the longitudinal case studies cited in Johnson (1992), dealing with second language writing, 'cognitive scaffolding' and language learning, reading strategies, and adult literacy, or the work of Hakuta (1976) and Wode (1976), and many case-based studies of learning strategies (for example, Oxford, 1990). These more individualistic studies do not follow the strictly nomothetic objectives of much SLA work, and are closer in orientation to the work of teachers.

We leave this section with the observation that SLA offers a great deal of fascinating and challenging study for teachers' practice. Every teacher will find his/her own areas of interest from sifting through the literature: for the record, these are just a few of ours:

- role of error correction and feedback
- can teaching cause errors?
- enhancement of learning by learners' control of topics
- delay in uptake of teaching input
- extent to which instruction can affect the 'natural' sequence of learning
- styles and strategies of individuals within a group.

We now turn to the question of how teachers might contribute, via cases, to our understanding of language learning, but also of other aspects of practice.

Case studies and the language teacher

As far as thematic content is concerned, we have already commented on the obvious congruence of interest of professional researchers and teachers in learners and learning. Stake draws a different and rather novel parallel that is particularly relevant to the study and public presentation of qualitative case research by equating the roles of teacher-learner with those of researcher-reader. He writes (1995: 92):

> Teaching is not just lecturing, not just delivering information; ... it is the arrangement of opportunities for learners to follow a natural human inclination to become educated.... It is important to realize

that, even though students do not learn all they are taught, they learn considerably more than they are taught.... The competent teacher anticipates unanticipated learning.... The classroom teacher soon knows each individual face and something about the mind behind it, but all too little.

This implies, then, a value-laden view of the case researcher's role, who is enjoined (by Stake at least) to offer the case to its readers for other kinds of interpretation and perspective, even persuasion about a point of view. (We will see later how it relates this to 'naturalistic' generalization.)

Teachers and learners

Where learners are concerned, teachers do not have to seek out cases: they are there in front of and around them, in daily proximity. Teachers spend their working lives dealing in different ways with individuals, and they need to understand those 'cases', not in the first instance to build theories and search for broader patterns, but to understand their learners' behaviours, learning styles, language development, successes, failures, attitudes, interests and motivation. As Berthoff puts it: 'We do not need new information; we need to think about the information we have' (1987: 92). They are, moreover, very well placed to do this over extended periods of time, making the longitudinal case study a natural format. Our learners are unique cases almost by definition, and our knowledge of them is particularistic and idiographic (Bolster, 1983, discussed in Chapter 2 of this book). Teachers study cases to enhance their own understanding; to share that understanding with others who may then carry out parallel work of their own; perhaps to change their teaching methodology; and sometimes to collaborate with a researcher, because teacher and researcher studies should be complementary, not incompatible (see, for example, the collaborative action research reported by Wallat et al., 1981).

Teachers are also in a position, as complete participants, to be sensitive to context and therefore to have an instinctive sense of how each case might be delineated as a 'bounded system'. It is useful to borrow here from role theory, where a 'focal person' is placed at the centre to show those factors that impinge on him/her (see Fig. 13.1). All these elements in various combinations affect learners in classrooms.

There are huge numbers of case studies in the professional literature, although many of them do not call themselves that. Between them they use all the available research methodology – surveys, interviews, questionnaires, observation, introspective techniques, test instruments, written documents and more. In general terms their rationale is to offer up instances, or collections of instances, for public scrutiny as a contribution to professional knowledge. We will look at two explicit case study

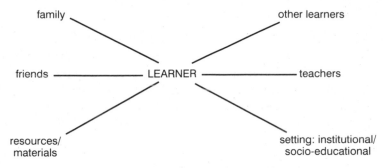

Fig. 13.1 (Adapted from Handy, 1985)

examples in a little more detail: each of them tells us something about method, and the varying degrees to which boundary definitions are taken into account.

1. The case of Q (McDonough and McDonough, 1993)

Q was an adult learner who needed to do English for his later academic study. He was a student of one of the present authors over several months. His level on arrival could roughly be described as intermediate, though his initial reluctance to participate in class or engage with English made it difficult to tell. The starting point for the case study was the teacher's diary, which expressed considerable frustration at his passivity. The case study emerged from this, and was not consciously planned in advance. In outline, the study proceeded as follows.

Timing: over six months, with subsequent follow-up

Methods: Teacher's diary including notes on Q's classroom
(triangulated) performance
Q's diary and class work
Reports from other teachers
Interviews with Q
Interviews with his future academic supervisor
Language test results

Case report: Shown to Q in full and checked by him for accuracy
Permission to use in public report if anonymized

Thematic context A contribution to methods of student evaluation
and outcomes: Particularistic understanding of one learner: affective factors, the process of acculturation and its interaction with language learning; his attitude to learning English; his uptake (or not) of instructional input.

2. The case of Marcos (James, 1984)

Marcos was a Brazilian postgraduate and James the language tutor who provided the English language supervision on a 1:1 basis over many months as Marcos was writing his Ph.D. The case study offers a fascinating and detailed insight into a student's language development as he attempted to express complex arguments. Through reading, negotiation of meaning, discussion and observation, James found three categories of mistake, shown here in summary form:

- leading to breakdown in meaning
- leading to blurring of meaning
- distracting the reader from the meaning conveyed

(each of which is exemplified in detail in the paper).

In some ways the case of Marcos, focusing as it does on very specific aspects of language learning, is more 'bounded' than that of Q. However, readers come to understand some of the factors affecting the way this student writes, including the demands of the British academic culture in which he has chosen to study, his previous language training, his beliefs about mother-tongue interference, the style of his discipline (sociology), and the Marxist environment of his Brazilian university. We also learn about the attitudes of the tutor studying the case.

Both cases cited here illustrate how teachers, working from the inside, can confine their attention to aspects that are relevant to the research problem, thus making judgements as to the boundaries of the particular case.

Other kinds of case

For a language teacher, the learner virtually self-presents as an object of study: however, there are other kinds of case that teachers are well placed to investigate. One, of course, is themselves (or their peers): readers are referred to the chapter on diaries for some examples of how this might be done, although the possibilities extend beyond the application of just one technique. It is in fact worth observing that there are relatively few reported case studies of teachers, so perhaps a shift of focus is due. Beyond this, as we have noted, cases do not have to be human, except in the sense that everything we are dealing with is a human construct. There is only space here to enumerate briefly three categories which fit both within the definition of research adopted in this book, and the notion of 'case'. All three areas have an enormous literature. They are of particular relevance to teachers because, from a case study perspective, they are concerned with the investigation of local meanings in specific contexts.

1. Evaluation

'All evaluation studies are case studies' (Stake, 1995: 95). This is the biggest industry of all in education. In our own field, programme evaluation has become increasingly important: discussion and exemplification can be found in Rea-Dickins and Germaine (1992). There is a standard distinction between *summative* and *formative* modes of evaluation, the former concerned with the end-product and the latter with the ongoing process of course development. These intersect with a range of available quantitative and qualitative techniques, including measurement scales, questionnaires and interviews. Educationalists further distinguish between *autocratic, bureaucratic* and *democratic* evaluation (Norris, 1990). An example of a 'democratic' evaluation (in the USA) is afforded by *Bread and Dreams* (MacDonald and Kushner, 1983), which is called by the authors a 'case study' in which the word 'case' comes to represent both the school and the study itself. From a teacher-researcher point of view, there is a natural affinity with a format that gives them some ownership of the study and that can handle the perceptions of everyone involved as they change and develop over time. It is for this reason that Elliott (1991) sees a close link between evaluation case studies and the tenets of action research.

2. Needs analysis

The analysis of learner needs has received most attention in the field of English for Specific Purposes (ESP) because of the largely instrumental nature of these kinds of courses. Needs analyses may be carried out by an external consultant, or by a teacher/course designer. Being concerned with specific groups/individuals in specific contexts, they provide a central manifestation of a 'case' in EFL. A representative example can be found in Markee (1986), who conducted a needs analysis in a complex language situation at Khartoum Polytechnic: like James' Marcos, the Sudanese case also raises issues of more general interest as well as being a fascinating 'intrinsic' study in itself. Much needs analysis has an action-research ethos because it leads necessarily to the construction of appropriate programmes, though cases can also contribute to broader needs-analysis research by modifying and testing out procedural models (see Hutchinson and Waters, 1987). The techniques most used are questionnaires and interviews, carried out with learners at various stages, language teachers, specialist staff, employers and administrators.

3. Programme design and development

This sits logically between needs analysis and evaluation, and can be seen most usefully as a case when it is part of a whole package, beginning with fact finding (needs analysis), through choice of approach and design parameters (design) to reflection on their appropriacy (evaluation). To extend

Nunan's (1992b) justification of evaluation as research, programme construction therefore contains questions, data and interpretive analysis. Jordan's (1983) *Case Studies in ELT* provides a useful survey of this perspective.

The controversy of case study

At the end of his case study of Marcos, James writes: 'It would be tempting to speculate what lessons one might draw ... I shall, however, resist this temptation. For one thing, it is dangerous to generalize from one case study' (1984: 112). It is the intrinsic, naturalistic case study in particular that has been accused of failing to meet the conventional research criteria of generalizability and external validity. The debate is very wide-ranging, and we can only scratch the surface here.

The one-off case study, it is said by its critics, deals by definition with an individual (language learner, programme, child, and so on) in context: however interesting in itself, the research design has failed to build in features such as sampling or experimental treatment that would allow extrapolation to a wider population. If a researcher is seeking typicality or is primarily concerned with theory-building, then the charge has some force. Atkinson and Delamont – in a paper that refers directly to *Bread and Dreams* (MacDonald and Kushner, 1983),– are particularly vociferous in their criticisms, claiming that much case study research is a 'methodological cop-out'. They are concerned about what they see as imprecise definitions and the vagueness of the unit of analysis as a 'bounded system'; about the number of definitions that say what a case is not; and about an over-focus on ethics and political issues at the expense of theory and method. They are firmly against a series of one-offs because 'theory cannot be left to accumulate' (1986: 251).

There are a number of counters to this kind of critique (and, of course, counter-criticisms as well), and the title of one well-known collection – *Towards a Science of the Singular* (Simons, 1980) – is a clear indication of the attitude of proponents of naturalistic case study research. Some appear to be against generalization altogether. Cronbach, talking about changeability and therefore problems with 'fixing' generalizations, puts it like this: 'The trouble, as I see it, is that we cannot store up generalizations and constructs for ultimate assembly into a network. It is as if we needed a gross of dry cells to power an engine and could only make one a month. The energy would leak out of the first cells before we had half the battery completed. So it is with the potency of our generalizations' (quoted in Eisner and Peshkin, 1990: 178). At the level of principle, many writers argue for the value of aggregated case studies so that (rather like case law) a body of knowledge is gradually accumulated that can inform further studies. This is not the strict replication requirement of the positivist paradigm, though Kennedy (1979), proposing a methodology for sampling the attributes of single cases, comes very close. The teacher researcher, like James, offering his or her findings to a wider professional audience, is essentially inviting the collection of further such data which might confirm the outcome of the original case – Lincoln and Guba's (1985) 'transferability'. Stake (1995) proposes a distinction between 'petite' generalizations from a few cases in a particular situation, and 'grand' generalization, where a case may contribute either by confirmation or conversely by showing dissimilarity with established findings, thus undermining them. A case study may also help to form questions, not just lead to answers. In our own field it may well be that generalizations from applied linguistics contribute to teachers' unease about the relevance of such research, and their own daily contact with the idiographic, formulated in case study terms, could offer an important alternative perspective.

Stake also invokes a notion of 'naturalistic generalization' (a concept not universally accepted even by researchers of the same persuasion). It is in a sense another name for learning from and applying the work of others, and is to be distinguished from the conventional notion of 'explicated' or 'propositional' generalization. 'Naturalistic generalizations are conclusions arrived at through personal engagement in life's affairs or by vicarious experience so well constructed that the person feels as if it happened to themselves' (1995: 85). In other words, readers generalize by virtue of interpreting the case as put to them by the researcher. Operationally at least this is a useful notion for the teacher studying and then going public with data from a single case: for us, James' analysis of Marcos' language is illuminating for our own situation, despite his modest claims as to its transferability.

Finally, it is useful to set out the advantages of qualitative case study research proposed by Adelman et al. (1980: 59–60), because in our view they summarize the main reasons why this is a 'user-friendly' research format for the teacher to undertake:

1. Case study data is 'strong in reality'.
2. Case studies allow generalizations about an instance, or from that to a class.
3. They recognize the complexity of 'social truths' and alternative interpretations.
4. They can form an archive of descriptive material available for reinterpretation by others.
5. They are a 'step to action' (for staff/institutional development; for formative evaluation).
6. They present research in an accessible form.

Conclusion

This chapter has drawn together a wide range of types of study under the heading of 'case'. Various ways of defining the essential attributes of case-study research have been explored, looking both at what counts as a 'case' and what methods of 'study' are appropriate and used. Several ways of classifying case studies were presented, which demonstrate how broad and useful this research genre has been. Research methodology has used both quantitative and qualitative techniques, and focused, predecided questions as well as 'emergent' designs. The central section of the chapter gave a range of examples of case studies, first in second language acquisition research, and second in research about language teaching, both concerning individual teachers and learners and broader issues such as needs analysis, evaluation and programme development. Finally the chapter critically discussed some of the crucial issues surrounding case study, but finished on an optimistic note, reviewing the reasons for recommending case study methodology in our field.

Discussion notes

1. The contextual factors taken into account differ in the cases of Q and Marcos: they are 'bounded' in different ways. If you undertook a case study of an individual learner, how would you go about defining that learner as a 'bounded system'? What would you leave in/out?
2. Do you think it sufficient if a case study is just of intrinsic interest in a local context? If so, what is its value?
3. Selecting a possible case (learner, yourself, colleague, programme, set of materials), sketch out a research design to show what methods and techniques would be most appropriate.

14

Mixing research methods

Introduction

In the course of this book, both by implication and from time to time explicitly, we have touched on the use of research methods in combination with others. By and large, however, the preceding chapters have essentially treated these methods and techniques as discrete, in order to bring out their main characteristics and applications (rather like discussing individual language skills before considering ways in which they might be integrated, though the parallel should not be pushed too far). Case study research is an obvious exception, being more likely than not to amalgamate two or more procedures – interviews, diaries, observations, and so on.

Following on, then, from that discussion, this final chapter focuses on the principles and methodology of mixing research procedures. It is patently impossible, and unhelpful, to cover all possible permutations for linking two or more methods: the chapter is therefore divided into two main sections. First of all, we look in general terms at some of the issues raised by methods mixing and at some of its manifestations. Second, the book goes full circle as it were by picking up on a few of the teacher case studies outlined earlier in terms of research *potential*, this time, however, converting that potential into *actual* research undertaken. The purpose is simply to illustrate just a few of the many possibilities.

Principles in mixing methods

The different ways in which research methods can be combined have a number of implications, which are subsumed here under two main headings: one concerns scale, the other level. We take each of these dimensions in turn.

Scale

As with any research project, a multimethod approach can also occur on a continuum from, at one end, a microstudy carried out by an individual to a large-scale undertaking at the other. It would be simplistic and misleading to suggest that teacher research necessarily takes place on a smaller canvas, and certainly there is no equation such that:

professional researcher = large-scale work
teacher researcher = small-scale work.

However, the nature of teacher involvement in research is likely to differ depending on the scale of its conception, and direct teacher initiation of research will probably fit more comfortably in the localized context of personal professional experience.

At the macro end of the spectrum, there are many instances of research in education and in language teaching and learning involving quite large numbers of people that is both multimethod and multisite. In Johnson's definition: '*Multisite, multimethod, large-scale research* refers to large studies in which a team of collaborating researchers collects data from a number of sites and employs a variety of both qualitative and quantitative data-collection and analysis strategies' (1992: 192). Moreover, this kind of research may also be linked to evaluation studies, and have implications for educational policy decisions. There may well be considerable funding involved, with sponsoring bodies having quite definite expectations as to research outcomes. To mix metaphors as well as methods, the holders of the purse-strings will probably want a stake in calling the tune, and it is still sometimes the case that a quantitative/survey methodology is more likely to attract funding because its parameters appear to be more clear-cut and the timescale more predictable than with an ethnographic/qualitative project.

There are many examples of large-scale multimethod research that can quite readily be found in the educational and applied linguistic/language teaching literature. Here are just a few of them.

1. Humanities Curriculum Project (HCP).
2. Ford Teaching Project (FTP).

Both of these projects took place in British schools in the 1970s, and are described at length in Elliott (1991). They are notable from our point of view because, although initiated by university-based teacher educators (HCP by Stenhouse), they were informed by a commitment to an 'emancipatory' principle that centrally involved teachers (and pupils) in large-scale action research.

3. L2 methods comparisons, such as the well-known if not entirely successful Pennsylvania project comparing grammar-translation and audio-lingual approaches.
4. Evaluation of bilingual education programmes.

These are both reported in Johnson (1992).

5. The large-scale, nationally funded Australian Migrant English Program (AMEP), which has over the years involved large numbers of teachers in investigating and evaluating curriculum and policy development and change (Burns and Hood, 1995; Nunan, 1988).

6. Large-scale multimethod multitrait research has been conducted by language testers to investigate some of the core theoretical concepts of language testing. Bachman and Palmer (1982) investigated the 'Unitary Competence Hypothesis' and the different testing methods used to evaluate it. This was partly motivated by the wish to dissociate testing particular skills from particular test types in order to get a 'purer' measure of the underlying competence.

7. A very interesting project investigating reading test validity was conducted by Anderson *et al.* (1991), which related three kinds of information: student performance on test items, verbal reports of student strategies for finding the answers, and theoretical classifications of the questions in terms of their logical status. The study therefore combined qualitative and quantitative data in an area traditionally associated with quantitative evaluation only.

In many large-scale projects, of course, teachers are part of the research scenery, investigated rather than themselves doing the investigating. In many more, however, teachers have become increasingly involved, not on the whole as initiators but certainly as active participants, and often in collaborative modes – academic with teacher, teacher with teacher under the aegis of a project director. (See Brindley's 'research agenda', 1990, for an extended discussion of collaborative research possibilities.)

In principle, no method is excluded from this kind of research, though it is useful to note here Johnson's list of the more common data-collection techniques, applicable particularly but not only to evaluation studies (1992: 196):

- site visits
- observations
- interviews
- questionnaires
- test data
- documents
- quantitative data.

Teachers are more likely to have scope to generate research further along the continuum and away from large-scale, often longitudinal projects using full-time professional researchers and frequently involving very time-consuming funding applications to government agencies and research councils and the like. It is difficult to be specific about central points on continua, but the kind of medium-scale research probably using more than a single method can be illustrated by the following.

1. Replicated or follow-up studies, such as the accumulation of case study research outlined in Chapter 13, where one teacher's research reported in a public forum is picked up on by teachers in other institutions.
2. School-based/local collaborative action-research projects.

Yet smaller-scale research will be carried out by individual practitioners in their own context. We have met a couple of examples in the course of this book, and the theme will be explored again in the final section of this chapter. Here is a brief list of examples.

1. Using questionnaires and selective interviewing in needs analysis.
2. Combining observation and documentary evidence in programme evaluation.
3. Using test data, experiment and self-reporting in research on reading comprehension.
4. Mixing diaries, interviews, documents, all from different sources, in case studies of individuals.
5. Student course evaluation by prompted focus group discussion at the end of the course with diaries written during the course.
6. Using lesson transcripts and test scores to investigate the effects of different error-correction strategies.
7. Investigating listening strategies by qualitative analysis and implicational scaling to discover the hierarchy of strategic choice.

Level

A mixed-method approach to research raises some key questions as to the level at which that mix takes place, or might legitimately do so. At the broader *paradigm* level, there has been a considerable degree of controversy: is a researcher who deliberately chooses, say, a survey approach alongside narrative introspection, with the explicit aim of exploring reality from different perspectives, doing some kind of epistemological damage? Is it even logically impossible as an approach to research? Some people hold the view that quantitative and qualitative paradigms do not mix well: as we noted earlier, Lincoln and Guba (1985), for example, argue strongly that they virtually represent different world views. Others consider that the distinction is overstated, and that 'there is ... no necessary link between choice of method and logic of enquiry' (Brannen, 1992b: 10). Hammersley (1992) is likewise concerned to 'deconstruct the qualitative–quantitative divide' from a conviction that competing paradigms (indeed, the whole notion of a 'paradigm') unhelpfully obscure diversity and complexity. He argues that the following seven polarizations (which were touched on in Part 1 of this book) are in fact simplistic.

1. Qualitative versus quantitative data
2. Natural versus artificial settings
3. Meanings versus behaviour
4. Adoption versus rejection of natural science model
5. Inductive versus deductive
6. Cultural patterns versus scientific laws
7. Idealism versus realism.

He expresses his position on the appropriacy of linking paradigms in the following terms (1992: 52):

the distinction between quantitative and qualitative approaches does not capture the full range of options that we face, and ... misrepresents the basis on which decisions should be made. What is involved is not a crossroads where we have to go left or right. A better analogy is a complex maze where we are repeatedly faced with decisions, and where paths wind back on one another. The prevalence of the distinction between qualitative and quantitative approaches tends to obscure the complexity of the problems that face us and threatens to render our decisions less effective than they might otherwise be.

At the level of *technique*, the debate has raged somewhat less fiercely, and it is more likely to be accepted that the numerical and interpretive can in principle be used in combination. As we have seen, qualitative data may in fact be counted and quantified (as in content analysis, for example); and reliability is arguably enhanced by pluralism in methodology. Triangulation is obviously very important when methods are combined. Brannen makes the common-sense point that, in reality, 'the practice of research is a messy and untidy business which rarely conforms to the models set down in methodology textbooks.... The cart often comes before the horse.... Researchers are often required to conduct balancing acts between a number of pragmatic considerations' (1992b: 3–4). She then sets out the different possible relationships between quantitative-qualitative in a practical research undertaking. In summary form, these are as follows.

1. Where qualitative methods play a subsidiary role

a. They can act as a source of 'hunches' which are then tested by quantitative work.
b. They can be used to pilot research instruments.
c. They may help in data interpretation.

2. Where quantitative methods play a subsidiary role

a. They provide quantified background data to contextualize small-scale projects (e.g. official statistics).
b. They may test hypotheses derived from qualitative work.
c. They can provide a basis for case sampling.

3. Where qualitative and quantitative methods have equal weight

a. In separate but linked studies.
b. Integrated in one study.
c. Conducted simultaneously or consecutively.

From a data-analysis and interpretation point of view, the last group is both the most interesting and the most problematic. Collapsing for the moment the distinction between 3a and 3c, there are published studies which use different methods from different traditions to study the same phenomena. In research on the two issues mentioned here as examples, work in the two traditions to a certain extent confirmed the conclusions from the other in one case, and in the other the results were quite discrepant. The first example is from training in first language composition skills development at college level in the USA. The issue was strategies and kinds of revision used by these trainee academic writers. Faigley and Witte (1981) performed an extensive text analysis of the products of writers gradually refining their texts. This process/product study confirmed many of the findings of an earlier study by Sommers (1980) which had used an extensive and very detailed interviewing method.

The second example is about the issue of the effectiveness of feedback by teachers on written work produced by L2 writers. A think-aloud study of strategies for processing feedback by Cohen and Cavalcanti (1990) cast considerable doubt on the effectiveness of feedback because of the high proportion of teachers' comments that the students reported they had not understood or did not know how to handle. The quasi-experimental study by Fathman and Whalley (1990) mentioned in Chapter 10, on the other hand, showed that feedback did have measurable beneficial effects, and gave a much more positive outcome. Such a discrepancy, whether due to research method, context or theory, is naturally a spur to further research.

An example of 3b in the area of testing research was given earlier in this chapter, Anderson *et al.* (1991). It is worth mentioning again in this context because the data analysis, which was both interpretive and statistical, required counting respondents' frequency of mention of certain strategies and comparing the frequencies with item analysis of the test questions – to find, for example, what strategies were used most with easy and difficult items, among other things. Another example where both qualitative and quantitative methods were used is Tonkyn *et al.* (1993). This study of English for Academic Purposes teachers' predictions of academic success of their students in a British university used a variety of data sources: mainly questionnaires from students and tutors, teachers' reports, and interviews with academic tutors and EAP teachers. The method of analysis was entirely numerical, counting the frequencies of results from the questionnaires, and analysing the reports and the interviews also by counting frequency of mention of a whole range of factors. These two pieces of research demonstrate both the complications and the rewards of attempting to integrate qualitative and quantitative data and subject both to a common method of analysis.

In the end, individual researchers will have to make up their own minds about the degree to which the techniques they select represent a particular view of that part of the social world they have chosen to investigate. Questions of principle are most likely to come into play at the initial stage of conception of the research, and techniques to slot into place as detailed planning unfolds. It is nevertheless important that implications of particular methods choice are fully understood, and that research does not happen 'blindfold' just because of familiarity with, or preference for, certain techniques.

In the next and final section we follow up five of the teachers introduced in Chapters 1 and/or 5, and describe the research in which they have become involved followed by a short commentary.

Teachers' research: some continuing case studies

Table 14.1 provides a summary tabulation of the teachers' working situations, the main features affecting research possibilities for them, and, where applicable, any research undertaken so far.

We now suppose that each of them carried on (or started) their research in a number of different ways:

Kenji Matsuda

Findings:	The textbook analysis yielded a very small number of techniques, mainly (i) translation of supposedly difficult lexical items, and (ii) picture descriptions.
Teaching techniques tried:	(i) English-English dictionary explanations, (ii) oral explanations in English, and (iii) blank-filling of 'learnt' items in texts.
Tests:	Showed that (i) blank-filling was useful at all levels, (ii) more elementary students recalled more with translation.

Table 14.1

	K. Matsuda	A. Barker	I. Petrov	C. Turner	F. Jones
Main characteristics	School 18 hrs p/wk plus other duties 35 in class AET nsp colleague	Language school 25 hrs p/wk Nursing background	University English for Engineering 16–20 in class/mixed levels	Special needs Some ESL children Peripatetic Works with groups and individuals	University EAP Postgraduates
Context features	Ministry–initiated syllabus Local teachers' group Six months' UK training	Introduction of ESP Membership of ARELS and teachers' association Time remission	Change in status of English Writes own materials Resources limited	Works in several schools Access to parents, other teachers, school records	Research as part of contract Conferences
Research begun	Techniques for teaching vocabulary	Contacts made with hospital to collect language data	Questionnaires Diaries Interviews	Learning styles Data collection Updating	Student expectations Questionnaire

Follow-up: Some colleagues teaching at other levels tried the same techniques. Translation appears to be less facilitating as proficiency increases.

KM has been asked to give talks on vocabulary teaching to predeparture teachers going to UK on training programmes.

Summary of research methods: Coursebook analysis.
Frequency tabulation.
Tests.
Comparative data.

Ann Barker

Data collection: Different kinds of written documents made available.
Spoken data could not be recorded because of confidentiality, but AB was allowed to 'listen in' and take notes.

Analysis: Language analysis of written texts.
Some more informal comparison with spoken data.

Follow-up: Data collected from other medical personnel for comparison/contrast in terms of language and content.
Resource bank of pedagogic materials set up in the school for use on its medical English courses.
AB has been given some remission from teaching in order to do the research and materials development. She has also given reports at ARELS workshops and written an article for *Modern English Teacher.*

Summary of research methods: Collection of written data from different professional areas.
Data comparison (i) between content areas, (ii) between spoken and written language.
Various methods of text and discourse analysis.

Irina Petrov

Research idea: Needs analysis, materials development, and subsequent evaluation.

Procedure: Examination of the language needs of Engineering students in relation to present study and future jobs. Information is sought from current and past students, and from Engineering staff.

Analysis of attitudes to English classes and materials in use.

Piloting of some Units of new materials written by teaching team, and subsequent evaluation by learners.

Summary of research methods:	Questionnaires to three different groups. Selected structured interviews: staff and students. Follow-up evaluation via questionnaires and interviews. Peer observation using new pilot materials.

Carol Turner

Research focus: ESL children's language development over the school year using a small number of pupils.

Research instruments: Children's work from special class.
Selection of work from regular classes.
Personal teaching diary.
Interviews with parents and other teachers.
Regular measurement of progress via standardized tests.

Main findings: Language development differs widely between individuals depending on a range of factors, such as amount of exposure to English outside class, family support, degree of participation, and preferred learning modes.

Follow-up: More in-depth case studies.
Reading/attending in-service training on the language development of younger ESL learners.
By chance, CT's Local Education Authority has been approached by the local university to participate in a research project on second language acquisition. CT is able to share her own data with the research team, and also to assist in the administration of test instruments designed to elicit certain kinds of language data.

Frank Jones

Focus: Postgraduate EAP students' expectations and attitudes to study over an academic year period.

Findings: There are clear changes, and high/low points, in the attitudes, expectations and experiences of overseas students as the academic year progresses. This is verified by replicated studies conducted elsewhere.

Follow-up: Semi-structured interviews over the next year with volunteer students. An attempt is made to find people from different countries and studying a variety of subjects.

Data analysis: Interviews are transcribed and subjected to both content and language analysis. The questionnaire findings are confirmed to some extent, but there is also quite sharp differentiation between people's experiences making any generalization difficult.

Summary of research methods: Two questionnaires to large student populations (about 300).
Use of questionnaire in other institutions.
Semi-structured interviews ('member-checked' with interviewees for accuracy).

Commentary

These fictional, though not entirely imaginary, research stories illustrate a number of themes that have been discussed in various parts of this book.

Scale

These teachers are involved in research on various levels of scale. KM looked mainly at his own English classes, but, given normal class size in his country, he obtained data from over 100 learners from three classes, and then involved other colleagues in short-term trials of the teaching techniques he wanted to focus on. CT amassed a large amount of different sorts of data about a small number of her pupils, from them, from their parents, from herself, and from regular classes. FJ looked at a relatively large number of people entering and subsequently working in a medium-sized university with an annual entry of overseas students of between one and two thousand. Scale brings problems of record-keeping and data safety, but mainly of time-management and administration of the research project.

Collaboration

Some of our group have been ploughing their lonely research furrow, but some have been able to involve colleagues in the research in various ways. KM persuaded other teachers in his own and other schools to try out his techniques and tell him the results. IP was working as a member of a materials writing team, contributing in particular the needs analysis but also piloting draft materials in the classroom. CT's research came to the attention of some researchers, in the local university and she discussed it with them while collaborating with them in their own project. Research collaboration for these teachers came to mean two things: peer evaluation and mutual contributions, and sharing data.

Mixing methods

None of these teachers used only one data source in their research. All of them contrived to combine several kinds of data in the one project. AB looked at written documents from medical histories and performed content and linguistic analysis, made her own notes of case conferences, and looked at the way medical, nursing and administrative staff talked about and wrote about their patients in the hospital. IP used questionnaires and interviews in the needs analysis and arranged observation of each other's classes using the new materials by the project team.

Communication

Several of our group have already 'gone public' with their research, in the form of talks at teachers' workshops and even of a published article. IP's team is not so far advanced as to be able to publish articles, but she is hoping to get funding to attend an IATEFL conference at which she will give a paper. FJ has attended conferences where other researchers in the area have talked about their work, and when the comparison between the questionnaire and the interview findings is complete it will be written up as an article, perhaps even in the form of a higher degree thesis. AB has already published an article in a relevant journal and is hoping to do another one including some evaluation of the new materials. In these ways, their findings can be brought to a wider audience and can be subjected to critical analysis by their peers.

Description, evaluation and measurement

None of these teachers has chosen an explicit experimental or even quasi-experimental approach. The nearest to such a design was KM, measuring different outcomes following different teaching treatments. For several, their final data analysis involved quantitative methods as well as verbal data in various forms. All of them were attempting some kind of description of aspects of their own teaching contexts, either monitoring or evaluating a change in teaching practice; performing a needs analysis and developing new materials; attempting to uncover the range of attitudes and expectation underlying performance in tertiary education; or investigating language development in young learners. Their research benefited in each case from their own privileged knowledge of their teaching contexts, but the research also taught them a great deal about which previously they had held inaccurate assumptions.

Action research?

Only one, CT, was doing anything resembling full-scale action research, as represented by the action-research spiral (Chapter 2). Although she was only following a small number of pupils, she was doing so over quite a long timespan, a whole year, and looked at different data sources as they became relevant. However, some of the other projects were using action research in the weaker sense, and one feature in particular, the emergence of research issues, was a characteristic of several of them. The research question developed through the course of the research particularly for her, for AB, for IP and for FJ. As the issue at the heart of each project became clearer and they began to see different ways of looking at it, so the methods they chose to follow up the new leads changed. FJ turned from surveys using questionnaires to interviews; CT switched to in-depth case studies; IP moved from needs analysis to evaluation to collaborative evaluation by peers; AB moved outwards into other areas of medical discourse to illuminate her original problem and widen the scope of the materials resource bank.

Feedforward

These teachers got involved in research for a number of reasons: in response to an employment requirement, for personal professional development, to introduce innovations in their teaching methods. AB and FJ had time made available for their research through contract and remission of teaching duties; KM had his interest and motivation stimulated by a Government-sponsored period at a university in the UK; IP and CT were responding in their own ways to a need they had perceived. Their research and the results brought both personal benefits in terms of professional development and increased involvement in the issues, and also tangible 'feedforward' into the teaching contexts: things began to change. In three institutions, new teaching materials or new techniques for classroom exploitation of materials, and new workplans, were available and were gradually being taken up by other colleagues. CT's LEA began to take greater interest in her special-needs work, and a possibility of greater funding is on the horizon. FJ's university is reviewing its policies for recruitment and support of international students and he has brought the research to their attention already.

Conclusion

This chapter has pulled together for discussion and examination various suggestions made in other chapters about the true nature of the difference between normative and interpretive, quantitative and qualitative approaches. It has explored, with examples, albeit not comprehensively, practical ways of combining different data sources and methods of analysis in the interests of completeness of description, greater accuracy and sensitivity of interpretation. Some of the difficulties of mixing methods and triangulation have been addressed. Finally, we took a last look at some of the fictitious teacher researchers whose research careers we have been following off and on throughout the book, and we have attempted to personalize the discussion by narrative. Of course, in the real world, the positive outcomes described may not always happen; remission of time off teaching to do research may be cancelled because of adverse economic circumstances or trading position, and staff shortage; interesting results may be 'shelved' by authorities and no lasting development allowed to occur. However, these case histories show what can happen, and, since they are based on real acquaintances, we know they do happen.

Discussion notes

Taking a teaching situation with which you are directly or indirectly familiar, and using the following headings just as guidelines, sketch out a plan for a small-scale research project that would take it from inception at least to the data analysis stage:

- issue, problem, focus of interest
- source(s) of data (tests, learners, text, colleagues, other written data, and so on)
- overall rationale for and approach to research design
- preferred/appropriate research instruments
- method of data analysis
- timescale
- anticipated findings
- possible follow-up
- dissemination of findings.

Conclusion

The primary intention of this book has been to lay out the range of approaches, methods and techniques available for research by teachers of English as a foreign/second language, to give some indication of the underlying philosophies, to indicate what a rich menu of possibilities there is, to open up what 'doing research' might actually mean, and give some practical procedures for starting, generating research questions, looking at the history of issues, choosing methods, and bringing the work to the attention of a wider public.

We have illustrated this in three ways. First, we have described a substantial number of examples of research by teachers, mostly but not exclusively of English as a foreign language, which have appeared in print, commenting on the designs and methods used, and on the outcomes. Second, we have used examples by professional researchers in 'applied linguistics', which serve to demonstrate the methods in operation, often in large-scale work, but also the difficulties and shortcomings of such work from the practising teacher's point of view. Cross-fertilization, as we shall argue below, is, however, preferable to mutual ignorance. Third, we have followed a set of fictional but not imaginary teachers in action from their starting points in their contexts and their often highly constrained possibilities for doing research through some of their crucial decision-processes to when their research is nearly completed and they are looking for how to develop the next stage, and how to communicate it to other interested colleagues. We intend this narrative strand not to be comprehensive but to personalize the more general and inevitably theoretical discussion of research philosophies and methods.

The role of research by teachers

A very important theme in the book has been that of research by teachers being able to contribute to various kinds of practical outcomes, for example both the creation of knowledge and the development, monitoring and maintenance of innovations, in teaching methods as well as in class-room organization, curriculum development, materials and institutional cultures. The importance of this contribution by teachers can be seen at several points: in personal and professional development of the teacher, in bringing to bear the teacher's inside knowledge on problems that arise, and in the communication of that special information to the wider professional community of teachers and researchers. By developing the right questions, by taking up issues that arise directly from their experience of the interaction with learners, the teacher researchers can expand the general knowledge base in relevant ways, both contributing to and challenging the conventional wisdom.

Appropriate methodologies

Lest it be thought that such considerations are only relevant for a small group of privileged people in one native-speaker environment, we have made a point of illustrating many of our points with examples from countries other than Britain.

This raises an important issue which has received a great deal of discussion recently, the situation where methodologies are imported or exported from one educational environment to another. 'Appropriate methodology' as discussed by Holliday (1994) and by Budd (1995) refers mainly to the reaction against the wholesale adoption of (usually) communicative methodology in countries other than Britain, where it was developed in the early 1980s. Imported methodologies, especially when the traffic is from countries such as Britain and North America ('BANA') into countries where English is taught as a foreign language in tertiary, secondary and primary state education ('TESEP'), often do not match local conditions in terms of teacher training, usual levels of proficiency among the teachers, cultural attitudes to certain kinds of activities, acceptable roles for teachers and learners, class sizes, and so forth. Despite the difficulties involved in drawing Holliday's line, it is reasonable to ask how curriculum and methods development occurs in these various contexts. This is not a simple task: Clegg (1995: 133) shows how different the various contexts for language teaching are in just one country (Britain), and how difficult communication is between them, and what a long time coordinated development actually takes. There is a role here for research which is home-grown and sensitive to local context, initiated by teachers, conducted by teachers both working alone and in collaboration with others. Such research can aid, accelerate and give direction to the development of methodology and institutional forms for language teaching which are relevant to those local contexts. This is as true of Britain as it is of any other country. Holliday makes this point himself (1994: 9) but does not indicate how teachers in TESEP contexts can be given the skills necessary to accomplish such research.

Of course, as Holliday (1995) points out, the very idea of teacher research in the sense of this book, and the associated philosophy of the reflective practitioner, may itself be a BANA concept, and may have to fight hard to be accepted in those contexts which also find other BANA ideas like the communicative approach uncongenial. However, as he also points out, BANA countries do not have a monopoly on thoughtful practising teachers, and many teachers in those contexts have as much to contribute as BANA teachers (including, of course, expatriates working on British Council, Overseas Development Administration, and United States Information Service projects overseas). The opportunity for such contribution, however, depends on the vocabulary and assumptions of teacher research not being perceived as either yet another import or imposition, or as yet another foreign (or indeed alien) exclusive discourse to be received courteously but not collaborated with. An interesting insight into the process of introducing the methods of action research and qualitative research into schools in Eastern Europe (specifically the Czech republic) is given by Burešová (1996), who reports the gradual breaking-down of traditional attitudes to research both in the academic community and among the language teachers, to the benefit of applied research. However, such developments have to arise from a local perception of relevance and local access to the thinking and the methods of doing such research, rather than be 'flown in' by foreign 'experts'.

Development of criteria

We intend the book to be read as a contribution, not a final comment, to the development of appropriate criteria for research in English language teaching and applied linguistics. Fields are typically defined by topics and by methods of enquiry. They develop as the professional problems multiply, as the knowledge gained through research suggests new leads for research, as methods for research open up new ways of obtaining good-quality data. As we have seen, available research methodologies range from the precise, interventionist, objective, context-free experimental paradigm right across to the descriptive, interpretive, context-bound naturalistic paradigm. We have discussed teacher research in language teaching using elements from the whole range, and mixing methods. As the field develops, so will the practitioners come to agree on criteria for designing and accepting such research. The classical criteria are set out in Chapter 4: but as we saw there, new kinds of research have to develop their own arguments about the importance of those criteria and how they are worked out in actual practice. One dimension on which there is clearly movement is that referred to by Van Lier (1989) as 'openness', referring to ethnography. As Schecter and Ramirez (1992) note, teacher research tends to downplay aspects such as literature search and generalizability (notably those criteria looking outside the immediate environment except for applicability) but requires openness in the sense of clarity of decision process, and narrative about the teacher/researcher's own involvement in the process of obtaining the knowledge.

'Popularity' of various techniques

In this context it is interesting to note how teachers react when asked what kinds of research they found most congenial and what they feel they could do in their typical teaching context. In a small-scale survey of participants in a research methods class for MA students on a course for experienced teachers, one of the authors found that the 'top four' topics were:

- classroom observation
- questionnaires
- case studies
- ethnography.

Perhaps surprisingly, action research featured fairly low in rank order, down with experimental methods. This is probably because it is perceived as very time-consuming and large-scale in nature. Research training courses clearly have to bear in mind two sets of needs, which do not necessarily overlap: those of people who are confronted perhaps for the first time with difficult numerically evaluated experiments and quasi-experiments (because such a large part of the applied linguistics and second language acquisition literature uses these methods), and also those of the teachers when they return to work and wish to make their contribution to the field and do empirical work to introduce innovation in their own teaching environments. Research by teachers *in situ* does not have to be constrained to use only a narrow range of techniques for want of guidelines in how to expand that range. We have tried to show that a wide spectrum of fieldwork techniques is available, and a matching range of techniques of analysis, in many cases with useful off-the-peg computational aids for both quantitative and qualitative evaluation.

Teacher research and higher-degree research

At several points in our text we have mentioned the different demands, and criteria, of teacher research and research performed in pursuit of higher academic degrees such as MA, MPhil and PhD. Apart from scale (a PhD thesis is after all a book-length treatise), there are clearly other issues at stake in the comparison, which bear upon the notion of compatibility between the two. One is the role of scholarship and literature review.

While we have argued, under the heading of cross-fertilization, that knowledge of the history of issues and of previous ways of tackling them is beneficial to teacher research, it is also evident that 'university' research demands a particular style and format for such a review, and the reason is not solely derived from the principles of good research; it also has to do with entry to a particular profession and demonstration of a skill of scholarship that is expected of members of that profession. The academic community – in our view rather unfortunately – has tended to promote a particular view of research, namely the dominant positivist and experimental paradigm, at the expense of others. Teachers have to demonstrate other skills in order to be accepted in their profession.

Another issue is the commonplace dislocation from context usually suffered by postgraduate students doing research, especially if they are from overseas. Their research projects, often despite their own first inclinations, cannot be based within their own teaching contexts because they cannot stay in those contexts while studying for their degree. Consequently research degrees are frequently different in aim and conception to the kind of research considered mainly in this book. This is not necessarily a healthy situation; however, there are developments in the university system which allow research by practising teachers to be counted towards degree awards: part-time study incorporating action research in the teachers' schools, distance learning with local supervision, split-site registration for PhD work carried out in another country. Increasingly, communication between university and degree aspirant uses modern electronic means – fax and e-mail. Such interaction between different elements of the profession can only increase interdependence within the research community, and will slowly help to establish the kind of development of appropriate research methodology, criteria, means of dissemination and mutual cooperation envisaged by this book.

Evaluations of teacher research

Earlier in the book we referred to Shecter and Ramirez's (1992) useful article describing a meta-analysis of a number of teachers engaged in action research of various types. That article, however, did not attempt to evaluate the effectiveness of the activity. There have been remarkably few such evaluations in the language teaching literature; there has been a great deal of enthusiasm for promoting such involvement in research, and those involved have often commented, as do Schecter and Ramirez's teachers, very positively on the personal and professional development prospects that they have experienced as a result of doing the research. A study by Morrow and Schocker (1993) demonstrated just how powerful the involvement of teachers on a teacher development course in the evaluation of the course by various means became: involvement through group discussions, individual interviews and written feedback promoted reflection, interest and sheer amounts of time being devoted to the activities and the course, even at four o'clock on a Friday afternoon! But involvement and positive attitudes on a short course are one thing, evaluation of a long-term research project another. One paper that attempted such an evaluation was Roberts' 'Evaluating the impacts of teacher research' (1993; see Chapter 2). This study reports on two teacher-research projects, both involving collaboration with a university in different ways. In one, teachers in state schools collaborated in classroom research as part of the work they needed to do to qualify for MA degrees; in the other, ELT staff collaborated on a mixed-ability teaching project doing action research in a state school in Israel. In both projects, there was considerable support and enthusiasm among the participants for doing research as a means of professional development, but the picture also contained some difficulties. For example, where teachers are working towards degree awards, there are increased and for some intolerable pressures of workload; there are also difficulties with colleagues who sometimes resent the added status their collaboration might bring not to them but to those engaged in the research; there are frustrations where the research is not seen to be taken up and used in the school after it has been completed.

Roberts drew several interesting conclusions, which are worth repeating here by way of closing the circle: that action research does promote reflectivity, but is not the only way of doing this; that research alone will not change contexts, but that opportunities for change necessarily depend also on the power of the teacher researchers to implement the change; that doing research gives teachers new ways of responding to problems; and that, despite the frustrations, most teachers who engage in this activity develop very positive attitudes and do experience (and report) the sense of personal and professional development that has been referred to several times in this text.

Involvement can itself have strong effects even if the research is not completed. Naidu et al. (1992) write about an action-research project which decisively affected the participating teachers, although, at the time their article was written, they had not completed the observation phase of their plan nor analysed any of the field records of the observations they had performed. The article documents their use of structured talking sessions involving the four teachers discussing in a planned and disciplined fashion their experience of heterogeneity in teaching English in large classes. Arranging and maintaining the discussion sessions in the middle of full teaching loads was a non-trivial problem in itself. This led to a new, shared understanding of the issues in their teaching practices, which in turn led to an observation and analysis plan. However, they were so struck by the effect on themselves of the discussions they decided to write that up as an independent topic. Incidentally, they comment that, although they had some familiarity with work elsewhere on the issue of large classes, they found that considering points arising from the work of others at that juncture clouded their developing perceptions of their own issues, and thought that the proper place for considering 'the literature' would be after, not before, they had formulated and analysed their own points of view. This comment is congruent with, and perhaps helps to explain, the attitudes to the history of issues in other people's work which have been mentioned above in connection with research work by teachers.

Naturally, in evaluating the success of research by teachers in promoting and implementing innovation one should not forget that the capacity for any kind of research to do this is limited. Indeed, the pressures for conservatism and against change in education are strong. The application of any kind of research is subject to political pressures which may emanate from students, colleagues, senior administrators, external agents (such as producers and suppliers of teaching materials and other resources) and wider structures with power over the decisions of the particular institution.

And finally …

A teacher once queried, after reading copious amounts of research in language teaching and about language-research methods, whether research can ever 'get to the bottom' of the complications in a teaching situation or whether teachers were condemned to 'shoot in the dark' for ever. To claim that research will enlighten everything would be too positivistic; to claim that the normal process of questions throwing up further questions was eternal darkness would be too nihilistic. What is clear is that research, properly conducted, with due regard for context and for the development of theory, using appropriate methods from the full range available, asking carefully formulated questions, interpreting with imagination but with an honest judgement of plausibility, will increase our understanding of the many issues in language education and enable us to produce professional answers with confidence to professional problems as they arise.

Appendix

Addresses of organizations

British Association for Applied Linguistics
c/o Multilingual Matters
Frankfurt Lodge
Clevedon Hall
Victoria Road
Clevedon
Avon BS21 7SJ
UK

The British Council
Medlock St
Manchester M15 4PR
UK

Centre for Information on Language Teaching (CILT)
20 Bedfordbury
London WC2N 4LB
UK

Classroom Action Research Network (CARN)
School of Education
University of East Anglia
Norwich NR4 7TJ
UK

Educational Research Information Center (ERIC)
Clearinghouse on Languages and Linguistics
Center for Applied Linguistics
118 22nd Street NW
Washington DC 20037
USA

International Association of Teachers of English as a Foreign Language
(IATEFL)
3 Kingsdown Chambers
Kingsdown Park
Tankerton
Whitstable
Kent CT5 2DJ
UK

TESOL
1600 Cameron St, Suite 300
Alexandria, VA 22314–2751
USA

Electronic addresses

Birkbeck College Virtual Library
http: //www.bbk.ac.uk. Departments/Applied Linguistics/Virtual Library.html

British Council
http: //www.open.gov.uk/bc/bcchom01.html

ERIC
e–mail:
askeric@ericir.syr.edu

IATEFL
http: //www.man.ac.uk/iatefl

TESL-EJ
LISTSERV@CMSA.BERKELEY.EDU
Type the following message:
SUB TESLEJ-L first name second name

TESL-L
LISTSERV@CUNYVM.BITNET
or
LISTSERV@CUNYVM.CUNY.EDU
Type the following message:
SUB TESL-L first name second name

TESOL
e–mail:
tesol@tesol.edu

Journals

Applied Linguistics
Oxford University Press
Walton St
Oxford OX2 6DP
UK

EL Gazette
10 Wrights Lane
London W8 6TA
UK

ELT Journal
Oxford University Press
Walton St
Oxford OX2 6DP
UK

English for Specific Purposes
Pergamon Press plc
Headington Hill Hall
Oxford OX3 0BW
UK

International Journal of Applied Linguistics
Novus Press
P O Box 748 Sentrum
N1066 Oslo
Norway

International Review of Applied Linguistics
Julius Groos Verlag
Postfach 10 24 23
69014 Heidelberg
Germany

Language Awareness
Multilingual Matters
Frankfurt Lodge
Clevedon Hall
Victoria Road
Clevedon
Avon BS21 7SJ
UK

Language Learning
178 Henry S Frieze Building
105 South State Street
Ann Arbor
Michigan 48109–1285
USA

Language Teaching
Cambridge University Press
The Edinburgh Building
Shaftesbury Road
Cambridge CB2 2RU
UK

Language Teaching Research
Arnold
A member of the Hodder Headline Group
338 Euston Road
London NW1 3BH
UK

Linguistics and Language Behavior Abstracts
Sociological Abstracts Inc.
7428 Trade St
San Diego
CA 92121–2479
USA

Modern English Teacher
Macmillan
25 Eccleston Place
London SW1 W9NF
UK

Practical English Teacher
Pilgrims Language Courses
8 Vernon Place
Canterbury
Kent CT1 3NG
UK

Prospect
NCELTR
Macquarie University 2109
Sydney
Australia

RELC Journal
RELC
30 Orange Grove Road
Singapore

Second Language Research
Arnold
A member of the Hodder Headline Group
338 Euston Road
London NW1 3BH
UK

Studies in Second Language Acquisition
Cambridge University Press
The Edinburgh Building
Shaftesbury Road
Cambridge CB2 2RU
UK

System
Elsevier Science Ltd
The Boulevard
Langford Lane
Kidlington
Oxford OX5 1GB
UK

TESOL Quarterly
TESOL
1600 Cameron St, Suite 300
Alexandria, VA 22314–2751
USA

The Teacher Trainer
Pilgrims Language Courses
8 Vernon Place
Canterbury
Kent CT1 3NG
UK

References

ADELMAN, C. 1991: Talk on action research given at the Centre for Applied Research in Education (CARE), University of East Anglia (March).

JENKINS, D. and KEMMIS, S. 1980: Rethinking case study: notes from the second Cambridge conference. In Simons (1980: 45–61).

ALDERSON, J. C. 1991: Bands and scores. In Alderson and North (1991: 71–86).

and NORTH, B (eds) 1991: *Language testing in the 1990's: the communicative legacy.* Review of ELT, 1 (1). London: Macmillan, Modern English Publications in association with the British Council.

ALLWRIGHT, D. 1980: Turns, topics and tasks: patterns of participation in language learning and teaching. In Larsen-Freeman, D. (ed.), *Discourse analysis in second language research.* Rowley, Mass.: Newbury House, 165–87.

1988: *Observation in the language classroom.* London: Longman.

1993: Integrating 'research' and 'pedagogy': appropriate criteria and practical possibilities. In Edge and Richards (1993: 125–35).

and BAILEY, K. M. 1991: *Focus on the language classroom.* Cambridge: Cambridge University Press.

ANDERSON, N. J., BACHMAN, L., PERKINS, K. and COHEN, A. 1991: An exploratory study into the construct validity of a reading comprehension test: triangulation of data sources. *Language Testing* 8(1), 41–66.

APPEL, J. 1995: *Diary of a language teacher.* Oxford: Heinemann.

ARNDT, V. 1987: Six writers in search of texts: a protocol-based study of L1 and L2 writing. *ELT Journal* 41(4), 257–67.

ATKINSON, P. and DELAMONT, S. 1986: Bread and dreams or bread and circuses? A critique of 'case study' research in education. In Hammersley (1986: 238–55).

BACHMAN, L. and PALMER, A. 1982: The construct validation of the F.S.I. oral interview. *Language Learning* 31(1), 67–86.

BAILEY, K. M. 1983: Competitiveness and anxiety in adult second language learning: looking *at* and *through* the diary studies. In Seliger, H. W. and Long, M. H. (eds), *Classroom-oriented research in second language acquisition.* Rowley, Mass.: Newbury House, 67–103.

1990: The use of diary studies in teacher education programs. In Richards and Nunan (1990: 215–26).

and OCHSNER, R. 1983: A methodological review of the diary studies: windmill tilting or social science? In Bailey, K. M., Long, M. H. and Peck, S. (eds), *Second language acquisition studies.* Rowley, Mass.: Newbury House, 188–98.

BASSEY, M. 1986: Does action research require sophisticated research methods? In Hustler *et al.* (1986: 18–24).

BEEBE, L. M. (ed.) 1988: *Issues in second language acquisition: multiple perspectives.* Rowley, Mass.: Newbury House.

BELLELI, L. 1993: How we teach and why: the implementation of an action research model for in-service training. In Edge and Richards (1993: 65–75).

BERTHOFF, A. E. 1987: The teacher as REsearcher. In Goswami and Stillman (1987: 28–38).

BIALYSTOK, E. 1990: *Communication strategies.* Oxford: Blackwell.

BLACKIE, D. 1995: The Internet: what's in it for an EFLer? *IATEFL Newsletter* 129, 10–11.

BLOCK, E. 1986: The comprehension strategies of second language readers. *TESOL Quarterly* 20(3), 463–94.

   1992: See how they read: comprehension monitoring of L1 and L2 readers. *TESOL Quarterly* 26(2), 319–43.

BLUE, G. (ed.) 1993: *Language, learning and success: studying through English.* London: Macmillan. Modern English Publications in association with the British Council.

BOLSTER, A. S. 1983: Towards a more effective model of research on teaching. *Harvard Educational Review* 53(3), 294–308.

BOOMER, G. 1987: Addressing the problem of elsewhereness. In Goswami and Stillman (1987: 4–12).

BRANNEN, J. (ed.) 1992a: *Mixing methods: qualitative and quantitative research.* Brookfield: Avebury.

   1992b: Combining qualitative and quantitative approaches: an overview. In Brannen (1992a: 3–37).

BRINDLEY, G. 1990: Towards a research agenda for TESOL. *Prospect* 6(1), National Centre for English Language Teaching and Research, Macquarie University, Sydney, 7–26.

   1991: Assessing achievement in a learner-centred curriculum. In Alderson and North (1991: 153–66).

BROWN, C. 1984: Two windows on the classroom world: diary studies and participant observation differences. In Larsen, P., Judd, E. and Messerschmidt, D. (eds), *On TESOL '84: a brave new world for TESOL.* Washington DC: TESOL, 121–34.

BROWN, J. D. 1988: *Understanding research in second language learning: a teacher's guide to statistics and research design.* Cambridge: Cambridge University Press.

BRUMFIT, C. and MITCHELL, R. (eds) 1989: *Research in the language classroom.* London: Modern English Publications in association with the British Council.

BRYANT, I. 1993: 'These are the facts': some informal ideas about practice. *Action Researcher* (introductory issue), 3–4.

BUDD, R. (ed.) 1995: Appropriate methodology: from classroom methods to classroom practice. *The Journal of TESOL France*, 2(1).

BUREŠOVÁ, V. 1996: Any takers for classroom research? *Teacher Development.* Newsletter of the IATEFL Teacher Development SIG, No. 31, 8–10.

BURNS, A. 1995: Teacher researchers: perspectives on teacher action research and curriculum renewal. In Burns and Hood (1995: 3–20).

   and HOOD, S. (eds) 1995: *Teachers' voices: exploring course design in a changing curriculum.* National Centre for English Language Teaching and Research, Macquarie University, Sydney.

BURTON, J. and MICKAN, P. 1993: Teachers' classroom research: rhetoric and reality. In Edge and Richards (1993: 113–21).

CALDERHEAD, J. (ed.) 1987: *Exploring teachers' thinking*. London: Cassell.

CAMPBELL, D. T. and STANLEY, J. C. 1963: Experimental and quasi-experimental designs for research on teaching. In Gage, N. L. (ed.), *Handbook of research on teaching*. Chicago: Rand McNally, 171–246.

CANE, B. and SCHROEDER, C. 1970: *The teacher and research*. Slough: National Foundation for Educational Research (NFER).

CARR, W. and KEMMIS, S. 1986: *Becoming critical*. London and Philadelphia: The Falmer Press.

CARRELL, P. L. 1989: Metacognitive awareness and second language reading. *The Modern Language Journal* 73(2), 121–34.

and EISTERHOLD, J. C. H. 1983: Schema theory and ESL reading pedagogy. *TESOL Quarterly* 17(4), 553–73.

PHARIS, B. G. and LIBERTO, J. C. 1989: Metacognitive strategy training for ESL reading. *TESOL Quarterly* 23(4), 647–78.

CARROLL, B. J. and WEST, R. 1989: *ESU framework: performance scales for English language examinations*. Harlow: Longman and English Speaking Union.

CASANAVE, C. P. and HUBBARD, P. 1992: The writing assignments and writing problems of doctoral students: faculty perceptions, pedagogical issues, and needed research. *English for Specific Purposes* 11(1), 33–49.

CHAMOT, A. U. 1995: The teacher's voice: action research in your classroom. *ERIC/CLL News Bulletin* 18(2), Washington, DC: Center for Applied Linguistics.

CHAUDRON, C. 1988: *Second language classrooms: research on teaching and learning*. Cambridge: Cambridge University Press.

CLEGG, J. 1995: Language education in schools and the role of British EFL. In Budd (1995: 133–46).

COHEN, A. D. 1984: On taking language tests: what students report. *Language Testing* Vol. 1, 70–81.

1992: *Language learning*. Rowley, Mass.: Newbury House.

1995: Verbal reports as a source of insights into second language learning strategies. Paper given at the University of Essex.

and APHEK, E. 1981: Easifying second language learning. *Studies in Second Language Acquisition* 3(2), 221–36.

and CAVALCANTI, M. L. 1990: Feedback on compositions: teacher and student verbal reports. In Kroll (1990: 155–77).

COHEN, L. and MANION, L. 1989: *Research methods in education*. London: Routledge (3rd edition).

COOK, V. J. 1986: The basis for an experimental approach to second language learning. In Cook, V. J. (ed.), *Experimental approaches to second language learning*. Oxford: Pergamon.

CORTI, L. 1993: Using diaries in social research. *Social Research Update*, Issue 2. Guildford: University of Surrey.

CRIPER, C. and DAVIES, A. 1988: *Research report 1(i): ELTS validation project report*. London and Cambridge: The British Council and University of Cambridge Local Examinations Syndicate.

CROOKES, G. 1993: Action research for second language teachers: going beyond teacher research. *Applied Linguistics* 12(2), 130–44.

CRYSTAL, D. 1991: *A dictionary of linguistics and phonetics*. Oxford: Blackwell (3rd edition).

1995: *The Cambridge encyclopaedia of the English language*. Cambridge: Cambridge University Press.

DADDS, M. 1995: Finding your 'self' in action research. Paper presented at the second Teachers Develop Teachers Research conference, Cambridge, January 1995.

DAY, R. R. 1990: Teacher observation in second language teacher education. In Richards and Nunan (1990: 43–61).

DENZIN, N. K. 1970: The methodologies of symbolic interactionism: a critical review of research techniques. In Stone, G. P. and Faberman, H. A. (eds), *Social psychology through symbolic interaction*. Waltham, MA: Ginn-Blaisdell, 447–65.

1978: *The research act: a theoretical introduction to sociological methods*. New York: McGraw-Hill (2nd edition).

and LINCOLN, Y. (eds) 1994: *Handbook of qualitative research*. Thousand Oaks, CA: Sage.

DOUGHTY, C. and PICA, T. 1986: Information gap tasks: do they facilitate second language acquisition? *TESOL Quarterly* 20(2), 305–25.

EDGE, J. and RICHARDS, K. (eds) 1993: *Teachers develop teachers research*. Oxford: Heinemann.

EFL SERVICES LTD., 1992: *Students talking*. Elsworthy: EFL Services Ltd.

EISNER, E. and PESHKIN, A. (eds) 1990: *Qualitative enquiry: the continuing debate*. New York: Teachers College Press.

ELLIOTT, J. 1991: *Action research for educational change*. Milton Keynes and Philadelphia: Open University Press.

and ADELMAN, C. (eds) 1975: *Ways of doing research in one's own classroom*. Cambridge: Cambridge Institute of Education.

ELLIS, M. 1993: Introducing reflective practice: an experimental project in Silesia, Poland. In Edge and Richards (1993: 102–12).

ELLIS, R. 1985: *Understanding second language acquisition*. Oxford: Oxford University Press.

1990: *Instructed second language acquisition*. Oxford: Blackwell.

1994: *The study of second language acquisition*. Oxford: Oxford University Press.

ELTON, L. 1995: Research and teaching in higher education. In Gilpin, A. (ed.) *Proceedings of the fourth annual seminar*, Institute for English Teacher Development in Higher Education, p. 8.

ENRIGHT, L. 1981: The diary of a classroom. In Nixon (1981: 37–51).

ERICKSON, F. 1986: Qualitative methods in research on teaching. In Wittrock, M. C. (ed.), *A handbook of research on teaching*. New York: Macmillan, 119–61.

and SCHULTZ, J. 1981: What is a context? Some issues and methods in the analysis of social competence. In Green and Wallat (1981: 147–60).

ERICSSON, K. A. 1988: Concurrent verbal reports on text comprehension. A review. *Text* 8, 295–325.

and SIMON, H. A. 1987: Verbal reports on thinking. In Faerch, C. and Kasper, G. (eds), *Introspection in second language research*. Clevedon: Multilingual Matters, 24–53.

and SIMON, H. A. 1993: *Protocol analysis: verbal reports on data*. Cambridge, MA: MIT Press (revised edition).

FAIGLEY, L. and WITTE, S. 1981: Analysing revision. *College Composition and Communication* 32, 400–14.

FANSELOW, J. F. 1977: Beyond Rashomon: conceptualizing and describing the teaching act. *TESOL Quarterly* 11(1), 17–39.

FATHMAN, A. K. and WHALLEY, E. 1990: Teacher response to student writing: focus on form v. content. In Kroll (1990: 178–90).

FITZPATRICK, F. 1995: Peering at your peers. *The Teacher Trainer* 9(2), 14–16.

FLANDERS, N. 1970: *Analysing teaching behaviour*. Reading, MA: Addison-Wesley.

FREIRE, P. 1972: *The pedagogy of the oppressed*. Harmondsworth: Penguin.

FRÖHLICH, M., SPADA, N. and ALLEN, J. P. B. 1985: Differences in the communicative orientation of L2 classrooms. *TESOL Quarterly* 19(1), 27–57.

GAGE, N. L. (ed.) 1963: *Handbook of research on teaching*. Chicago: Rand McNally.

GAIES, S. and BOWERS, R. 1990: Clinical supervision of language teaching: the supervisor as trainer and educator. In Richards and Nunan (1990: 167–81).

GARDNER, R. C. and MACINTYRE, P. 1993: On the measurement of affective variables in second language learning. *Language Learning* 43(2), 157–94.

GASS, S. M. and SCHACHTER, J. 1989: *Linguistic perspectives on second language acquisition*. Cambridge: Cambridge University Press.

GEERTZ, C. 1973: *The interpretation of cultures*. New York: Basic Books.

GIROUX, H. 1988: *Teachers as intellectuals: towards a critical pedagogy of learning*. Massachusetts: Bergin and Garvey Publishers.

GOOD, T. L. and BROPHY, J. E. 1978: *Looking in classrooms*. New York: Harper and Row (2nd edition).

GOSWAMI, D. and STILLMAN, P. R. (eds) 1987: *Reclaiming the classroom: teacher research as an agency for change*. Portsmouth, NH: Boynton/Cook Publishers.

GREEN, J. L. and WALLAT, C. (eds) 1981: *Ethnography and language in educational settings*. Norwood, NJ: Ablex.

GREEN, P. S. (ed.) 1975: *The language laboratory in school performance and prediction: the York Study*. Edinburgh and New York: Oliver and Boyd.

GUILFORD, J. P. and FRUCHTER, B. P. 1973: *Fundamental statistics in psychology and education*. New York: McGraw-Hill.

HAKUTA, K. 1976: A case study of a Japanese child learning English as a second language. *Language Learning* 26(2), 321–51.

HAMMERSLEY, M. (ed.) 1986: *Controversies in classroom research*. Milton Keynes and Philadelphia: Open University Press.

1989: *The dilemma of qualitative method: Herbert Blumer and the Chicago School*. London: Routledge.

1992: Deconstructing the qualitative-quantitative divide. In Brannen (1992a: 39–55).

and ATKINSON, P. 1983: *Ethnography: principles in practice*. London and New York: Tavistock.

HANDAL, G. and LAUVÅS, P. 1987: *Promoting reflective teaching: supervision in action*. Milton Keynes: Society for Research into Higher Education (SRHE) and Open University Press.

HANDY, C. B. 1985: *Understanding organizations*. London: Penguin Books (3rd edition).

HATCH, E. and FARHADY, H. 1982: *Research design and statistics for applied linguistics*. Rowley, Mass.: Newbury House.

HITCHCOCK, G. and HUGHES, D. 1995: *Research and the teacher*. London and New York: Routledge (2nd edition).

HOLLIDAY, A. 1994: The house of TESEP and the communicative approach: the special needs of state English language education. *ELT Journal* 48(1), 3–11.

1995: A post-communicative era? Method versus social context. In Budd (1995: 147–57).

HOLLY, M. L. 1984: *Keeping a personal-professional journal*. Deakin: Deakin University Press.

HOPKINS, D. 1993: *A teacher's guide to classroom research*. Buckingham and Philadelphia: Open University Press (2nd edition).

HOSENFELD, C. 1976: Learning about learning: discovering our students' strategies. *Foreign Language Annals* 9(2), 117–29.

1979: Cora's view of learning grammar. *Canadian Modern Language Review* 35, 602–7.

HUSTLER, D., CASSIDY, A., and CUFF, E. C. (eds) 1986: *Action research in classrooms and schools.* London: Allen and Unwin.

HUTCHINSON, B. and WHITEHOUSE, P. 1986: Action research, professional competence and school organization. *British Educational Research Journal* 12(1), 85–94.

HUTCHINSON, T. and WATERS, A. 1987: *English for specific purposes: a learning-centred approach.* Cambridge: Cambridge University Press.

JAMES, K. 1984: The writing of theses by speakers of English as a foreign language: the results of a case study. In Williams, R., Swales, J. and Kirkman, J. (eds), *Common ground: shared interests in ESP and communication studies.* ELT Documents 117, Oxford: Pergamon, in association with the British Council, 99–113.

JARVIS, J. 1992: Using diaries for teacher reflection on in-service courses. *ELT Journal* 46(2), 133–43.

JOHNSON, D. M. 1992: *Approaches to research in second language learning.* New York and London: Longman.

JOHNSON, H. and JOHNSON, K. Forthcoming: *Handbook of applied linguistics.* Oxford: Blackwell.

JONES, F. R. 1994: The lone language learner: a diary study. *System* 22(4), 441–54.

JORDAN, R. R. (ed.) 1983: *Case studies in ELT.* London and Glasgow: Collins.

1993: Study skills: experience and expectations. In Blue (1993: 70–9).

KEMMIS, S. 1991: Improving education through action research. In Zuber-Skerritt, O. (ed.), *Action research in higher education.* Brisbane: Griffith University, 57–75.

KENNEDY, M. M. 1979: Generalizing from single case studies. *Evaluation Quarterly* 3(4), 661–78.

KROLL, B. (ed.) 1990: *Second language writing.* Cambridge: Cambridge University Press.

LINCOLN, Y. S. and GUBA, E. G. 1985: *Naturalistic enquiry.* Beverley Hills, CA: Sage.

LLEWELYN, S. 1995: Topics, text-types and grammar: making the links. In Burns and Hood (1995: 67–74).

LOMAX, P. (ed.) 1990: *Managing staff development in schools: an action-research approach.* Clevedon, Philadelphia: Multilingual Matters.

LONG, M. 1983: Does second language instruction make a difference? A review of the research. *TESOL Quarterly* 17(3): 359–82.

LOW, G. 1991: Talking to questionnaires: pragmatic models in questionnaire design. In Adams, P., Heaton, B. and Howarth, P. (eds), *Sociocultural issues in English for academic purposes.* London: Macmillan. Modern English Publications in association with the British Council, 118–34.

MACDONALD, B. and KUSHNER, S. (eds) 1983: *Bread and dreams: a case study of bilingual schooling in the USA.* Norwich: Centre for Applied Research in Education, University of East Anglia.

MACKAY, R. and MOUNTFORD, A. (eds) 1978: *English for specific purposes.* London: Longman.

MALAMAH-THOMAS, A. 1987: *Classroom interaction.* Oxford: Oxford University Press.

MALMKJAER, K. 1993: *A linguistics encyclopaedia.* London: Routledge.

MARKEE, N. 1986: Towards an appropriate technology model of communicative course design. *English for Specific Purposes* 5(2), 161–72.

MARSHALL, C. and ROSSMAN, G. B. 1989: *Designing qualitative research.* Newbury Park: Sage.

McDONOUGH, J. 1994: A teacher looks at teachers' diaries. *ELT Journal* 48(1), 243–52.
and McDONOUGH, S. 1990: What's the use of research? *ELT Journal* 44(2), 102–9.
and McDONOUGH, S. 1993: From EAP to chemistry: risking the anecdotal. In Blue (1993: 132–40).
and SHAW, C. 1993: *Materials and methods in ELT*. Oxford: Blackwell.
McDONOUGH, S. H. 1995: *Strategy and skill in learning a foreign language*. London: Edward Arnold.
McLAUGHLIN, B. 1987: *Theories of second language learning*. London: Edward Arnold.
McNIFF, J. 1988: *Action research: principles and practice*. London: Macmillan.
MILES, M. B. and HUBERMAN, A. M. 1994: *Qualitative data analysis*. Thousand Oaks, CA: Sage (2nd edition).
MORROW, K. and SCHOCKER, M. 1993: Process evaluation in an INSET course. *ELT Journal* 47(1), 47–55.
MURPHY, R. and TORRANCE, H. (eds) 1988: *Evaluating education: issues and methods*. London: Paul Chapman, in association with The Open University.
MURPHY O'DWYER, L. M. 1985: Diary studies as a method for evaluating teacher training. In Alderson, J. C. (ed.), *Evaluation*. Lancaster Practical Papers in English Language Education, Vol. 6. Oxford: Pergamon Press, 97–128.
NAIDU, B., NEERAJA, K., RAMANI, E., SHIVAKUMAR, J. and VISWANATHA, V. 1992: Researching heterogeneity: an account of teacher-initiated research into large classes. *ELT Journal* 46(3), 252–63.
NAIMAN, N., FRÖHLICH, M. and STERN, H. H. 1975: *The good language learner*. Ontario Institute for Studies in Education: Modern Language Centre, Department of Curriculum.
NISBETT, R. E. and WILSON, T. D. 1977: Telling more than we can know: verbal reports on mental processes. *Psychological Review* 84, 231–59.
NIXON, J. (ed.) 1981: *A teacher's guide to action research*. London: Grant McIntyre.
NORRIS, N. 1990: *Understanding educational evaluation*. London: Kogan Page in association with CARE.
NUNAN, D. 1988: *The learner-centred curriculum*. Cambridge: Cambridge University Press.
1989: The teacher as researcher. In Brumfit and Mitchell (1989: 16–32).
(ed.) 1992a: *Collaborative language learning and teaching*. Cambridge: Cambridge University Press.
1992b: *Research methods in language learning*. Cambridge: Cambridge University Press.
O'MALLEY, J. M. and CHAMOT, A. U. 1990: *Learning strategies in second language acquisition*. Cambridge: Cambridge University Press.
OPEN UNIVERSITY/SCHOOLS COUNCIL 1981: *Curriculum in action: practical classroom evaluation*. Milton Keynes: Open University Press.
OXFORD, R. 1990: *Language learning strategies: what every teacher should know*. Rowley, Mass.: Newbury House.
PARKINSON, B. and HOWELL-RICHARDSON, C. 1989: Learner diaries. In Brumfit and Mitchell (1989: 128–40).
PEAL, E. and LAMBERT, W. 1962: *The relation of bilingualism to intelligence*. Washington: American Psychological Association. Psychological Monographs: General and Applied, 76 (546).
PECK, A. 1988: *Language teachers at work: a description of methods*. London: Prentice Hall.
PENNINGTON, M. C. 1990: A professional development focus for the language teaching practicum. In Richards and Nunan (1990: 132–52).
PERL, S. 1981: Coding the composing process: a guide for teachers and researchers. Manuscript written for the National Institute of Education, Washington, DC, USA, ED 240609.

PEYTON, J. K. and STANTON, J. (eds) 1991: *Writing our lives*. Englewood Cliffs, NJ: Prentice-Hall/Regents.

PICKETT, G. D. 1978: *The foreign language learning process*. London: British Council English Teaching Information Centre.

PLUMMER, K. 1983: *Documents of life*. London: Allen and Unwin.

PORTER, P. A., GOLDSTEIN, L. M., LEATHERMAN, J. and CONRAD, S. 1990: An ongoing dialogue: learning logs for teacher preparation. In Richards and Nunan (1990: 227–40).

POULISSE, N., BONGAERTS, T. and KELLERMAN, E. 1987: The use of verbal reports in the analysis of compensatory strategies. In Faerch, C. and Kasper, G. (eds) *Introspection in second language research*. Clevedon: Multilingual Matters, 213–29.

POWELL, R. C. 1992: 'More than just a hobby': language teachers' perceptions of involvement in a curriculum development project. *System* 20(4), 493–506.

PROGOFF, I. 1975: *At a journal workshop*. New York: Dialog House Library.

RAIMES, A. 1983: *Techniques in teaching writing*. New York and London: Oxford University Press.

RAMANI, E. 1987: Theorising from the classroom. *ELT Journal* 41(1), 3–11.

REA-DICKINS, P. and GERMAINE, K. 1992: *Evaluation*. Oxford: Oxford University Press.

RICHARDS, J. C. 1985: *The context of language teaching*. Cambridge: Cambridge University Press.

    and LOCKHART, C. 1994: *Reflective teaching in second language classrooms*. Cambridge: Cambridge University Press.

    and NUNAN, D. (eds) 1990: *Second language teacher education*. Cambridge: Cambridge University Press.

    and RODGERS, T. S. 1986: *Approaches and methods in language teaching*. Cambridge: Cambridge University Press.

RICHARDS, K. 1992: Pepys into a TEFL course. *ELT Journal* 46(2), 144–52.

RIVERS, W. 1964: *The psychologist and the foreign language teacher*. Chicago: University of Chicago Press.

ROBERTS, J. R. 1993: Evaluating the impact of teacher research. *System* 21(1), 1–19.

RUDDUCK, J. and HOPKINS, D. 1985: *Research as a basis for teaching: readings from the work of Lawrence Stenhouse*. London: Heinemann.

SAVILLE-TROIKE, M. 1989: *The ethnography of communication*. Oxford: Blackwell (2nd edition).

SCHECTER, S. R. and RAMIREZ, R. 1992: A teacher-research group in action. In Nunan (1992a: 192–207).

SCHMIDT, R. W. and FROTA, S. N. 1986: Developing basic conversational ability in a second language: a case study of an adult learner of Portuguese. In Day, R. R. (ed.), *Talking to learn: conversation in second language acquisition*. Rowley, Mass.: Newbury House, 237–326.

SCHÖN, D. A. 1983: *The reflective practitioner*. New York: Basic Books.

SCHUMANN, F. E. and SCHUMANN, J. H. 1977: Diary of a language learner: an introspective study of second language learning. In Brown, H. D., Crymes, R. H., and Yorio, C. A. (eds), *On TESOL '77: teaching and learning English as a second language – trends in research and practice*. Washington, DC: TESOL, 241–9.

SCHUMANN, J. H. 1993: Some problems with falsification: an illustration from SLA research. *Applied Linguistics* 14(3): 295–306.

SEEDHOUSE, P. 1995: Using the Internet for research purposes. *Research News*. Newsletter of IATEFL Research SIG No. 6, 10–11.

SELIGER, H. W. and SHOHAMY, E. 1989: *Second language research methods*. Oxford: Oxford University Press.

SEVIGNY, M. J. 1981: Triangulated enquiry – a methodology for the analysis of classroom interaction. In Green and Wallat (1981: 65–86).

SHARWOOD SMITH, M. 1994: *Second language learning: theoretical foundations.* Harlow: Longman.

SIMONS, H. (ed.) 1980: *Towards a science of the singular.* Occasional Papers 19, Centre for Applied Research in Education: University of East Anglia.

SKEHAN, P. 1989: *Individual differences in second language learning.* London: Edward Arnold.

SLIMANI, A. 1989: The role of topicalization in classroom language learning. *System* 17(2), 223–34.

SMITH, K. 1995: Guided and self-directed reflections in teacher training. Paper presented at the second Teachers Develop Teachers Research conference, Cambridge, January 1995.

SOMEKH, B. 1993: Quality in educational research – the contribution of classroom teachers. In Edge and Richards (1993: 26–38).

SOMMERS, A. 1980: Revision strategies of student writers and experienced adult writers. *College Composition and Communication* 31, 378–88.

SPOLKSY, B. 1989: *Conditions for second language learning.* Oxford: Oxford University Press.

STAKE, R. 1994: Case studies. In Denzin and Lincoln (1994: 236–47).

    1995: *The art of case study research.* Thousand Oaks, CA: Sage.

STENHOUSE, L. 1975: *An introduction to curriculum research and development.* London: Heinemann.

    1988: The conduct, analysis and reporting of case study in educational research and evaluation. In Murphy and Torrance (1988: 212–24).

STEVICK, E. W. 1980: *Teaching languages: a way and ways.* Rowley, Mass.: Newbury House.

STRICKLAND, D. S. 1988: The teacher as researcher: towards the extended professional. *Language Arts* Vol. 65, 754–64.

SWAN, J. 1993: Metaphor in action: the observation schedule in a reflective approach to teacher education. *ELT Journal* 47(3), 242–9.

TAYLOR, S. J. and BOGDAN, R. 1984: *Introduction to qualitative research methods.* New York: Wiley.

THORNBURY, S. 1991: Watching the whites of their eyes: the use of teaching practice logs. *ELT Journal* 45(2), 140–6.

TONKYN, A., LOCKE, C., ROBINSON, P. and FURNEAUX, C. 1993: The EAP teacher: prophet of doom or eternal optimist? EAP teachers' predictions of student success. In Blue (1993: 37–48).

TRANTER, D. 1986: Changing schools. In Hustler *et al.* (1986: 105–22).

TRIPP, D. 1993: *Critical incidents in teaching.* London: Routledge.

VAN LIER, L. 1988: *The classroom and the language learner.* London and New York: Longman.

    1989: Ethnography: bandaid, bandwagon, or contraband? In Brumfit and Mitchell (1989: 33–53).

WALKER, R. 1985: *Doing research: a handbook for teachers.* London: Methuen.

    1986: The conduct of educational case studies: ethics, theory and procedures. In Hammersley (1986: 187–219).

    and ADELMAN, C. 1976: Strawberries. In Stubbs, M. and Delamont, S. (eds) 1976: *Explorations in classroom observation.* Chichester: John Wiley, 133–50.

WALLACE, M. J. 1991: *Training foreign language teachers: a reflective approach.* Cambridge: Cambridge University Press.

WALLAT, C., GREEN, J. L., CONLIN, S. M. and HARAMIS, M. 1981: Issues related to action research in the classroom – the teacher and researcher as a team. In Green and Wallat (1981: 87–113).

WATSON-GEGEO, K.A. 1988: Ethnography in ESL: defining the essentials. *TESOL Quarterly* 22(4), 575–92.

WEIR, C. 1988: The specification, realization and validation of an English language proficiency test. In Hughes, A. (ed.), *Testing English for university study*.   London: Macmillan. Modern English Publications in association with the British Council, 45–110.

 and ROBERTS, J. R. 1994: *Evaluation in ELT*. Oxford: Blackwell.

WEITZMAN, E. A. and MILES, M. B. 1995: *Computer programs for qualitative data analysis*. Thousand Oaks, CA: Sage.

WENDEN, A. 1987: How to be a successful language learner. In Wenden, A. and Rubin, J. (eds), *Learner strategies in language learning*. Hemel Hempstead: Prentice Hall, 103–18.

WHITE, R. V. and ARNDT, V. 1991: *Process writing*. Harlow: Longman.

WIDDOWSON, H. G. 1978: *Teaching language as communication*. Oxford: Oxford University Press.

WODE, H. 1976: Developmental sequences in naturalistic L2 acquisition. *Working Papers in Bilingualism* Vol. 11, 1–31.

WOODS, A., FLETCHER, P. and HUGHES, A. 1986: *Statistics in language study*. Cambridge: Cambridge University Press.

WRIGHT, T. 1987: *Roles of teachers and learners*. Oxford: Oxford University Press.

Index